THE NEW SPACE ENCYCLOPEDIA

Claudia Martin and
Giles Sparrow

Picture Credits:
Key: b-bottom, t-top, c-center, l-left, r-right

Alamy: 14–15 (Ron Miller/Stocktrek Images), 40–41 (NASA Images), 68–69 (Mark Garlick/Science Photo Library), 70cl (Alan Dyer/Stocktrek Images), 72–73 (Walter Myers/Stocktrek Images), 80c (Encyclopedia Britannica/Universal Images Group North America), 84cr (World History Archive), 106–107, 240–241, 246–247 (NASA Photo), 118–119 (NASA/Science History Images), 138–139 (Photo Researchers, Inc), 152–153 (World History Archive), 158br (QAI Publishing/Universal Images Group), 164–165 (NASA/RGB Ventures/Superstock), 165cr (BJ Warnick/Newscom), 174–175 (NG Images), 208bc (Ashmolean Museum of Art and Archaeology/Heritage Images), 212c (Pictures from History/CPE Media Pte Ltd), 227tc (Trinity Mirrorpix), 234–235 (Associated Press/hkipix), 238–239 (NASA Archive), 242–243 (Science History Images), 242c (Pictorial Press Ltd), 248br (UPI); **alexfreire:** 198br; **Areong:** 62bc (NASA); **China News Service:** 156cr; **Department of Energy, Washington, DC, Office of Public Affairs:** 225br; **ESA:** 62cr (DLR/FU Berlin/J. Cowart), 90cr (2010 MPS for OSIRIS Team MPS/UPD/LAM/IAA/RSSD/INTA/UPM/DASP/IDA), 150–151, 188cr (D. Ducros), 184br (C Carreau); **ESO:** 39bl (Y Beletsky), 117br (Swinburne Astronomy Productions), 182br (Hubble Space Telescope), 194c (L Calçada), 203b (Y Beletsky), 230bl (M. Kornmesser); **EUMETSAT:** 150b; **Event Horizon Telescope Collaboration:** 230c; **Getty Images:** 8–9 (QAI Publishing/Universal Images Group), 112–113 (Ann Ronan Pictures/Print Collector), 114–115 (Roger Ressmeyer/Corbis/VCG), 139cl (Sovfoto), 151b (Detlef van Ravenswaay), 153tl (China National Space Administration/AFP), 154–155 (Adrian Mann/All About Space Magazine), 166–167 (Stefan Morrell), 172br (Jon Brenneis), 233cr (Dorling Kindersley), 237br (Ullstein Bild Dtl.); **TH Jarrett:** 169b (IPAC/SSC); **Keck Observatory:** 207cr (NRC-HIA, Christian Marois); **Library of Congress:** 218cl (New York World-Telegram and the Sun Newspaper Photograph Collection); **Matúš Motlo:** 12bl; **Max-Planck-Institut für extraterrestrische Physik:** 125b; **Alexander Mokletsov/RIA Novosti:** 236c; **NASA:** 3tr, 19br (NASA Goddard Photo and Video), 3br, 74bl (ESA, J. Clarke [Boston University], and Z. Levay [STScI]), 4tr, 157cr (John Frassanito & Associates), 5tr, 196b, 197tr (HST/ASU/J Hester et al.), 5br, 242bl (National Archives at College Park), 10c (ESA, N. Smith [University of California, Berkeley], and The Hubble Heritage Team [STScI/AURA]; credit for CTIO Image: N. Smith [University of California, Berkeley] and NOAO/AURA/NSF), 14bl (NASA Goddard Laboratory for Atmospheres and Yohkoh Legacy Data Archive), 19t, 78c (NASA Goddard Space Flight Center, Greenbelt, MD, USA), 19cr (TRACE), 22br, 87b, 200br (Hubble Space Telescope), 40bl (GSFC/Arizona State University), 50bl, 52cr, 53tc (Johns Hopkins APL/Carnegie Institution of Washington), 55b, 58–59, 58cr, 59c, 76cr, 84bl, 160br (JPL), 55tr, 118bc, 145bl, 146tr, 148br, 149tr, 151r, 157br (JPL–Caltech), 59br (JPL/Magellan Probe), 60cl (JPL–Caltech/MSSS), 60br (Viking 1), 62br (JPL/Malin Space Science Systems), 64cr (JPL–Caltech/Arizona State University), 64bl (World Wind), 66c (JPL–Caltech/University of Arizona), 66cr (JPL/University of Arizona), 70br (JPL–Caltech/Kevin M. Gill), 74cr (JPL–Caltech/SSI), 79br (JPL/Space Science Institute), 81bc (ESA and M. Showalter [SETI Institute]), 82cr (Erich Karkoschka, University of Arizona), 87cr (Voyager 2), 90cl (NEAR), 90c (USGS/JPL), 91bc (JPL/Processed by Kevin M. Gill), 92bl (JPL–Caltech/UCLA/MPS/DLR/IDA), 98c (ESA and M. Brown), 105tr, 119bl, 134–135, 134b, 135tr (NRAO/AUI/NSF/STScI/JPL–Caltech), 106bl, 139tr, 152bl, 152bc, 152br, 162br, 164br, 224bc, 240c, 241br, 243br, 246c (NASA Images), 111c (Robert Simmon/Chris Elvidge/NOAA/National Geophysical Data Center), 118bl, 119bc (Caltech, UC Berkeley, Albert Einstein Institute, Perimeter Institute for Theoretical Physics, National Science Foundation/Blue Waters), 118br (JPL–Caltech/K Gordon, ASU), 124–125, 124br, 127cr, 127bl, 128br, 143tr (JSC), 144–145 (Bill Stafford/JSC), 144br (Mark Sowa/JSC), 154cl (Johns Hopkins APL/Steve Gribben), 162cr (ESA/JPL/University of Arizona; processed by Andrey Pivovarov), 163bc (JPL/NOAO/Jason Perry), 166br (JPL–Caltech/SETI Institute), 168br, 173tr (WMAP Science Team), 176c (JPL–Caltech/Las Campanas Observatory), 179tr (CXC/Stanford/I Zhuravleva et al.), 180c (Spitzer Space Telescope), 182–183 (Chandra X-ray Observatory Center), 183cr (Fermi), 185c (NASA/CXC/CfA/M Markevitch et al./STScI/Magellan/ASU/D Clowe et al., ESO WFI), 186br (JPL/ASU), 189br (ESA/G Bacon/STScI), 190–191 (Digitized Sky Survey, Noel Carboni), 198c (AEI/ZIB/M Koppitz & L Rezzolla), 204c (ESA/S Larsen), 206b (ESA/ESO/L Ricci), 207tc (CXC/M Weiss), 224cr (Restored by Adam Cuerden), 232cl (Scan by J.L. Pickering), 234tl (Marshall Image Exchange), 234bc (Mercury-Redstone 3), 235tr (Davis Paul Meltzer), 238c (Gemini 8), 239c (Edwin E. Aldrin, Jr.), 247tr (Kennedy Space Center/Ben Smegelsky); **New York Public Library:** 210c (Abd al-Rahman al-Sufi); **NSO/NSF/AURA:** 14cr; **Science Photo Library:** 8cl (Paul D Stewart), 22–23 (Paul Wootton), 24–25, 48–49, 56cl, 212–213, 244–245 (Detlev Van Ravenswaay), 26br, 56–57, 62–63, 82–83, 89, 218–219, 220br, 228–229 (Mark Garlick), 26–27, 106, 160cl, 232–233 (NASA), 36–37 (Miguel Claro), 42br (Chris Butler), 50–51 (Alan Dyer/VWPICS), 52–53 (NASA/Johns Hopkins APL/Carnegie Institution of Washington), 54c (Juan Carlos Casado/StarryEarth.com), 56br (Lynette Cook), 64–65 (Walter Myers), 86–87 (Ron Miller), 88cr (NASA/JPL–Caltech), 94–95 (NASA/Johns Hopkins APL/Southwest Research Institute/Steve Gribben), 98–99 (M. Brown/CIT/NASA/ESA/STSCI), 98bl (Adam Nieman), 100cl (Jerry Lodriguss), 100br (Tim Brown), 102–103 (Jeff Dai), 108–109 (NASA/JPL–Caltech/R. Hurt [SSC]), 108r (NASA/JPL), 154br (ESA & NASA/Solar Orbiter/Spice Team), 158–159 (Julian Baum), 162–163 (David Ducros), 164c (Gregoire Cirade), 210–211 (Library of Congress), 216–217 (Canada-France-Hawaii Telescope/Jean-Charles Cuillandre), 216bl (Royal Astronomical Society), 224–225 (Claus Lunau), 226bl (Victor de Schwanberg), 228c (Robin Scagell), 230–231 (NASA/CXC/M. Weiss); **Shutterstock:** 3tl, 20bl (Natursports), 3bl, 38c (Muskoka Stock Photos), 4tl, 100–101 (Diego Hartog Rebello), 5tl, 178c (chainfoto24), 6–7 (Stefano Garau), 6cl (MaraQu), 6b (Viktar Malyshchyts), 6cr (NASA), 7t (tose), 7br (pixbox77), 9tc, 246br (Nerthuz/NASA), 9tcr (NASA Images), 9tr, 72c (Tristan 3D), 12cr, 31tr, 46cr, 48b, 69b, 118c, 172–173 (Designua), 10–11, 186c (Mopic), 10br (D1min), 11r (Erebor Mountain), 12–13 (Valentin Valkov), 13br (Azuzl), 16–17 (Bo Valentino), 16l, 34br (VectorMine), 17c (Aldona Griskeviciene), 17bl (Fouad A. Saad), 18cr (designer_an), 20–21 (Thanakrit Santikunaporn), 20ct (jflin98), 20cb (joelamfotohk), 21br, 46br (Alhovik), 22tl (seveniwe), 24b, 218b (Veronika By), 25bl (Redpixel.pl), 28–29, 70–71, 84–85, 96–97 (24K-Production/NASA), 28c, 30br, 109bc (Naeblys), 28br (Jane Kelly), 29bc (aphotostory), 30–31 (Fotos593), 30c (tinkivinki), 32–33 (Kedardome), 32c, 131, 133 (shooarts), 33bc (Brian Donovan), 34–35 (ArCaLu), 34c (AnnSky), 35tr (Nicolas Primola), 36c, 40cr (Siberian Art), 37bc (PhotoVisions), 38–39 (Anna Anikina), 38b (Plum Creek Aerial), 41br, 72br, 79tr, 82br (Blue bee), 42–43 (Pe3K/NASA), 44–45 (Soloviova Liudmyla), 44c (Inkoly), 45bl (Anna L. e Marina Durante), 46–47 (shuttertim82), 46c (mailbocy), 47tc (Aristokrates), 49tr (alexaldo), 51tr, 54br, 61br, 71br, 80br, 86br, 93br (Anatolir), 57br (Meggi), 60–61 (sakdam/NASA), 66–67, 160–161, 161cr (Dotted Yeti/NASA), 66br, 67tr (Kirius_Sirius), 68br (Whitelion61/NASA), 73br (ManuMata), 74–75 (3000ad/NASA), 75br, 85br (Golden Sikorka), 76–77 (bluecrayola), 77tc (Artsiom P/NASA), 77cr (Elena11/NASA), 78–79 (Stephane Masclaux), 80–81 (buradaki/NASA), 83cr, 94bl (Diego Barucco), 88bl (Claudio Caridi), 88bc (Meletios Verras), 90–91 (3d_vicka), 92–93 (Nostalgia for Infinity/NASA), 92cr (Marc Ward/NASA), 94cr (Lukas Bischoff Photograph), 96c (Vector Point Studio), 96br (gomolach), 97tr (Anna Sizova), 102cr, 198–199 (Vadim Sadovski), 102br (Marina_Maximova), 103bc (marcin jucha), 104–105 (Oscity), 104l (I Pilon), 104br (HelenField), 107tr (grimgram), 108br (ioanna_alexa), 110–111 (Yuriy Mazur), 110b, 220–221, 220cl, 226–227 (vchal), 112l (Zbiq), 113r (iryna1), 114b (Georgios Kollidas/R Hart), 115tr (VectorPot), 115cr (BlueRingMedia), 115br (Olga Rutko), 116–117 (EastVillage Images), 120–121, 121tr, 176–177, 180–181 (NASA), 121br (bhjary), 122–123 (IrinaK), 122br (Jennifer Stone), 123tr (Zern Liew), 126–127 (Vadim Sadovski/NASA), 127tr (bhjary), 128–129 (edobric), 130l (Marzolino), 131 b/g (Stephanie Frey), 132–133 b/g (Maria Starovoytova), 132l (Marzolino), 135br (Timothy Hodgkinson/NASA), 136–137, 214br (3Dsculptor), 136c (Fred Mantel), 136br (stoyanh), 137tr (Georgios Kollidas), 139br (Bon Appetit), 140–141, 140br, 141tr (Everett Historical), 141br (stoyanh), 142–143 (vicspacewalker), 143cr (Christopher Halloran), 143br (Andrew Rybalko), 146–147 (Stefan Ataman), 146–147 b/g (Viktar Malyshchyts), 146bl (Bannykh Alexey Vladimirovich), 146cr (Pavel L Photo and Video), 148–149 (Naeblys/NASA), 148bl, 149br (PavloArt Studio), 150c (Johan Swanepoel), 153br (RikoBest), 155tr (Alex Terentii), 156–157 (Merlin74/NASA), 158cl (3Dsculptor/NASA), 159bc (Raymond Cassel), 167br (Sebastian Kaulitzki), 168–169 (MaraQu), 170–171 (chaoss), 170bl (Igor Batrakov), 174br (vectortatu), 178–179 (Denis Belitsky), 181tl (Giovanni Benintende), 182cl (Igor Zh), 186–187 (breakermaximus), 187ct (Phongsak Meedaenphai), 188–189 (My Good Images), 191br, 195tr (sciencepics), 192–193 (ESA/NASA/Herschel/Hubble/DSS), 193tl (ESO/VPHAS+ Consortium/Cambridge Astronomical Survey Unit), 193tc (Egyptian Studio/NASA), 193tr (Ken Crawford Rancho Del Sol Observatory), 194–195 (Kalabi Yau), 194br, 196–197 (Jurik Peter), 199br (Catmando), 200–201 (Ken Crawford), 202–203 (Valerio Pardi), 204–205 (Tragoolchitr Jittasaiyapan), 206–207 (Giovanni Benintende), 208–209 (Chuta Kooanantkul), 209br, 215tr (Morphart Creation), 210bl (dore art), 212br (Prachaya Roekdeethaweesab), 213tc (Everett Collection), 214–215 (Miguel Regalado), 214cl (Helioscribe), 219tr, 222br (German Vizulis), 221tr, 227br (Naci Yavuz), 222–223 (Yuriy Mazur), 223bc (LuckyVector), 232br (Natata), 236–237, 236br (Mechanik), 238br (Nerthuz), 240br (Sergii Syzonenko), 244br (Axel Monse), 248–249 (Evgeniyqw); **Springel et al.:** 184–185; **Wellcome Collection:** 216c (A Diethe), 217br (Joseph Brown); **Wikimedia Commons:** 105cr (Vokrug Sveta), 113bl (Micheltb), 116c (z2amiller), 120cr (Lemuel Francis Abbott/National Portrait Gallery, UK), 123r (Arecibo Observatory), 167tl (SpaceX), 170tr, 202c (Henryk Kowalewski), 209tl (Bartolomeu Velho), 211br (Albrecht Dürer), 229tl (Mysid), 229br (With thanks to Roger W Haworth), 231br (With thanks to Borderline Rebel), 244c (Dyor), 245tr (Reuben Barton), 248cl (Courtesy Inspiration4/Dr. Sian Proctor), 249tr (Giuseppe De Chiara [Archipeppe68]).

Back cover: tl (Shutterstock/Claudio Caridi), tr (NASA Kennedy Space Center/Ben Smegelsky), c (NASA), bl (Shutterstock/biletskiyevgeniy.com), br (Shutterstock/Catmando).

Front cover: tl (Shutterstock/Sergii Syzonenko), tr (Shutterstock/Yurij Omelchenko), cl (Shutterstock/Andrei Armiagov), c (Shutterstock/Andrei Armiagov), cr (Shutterstock/Paopano), bl (Shutterstock/Nerthuz), b (Shutterstock/frestyle images), br (Shutterstock/lexaarts)

ARCTURUS

This edition published in 2024 by Arcturus Publishing Limited
26/27 Bickels Yard, 151–153 Bermondsey Street,
London SE1 3HA

Copyright © Arcturus Holdings Limited

All rights reserved. No part of this publication may be reproduced, stored in a retrieval system, or transmitted, in any form or by any means, electronic, mechanical, photocopying, recording or otherwise, without prior written permission in accordance with the provisions of the Copyright Act 1956 (as amended). Any person or persons who do any unauthorised act in relation to this publication may be liable to criminal prosecution and civil claims for damages.

ISBN: 978-1-3988-3690-7
CH010986US
Supplier 29, Date 1123, PI 00004801

Printed in China

Authors: Claudia Martin and Giles Sparrow
Designers: Lorraine Inglis and Amy McSimpson
Consultant: Dr. Helen Giles
Editor: Becca Clunes
Design manager: Jessica Holliland
Managing editor: Joe Harris

A note on large numbers:

1 million	1,000,000
1 billion	1,000,000,000
1 trillion	1,000,000,000,000
1 quadrillion	1,000,000,000,000,000
1 quintillion	1,000,000,000,000,000,000
1 sextillion	1,000,000,000,000,000,000,000
1 septillion	1,000,000,000,000,000,000,000,000

Contents

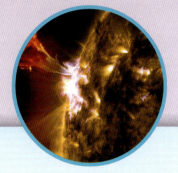

INTRODUCTION	6

CHAPTER 1:
The Solar System — 8
BIRTH OF THE SOLAR SYSTEM	10
OUR STAR	12
THE SUN'S STRUCTURE	14
SOLAR RADIATION	16
THE SOLAR CYCLE	18
SOLAR ECLIPSES	20
THE HELIOSPHERE	22
DEATH OF THE SUN	24

CHAPTER 2:
Earth and the Moon — 26
EARTH'S STRUCTURE	28
CHANGING PLANET	30
EARTH'S ORBIT	32
THE ATMOSPHERE	34
AURORAS	36
LIGHTS IN THE SKY	38
THE MOON	40
CRATERS AND SEAS	42
TIDES	44
WATCHING THE MOON	46

CHAPTER 3:
The Inner Planets — 48
MERCURY	50
MERCURIAN SURFACE	52
VENUS	54
VENUSIAN ATMOSPHERE	56
VENUSIAN VOLCANOES	58
MARS	60
WATER ON MARS	62
MARTIAN CANYONS	64
PHOBOS AND DEIMOS	66

CHAPTER 4:
The Outer Planets — 68
JUPITER	70
MOONS OF JUPITER	72
SATURN	74
RINGS OF SATURN	76
MOONS OF SATURN	78
URANUS	80
MOONS OF URANUS	82
NEPTUNE	84
MOONS OF NEPTUNE	86

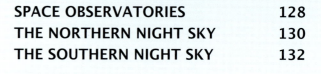

SPACE OBSERVATORIES	128
THE NORTHERN NIGHT SKY	130
THE SOUTHERN NIGHT SKY	132

CHAPTER 5:
Other Solar System Objects — 88
ASTEROID BELT	90
CERES	92
KUIPER BELT	94
PLUTO	96
SCATTERED DISK	98
COMETS	100
METEOR SHOWERS	102
METEORITE IMPACTS	104
NEAR-EARTH OBJECTS	106
FARTHEST REGIONS	108

CHAPTER 6:
Astronomy — 110
EARLY IDEAS	112
TELESCOPES	114
GIANT TELESCOPES	116
THE ELECTROMAGNETIC SPECTRUM	118
INFRARED TELESCOPES	120
RADIO ASTRONOMY	122
SPECIAL RAYS	124
HUBBLE SPACE TELESCOPE	126

CHAPTER 7:
Exploring the Universe — 134
ROCKETS	136
SPACE RACE	138
SPACE SHUTTLES	140
LAUNCHPADS	142
ASTRONAUT TRAINING	144
EARLY SPACE STATIONS	146
INTERNATIONAL SPACE STATION	148
SATELLITES	150
LANDING ON THE MOON	152
STUDYING THE SUN	154
MISSIONS TO MARS	156
MAPPING THE INFERIOR PLANETS	158
WATCHING THE GIANT PLANETS	160
DISTANT MOONS	162
SMALL OBJECTS	164
THE FUTURE	166

CHAPTER 8:
The Universe — 168
BIG BANG	170
EXPANDING UNIVERSE	172
GALAXIES	174
CRASHING GALAXIES	176
MILKY WAY	178

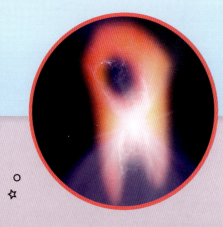

NEARBY GALAXIES	180
ACTIVE GALAXIES	182
DARK MATTER	184
ALIEN LIFE	186

CHAPTER 9:
Stars — 188
TYPES OF STAR	190
STAR BIRTH	192
STAR DEATH	194
NEUTRON STARS	196
BLACK HOLES	198
INTERSTELLAR SPACE	200
STAR GROUPS	202
GLOBULAR CLUSTERS	204
EXOPLANETS	206

CHAPTER 10:
Astronomers — 208
ABD AL-RAHMAN AL-SUFI	210
GALILEO GALILEI	212
ISAAC NEWTON	214
CAROLINE HERSCHEL	216
ANNIE JUMP CANNON	218
ALBERT EINSTEIN	220
EDWIN HUBBLE	222

KATHERINE JOHNSON	224
STEPHEN HAWKING	226
JOCELYN BELL BURNELL	228
ANDREA GHEZ	230

CHAPTER 11:
Astronauts — 232
ALAN SHEPARD	234
VALENTINA TERESHKOVA	236
NEIL ARMSTRONG	238
SALLY RIDE	240
MAE JEMISON	242
YANG LIWEI	244
PEGGY WHITSON	246
SIAN PROCTOR	248

GLOSSARY	250
INDEX	254

Introduction

Our Universe is a huge area of space made up of everything we can see in every direction. It contains a great number of different types of objects, from tiny specks of cosmic dust to mighty galaxy superclusters. Some of the most amazing of these objects are planets, stars and nebulae, galaxies, and clusters of galaxies.

Stars

A star is a dense (tightly packed) ball of gas that shines through chemical reactions in its core (middle). Our Sun is a star. Stars range from red dwarfs much smaller and fainter than the Sun, to supergiants a hundred times larger and a million times brighter.

Planets

A planet is a large ball of rock or gas that orbits (travels around) a star. In our Solar System there are eight "major" planets, several dwarf planets, and countless smaller objects. These range from asteroids and comets down to tiny specks of dust.

Nebulae

The space between stars is filled with mostly unseen clouds of gas and dust called nebulae. Where they collapse (fall in) and grow dense enough to form new stars, they light up from within.

Galaxies

A galaxy is a huge cloud of stars, gas, and dust, including nebulae, held together by a force called gravity. There are many different types of galaxy. This is because their shape, the nature of their stars, and the amount of gas and dust within them can vary.

This is our home galaxy, the Milky Way, seen from Earth. Our view of the Universe depends on what we can see using the best technologies that we have.

Galaxy Clusters

Gravity makes galaxies bunch together to form clusters that are millions of light-years wide. These clusters join together to form even bigger superclusters, which are the largest structures in the Universe.

Chapter 1

The Solar System

Eight planets, several smaller dwarf planets, and countless even smaller rocky, metal, and icy objects are orbiting (revolving around) the Sun. Six of the planets—as well as many dwarf planets and smaller objects—are themselves orbited by objects known as moons.

The Pull of Gravity

Gravity is a force that pulls all objects toward each other. The more massive the object, the stronger the pull of its gravity. The Sun's mass (weight) makes up 99.8 percent of the Solar System's mass. Its gravity is so immense that it holds the other Solar System objects in orbit.

> The planets and most other Solar System objects travel in the same direction that the Sun is rotating: counterclockwise (anticlockwise) as seen from above Earth's north pole.

Uranus

> The eight planets travel in roughly circular paths around the Sun's equator, all moving in the same plane, since they all formed from the same spinning disk of gas and dust.

English scientist Isaac Newton (1643-1727) figured out that the force that makes an apple fall from its branch to Earth is the same force that keeps the planets in their orbits.

8   **DID YOU KNOW?** The Sun's gravity is 28 times more powerful than Earth's gravity, so if you could stand on the Sun's surface, you would feel 28 times heavier than on Earth.

Planets, Dwarfs, and Moons

A planet is a large, rounded space object that orbits a star. Unlike a star, a planet does not produce its own light. A planet is massive enough for its gravity to have pulled it into a ball. Its gravity is also strong enough to clear other large objects out of its orbit. A dwarf planet orbits a star and is massive enough to be rounded, but it is not massive enough to clear its orbit. A moon may be bigger than a dwarf planet or even a planet, but it orbits a planet rather than a star.

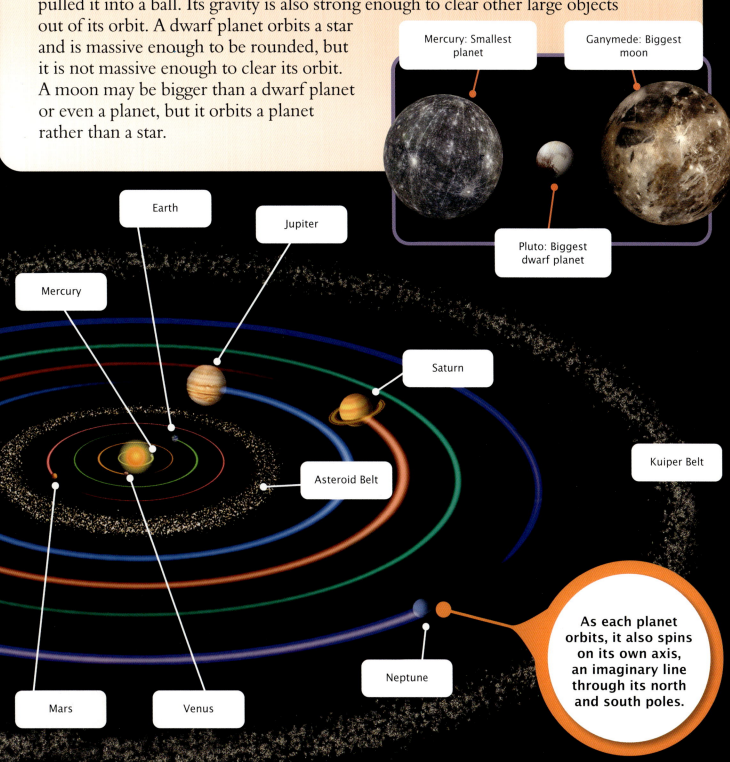

Mercury: Smallest planet

Ganymede: Biggest moon

Pluto: Biggest dwarf planet

Earth

Jupiter

Mercury

Saturn

Kuiper Belt

Asteroid Belt

Neptune

Mars

Venus

As each planet orbits, it also spins on its own axis, an imaginary line through its north and south poles.

Birth of the Solar System

The Solar System is 4.6 billion years old. It started to form when a thick cloud of dust and gas was shaken by the explosion of a nearby star. The cloud collapsed, forming a clump that slowly became the Sun and its orbiting planets.

The Sun Forms

As the clump grew in the cloud of dust and hydrogen and helium gas, the clump's increasing mass increased the pull of its gravity. The clump pulled more material toward it, forming a spinning sphere of more and more tightly packed matter. Finally, the pressure in the core of the sphere was so great that hydrogen atoms started to smash together, combining to form helium atoms. This released an immense amount of energy, so the sphere began to give off light and heat—making it a star.

Jupiter formed around 1 million years after the Sun, about 100 million years before Earth.

The Sun probably formed in a cloud such as this one, which is about 2 light-years long and 8,500 light-years from Earth.

SOLAR SYSTEM PROFILE

Diameter: Around 26.9 billion km (16.7 billion miles)
Mass: 333,466 Earths
Age: 4.6 billion years
Planets: 8 known
Dwarf planets: 9 known
Moons: At least 285 orbiting major planets

The Planets Form

A spinning disk of material, known as a protoplanetary disk, surrounded the brand-new star. Material in this disk began to clump together. Some clumps grew large enough for their own gravity to pull them into spheres, forming the planets, dwarf planets, and large moons.

The Sun started to glow around 10 million years after the cloud collapse that set off the Solar System's formation.

The protoplanetary disk around the young Sun spun counterclockwise (anticlockwise), the same direction in which the planets orbit today.

KEY

1. The newly formed Sun is surrounded by a protoplanetary disk.
2. Gaps form in the disk as protoplanets (clumps that are developing into planets) start to sweep up the dust and gas around them.
3. The protoplanets continue to grow as they clear the areas around their orbits.
4. The planets are fully formed, while smaller, leftover pieces become asteroids, comets, and small moons.

DID YOU KNOW? Several other stars formed in the same cloud as the Sun, but these sister stars drifted apart and are scattered through the Milky Way.

Our Star

The Sun is a middle-sized, middle-aged star. In every second, 600 million tons of hydrogen are fused into helium in the Sun's core, a process that changes 4 million tons of matter into energy. This energy, which we see as light and feel as heat, is the key source of energy for life on Earth.

A Ball of Plasma

Like all stars, the Sun is a ball of super-hot plasma. Plasma is one of the four forms that matter can take: solid, liquid, gas, and plasma. A material can move through these states as it gets hotter. For example, water changes from a solid (ice) to liquid (water) to gas (water vapor) as its atoms gain energy and start moving faster and more freely. Plasma is rare on Earth but common in the Universe. In a plasma, the atoms are so hot that they break apart, losing some of their electrons (see page 170). This makes a plasma electrically charged.

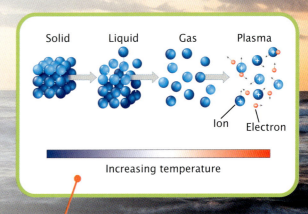

Electrons have a negative electric charge while protons have a positive electric charge. When atoms break apart in a plasma, the remaining portion of the atom, called an ion, has more protons than electrons, so it has a positive charge.

A Yellow Dwarf

The Sun is a type of star called a yellow dwarf. "Dwarf" tells us these stars are small compared to the largest stars, such as Betelgeuse, which is 764 times wider than the Sun. "Yellow" tells us that this type of star tends to shine with a yellow light because it is, for a star, medium hot. Hotter stars shine blue, while cooler stars shine red. However, brighter yellow dwarfs, including the Sun, actually shine white.

Despite being called a yellow dwarf, the Sun emits white light, as shown in this true image.

Around 73 percent of the Sun's mass is hydrogen, 25 percent is helium, and the rest includes oxygen, carbon, neon, and iron.

Never look directly at the Sun as its brightness can cause serious eye damage or even blindness.

From Earth, we are used to seeing the Sun and surrounding sky look yellow, orange, or red due to Earth's atmosphere scattering the Sun's white light so it appears yellower (see pages 16–17).

SUN PROFILE

Diameter: 1.39 million km (865,000 miles)
Mass: 332,950 Earths
Orbit around middle of Milky Way: Around 226 million years
Orbital speed: Around 864,000 km/h (536,865 miles per hour)
Rotation: Around 25 days
Rotation speed: Around 7,190 km/h (4,468 miles per hour)

DID YOU KNOW? The brightness of the Sun is equal to more than 4 septillion (4 followed by 24 zeros) household light bulbs.

The Sun's Structure

The Sun's core is where hydrogen is converted to helium, releasing energy in the form of tiny particles called photons. These packets of energy travel outward through the Sun's layers, before finally escaping into space from the star's surface, known as the photosphere.

Journey Through the Layers

From the core, photons must first travel through the Sun's radiation zone by a process called radiation: they bounce from atom to atom, losing a little energy with every bounce. It takes about 170,000 years for a photon to reach the Sun's next layer, the convection zone. Here, in the cooler, less-dense plasma, photons are carried by a process called convection: Like boiling water in a pan, hot bubbles of photon-carrying plasma rise to the photosphere. Finally, photons—which we see as light and feel as heat—stream into space.

This photo shows the photosphere's grainy appearance, which is caused by rising currents of plasma in the convection zone below. Each granule is up to 1,500 km (930 miles) across and lasts up to 20 minutes.

Captured using special instruments, this photo shows the Sun's corona extending far into space around the star.

Above the Surface

The Sun does not have a solid surface, but below the photosphere it is opaque (not see-through), making the photosphere the star's visible surface. Above the photosphere are layers of gas known as the chromosphere and corona. These layers of atmosphere are usually hidden by the brightness of the Sun's surface. Astronomers are not sure why, but the outer layer, the corona, is much hotter—at up to 1 million °C (1.8 million °F)—than the chromosphere, which is as cool as 3,500 °C (6,300 °F).

PHOTON PROFILE

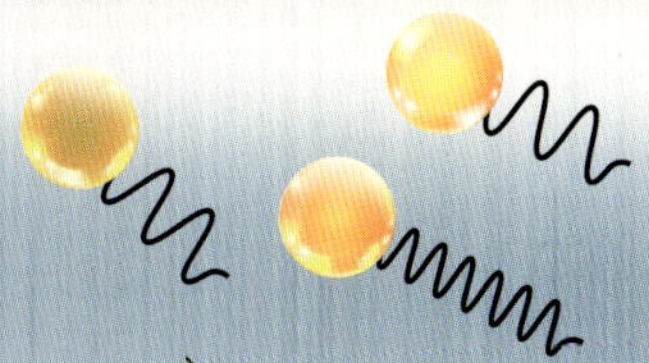

Diameter: Infinitely small
Mass: 0
Speed in empty space: 299,792,458 m/s (983,571,056 ft per second)
Lifetime: At least 1 quintillion (1 followed by 18 zeros) years
Number emitted by the Sun: At least 1 quattuordecillion (1 followed by 45 zeros) per second

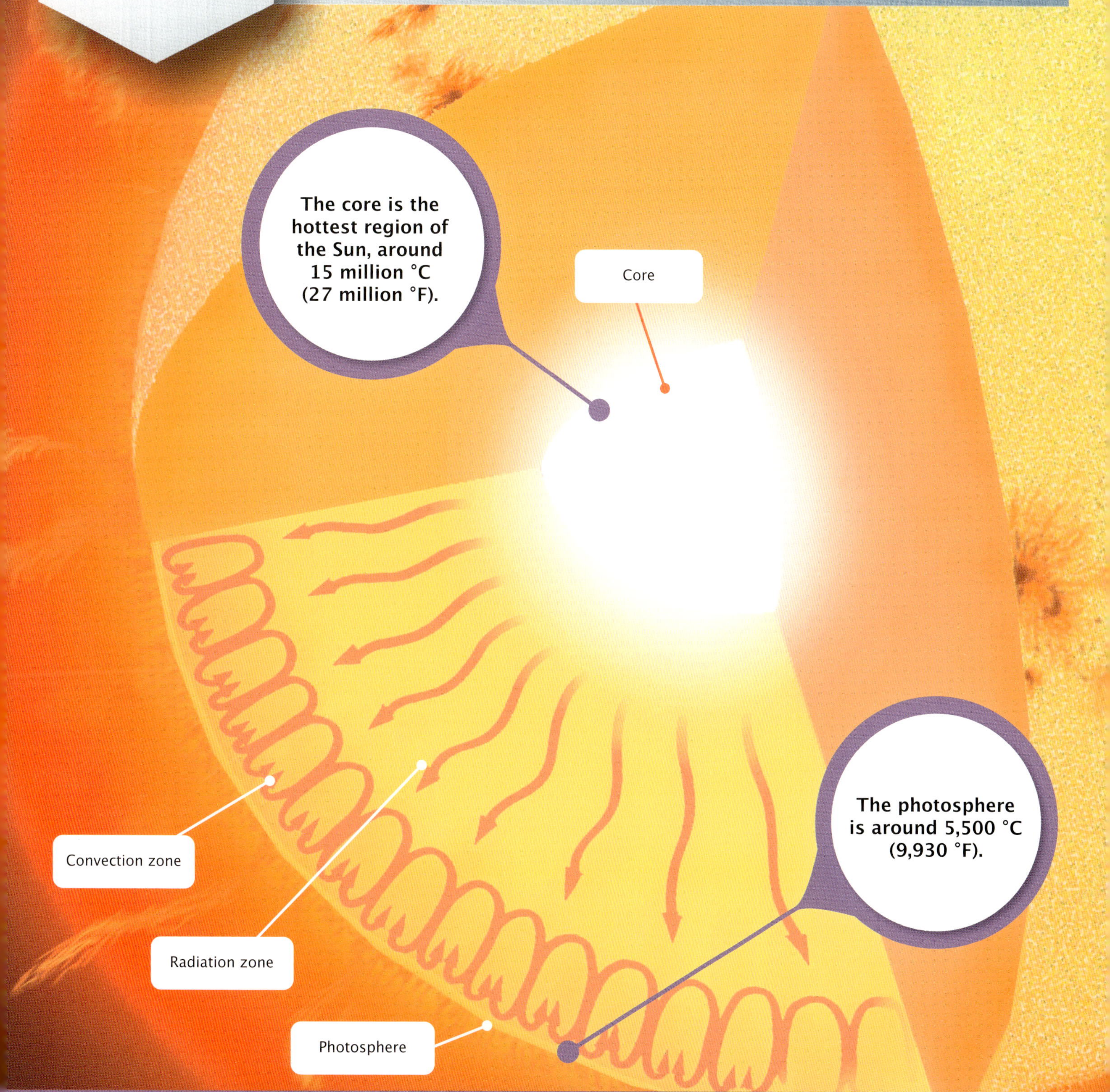

The core is the hottest region of the Sun, around 15 million °C (27 million °F).

Core

The photosphere is around 5,500 °C (9,930 °F).

Convection zone

Radiation zone

Photosphere

DID YOU KNOW? It takes 8 minutes for a photon to travel the 150 million km (93 million miles) from the Sun to Earth.

Solar Radiation

Solar radiation is the energy emitted by the Sun. The energy is emitted as photons, which travel in the form of waves. Different photons carry different amounts of energy and have different wavelengths: the distances between the crest of one wave and the next. Some wavelengths are visible to humans as light, but others are invisible.

The Electromagnetic Spectrum

The range of energy released by the Sun is known as the electromagnetic spectrum. At one end of the spectrum are low-energy photons, which have long wavelengths. At the opposite end are high-energy photons, which have short wavelengths.

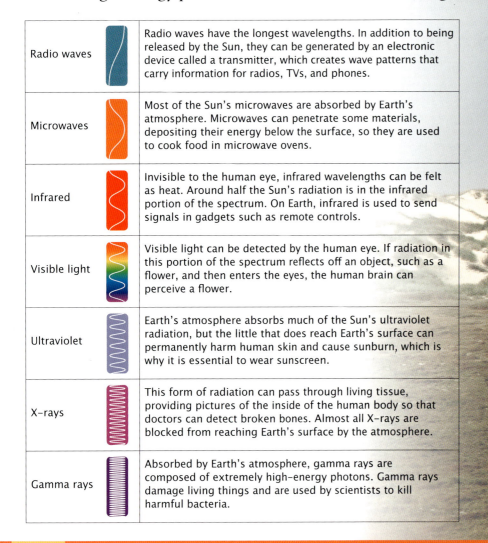

Sunlight usually looks white, but it is a mixture of all the shades of the rainbow.

When sunlight passes through raindrops, each wavelength of visible light is bent at a different angle, resulting in its separation into a rainbow.

Radio waves		Radio waves have the longest wavelengths. In addition to being released by the Sun, they can be generated by an electronic device called a transmitter, which creates wave patterns that carry information for radios, TVs, and phones.
Microwaves		Most of the Sun's microwaves are absorbed by Earth's atmosphere. Microwaves can penetrate some materials, depositing their energy below the surface, so they are used to cook food in microwave ovens.
Infrared		Invisible to the human eye, infrared wavelengths can be felt as heat. Around half the Sun's radiation is in the infrared portion of the spectrum. On Earth, infrared is used to send signals in gadgets such as remote controls.
Visible light		Visible light can be detected by the human eye. If radiation in this portion of the spectrum reflects off an object, such as a flower, and then enters the eyes, the human brain can perceive a flower.
Ultraviolet		Earth's atmosphere absorbs much of the Sun's ultraviolet radiation, but the little that does reach Earth's surface can permanently harm human skin and cause sunburn, which is why it is essential to wear sunscreen.
X-rays		This form of radiation can pass through living tissue, providing pictures of the inside of the human body so that doctors can detect broken bones. Almost all X-rays are blocked from reaching Earth's surface by the atmosphere.
Gamma rays		Absorbed by Earth's atmosphere, gamma rays are composed of extremely high-energy photons. Gamma rays damage living things and are used by scientists to kill harmful bacteria.

DID YOU KNOW? Most solar radiation is in the infrared, visible light, and ultraviolet parts of the electromagnetic spectrum.

Visible Light

The main source of visible light on Earth is the Sun, but it is also emitted by electric lights and flames. Visible light looks white, but it is made up of all the shades of the rainbow. Each shade has a different wavelength. Visible light can pass through some materials, such as glass and water, but not others. When light hits an opaque object, some wavelengths are absorbed and some are reflected. When we see an object of a particular shade, that wavelength of light is being reflected and the others are being absorbed.

A green object absorbs all wavelengths except green, which it reflects into human eyes.

A black object absorbs all wavelengths, so human eyes see it as black.

A white object reflects all wavelengths into human eyes, which see it as white.

SOLAR RADIATION WAVELENGTHS

Radio waves: 100,000 km to 1 m (62,000 miles to 3.3 ft)
Microwaves: 1 m to 1 mm (3.3 ft to 0.039 in)
Infrared: 1 to 0.00075 mm (0.039 to 0.00003 in)
Visible light: 0.00075 to 0.00038 mm (0.00003 to 0.000015 in)
Ultraviolet: 0.00038 to 0.000001 mm (0.000015 to 0.00000004 in)
X-rays: 0.000001 to 0.000000001 mm (0.00000004 to 0.00000000004 in)
Gamma rays: Less than 0.000000001 mm (0.00000000004 in)

The Solar Cycle

The Sun's appearance is not uniform or unchanging: With the help of special equipment, features such as sunspots, flares, and loops can be observed. These features are caused by the Sun's magnetic activity, which changes over an 11-year period known as the solar cycle.

This photograph of the Sun was taken by the Solar Dynamics Observatory, an Earth-orbiting satellite.

The Sun's Magnetic Fields

Magnetism is a force caused by the movement of electric charges. Since the Sun's plasma is electrically charged (see page 12), its movement creates powerful magnetism known as magnetic fields. As plasma rises and falls, the Sun's magnetic fields twist and tangle, creating eruptions of plasma and energy at the surface. Over an 11-year period, this activity peaks then dies away, as the magnetic fields smooth out again.

Magnetic fields attract or repel magnets, as well as affecting the movement of electrically charged particles, such as those in plasma.

SOLAR CYCLE 25

The 25th cycle since 1755, when monitoring began

Cycle began (last solar minimum): December 2019
Cycle ends (next solar minimum): Around 2030
Solar maximum: Around 2025
Estimated number of sunspots at solar maximum: Around 150 at one time

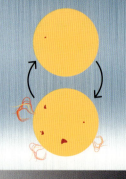

DID YOU KNOW? In 1859, an intense coronal mass ejection started electrical fires on Earth and caused intensely bright lights in Earth's atmosphere, known as auroras.

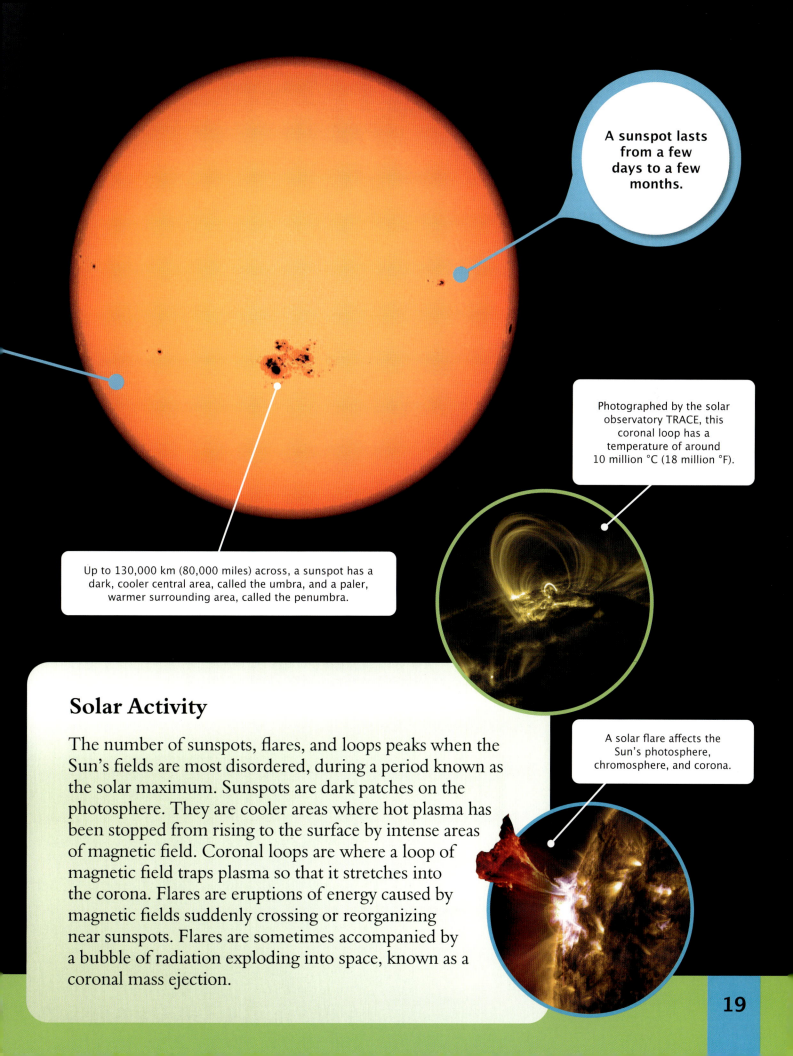

A sunspot lasts from a few days to a few months.

Up to 130,000 km (80,000 miles) across, a sunspot has a dark, cooler central area, called the umbra, and a paler, warmer surrounding area, called the penumbra.

Photographed by the solar observatory TRACE, this coronal loop has a temperature of around 10 million °C (18 million °F).

A solar flare affects the Sun's photosphere, chromosphere, and corona.

Solar Activity

The number of sunspots, flares, and loops peaks when the Sun's fields are most disordered, during a period known as the solar maximum. Sunspots are dark patches on the photosphere. They are cooler areas where hot plasma has been stopped from rising to the surface by intense areas of magnetic field. Coronal loops are where a loop of magnetic field traps plasma so that it stretches into the corona. Flares are eruptions of energy caused by magnetic fields suddenly crossing or reorganizing near sunspots. Flares are sometimes accompanied by a bubble of radiation exploding into space, known as a coronal mass ejection.

Solar Eclipses

A solar eclipse is when, as the Moon passes between Earth and the Sun, it partly or totally blocks the view of our star from a region of Earth's surface. Special eye protection or viewing equipment is essential when watching an eclipse to prevent permanent eye damage.

During a total solar eclipse, the sky darkens, the temperature falls, and birds may stop singing because they believe it is night-time.

Partial or Total

As the Moon orbits Earth, it passes between the Sun and Earth once every 27.3 days. Yet a total eclipse can be seen somewhere on Earth only every 18 months on average. This is because the Moon's orbit around Earth is tilted around 5 degrees away from Earth's orbit around the Sun, so the Moon does not frequently line up exactly with the Sun and Earth. In addition, the Moon's orbit is not exactly circular so—even when the Moon does line up—it may be too far from Earth to block the Sun's face entirely.

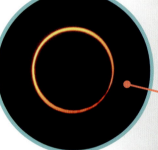

An annular solar eclipse is when the Moon lines up between the Sun and Earth but is too far away to cover the Sun's disk completely. Annular eclipses are about as common as total eclipses.

A partial solar eclipse is when the Moon partly covers the Sun's disk. Partial eclipses are a little more common than total eclipses.

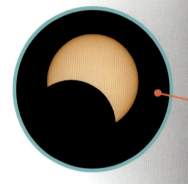

This photograph was taken the last time Venus transited the Sun, in 2012.

Transits

A transit of the Sun is when one of the planets that is closer to the star than Earth—Mercury and Venus—appears to cross its disk. The more distant planets cannot pass between Earth and the Sun. Mercury transits 13 or 14 times every century, always in May or November. The next Mercury transit will be in November 2032. Venus transits much more rarely, with the next taking place in 2117.

20

When the Sun's photosphere is completely covered, the glowing corona can be seen.

A total solar eclipse is visible from a narrow band across Earth's surface that falls in the path of the Moon's full shadow.

SOLAR ECLIPSES OF 21st CENTURY

Number: 224 (77 partial, 73 annular, 68 total, and 6 a combination of total and annular)
Most eclipses in a year: 4 (in 2011, 2029, 2047, 2065, 2076, and 2094)
Longest possible duration of a total eclipse at any location: 7 minutes 32 seconds
Only year with 2 total eclipses: 2057

Total eclipse
Partial eclipse

DID YOU KNOW? A particular town or city on Earth's surface is likely to experience a total solar eclipse only once every 360 to 410 years.

The Heliosphere

The heliosphere is a bubble-like region of space that surrounds the Sun, stretching far beyond the outermost orbiting planet. The heliosphere is filled by the solar wind, a stream of electrically charged particles that flows constantly from the Sun's corona.

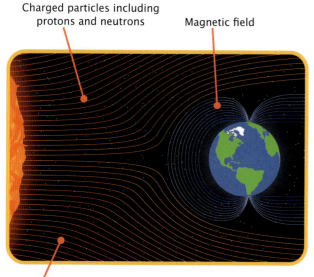

Earth's magnetic field makes most of the solar wind's high-energy particles flow around and beyond our planet.

The Solar Wind

The solar wind blows a bubble—also containing dust and hydrogen—in the interstellar medium, which is the matter that fills the space between the solar systems of a galaxy. The interstellar medium is composed of gas (mostly hydrogen and helium), dust, and high-energy particles. Earth is protected from the solar wind by its magnetic field (see pages 36–37).

Regions of the Heliosphere

The inner region of the heliosphere is where the solar wind blows fastest. This region ends at the termination shock. Beyond the termination shock is the heliosheath, an outer, stormy region of the heliosphere where the solar wind is buffeted by winds from outer space. The outer edge of the heliosphere is known as the heliopause. This is where the solar wind is no longer strong enough to push back the interstellar medium. Many astronomers define the heliopause as the edge of the Solar System.

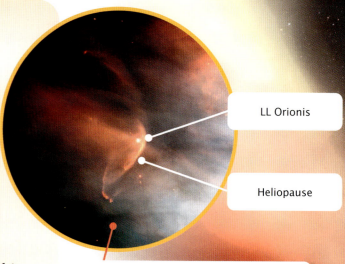

The Hubble Space Telescope took this photograph of the heliosphere of the star LL Orionis, which is believed to have a similar structure to the Sun's.

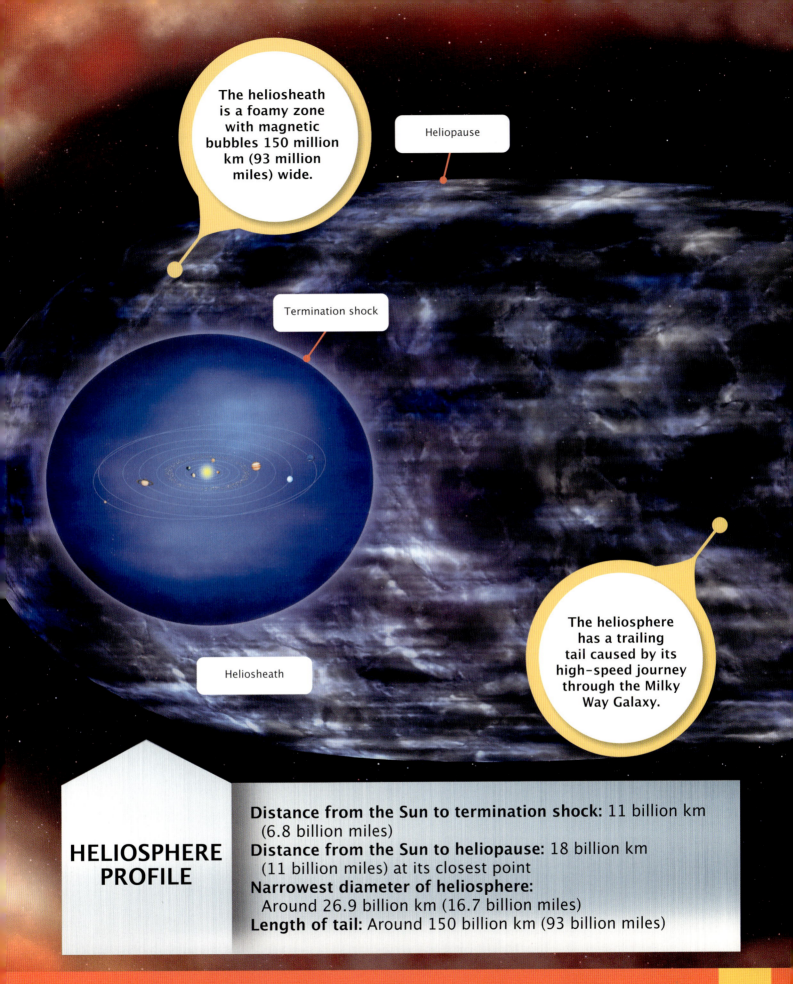

The heliosheath is a foamy zone with magnetic bubbles 150 million km (93 million miles) wide.

Heliopause

Termination shock

Heliosheath

The heliosphere has a trailing tail caused by its high-speed journey through the Milky Way Galaxy.

HELIOSPHERE PROFILE

Distance from the Sun to termination shock: 11 billion km (6.8 billion miles)
Distance from the Sun to heliopause: 18 billion km (11 billion miles) at its closest point
Narrowest diameter of heliosphere: Around 26.9 billion km (16.7 billion miles)
Length of tail: Around 150 billion km (93 billion miles)

DID YOU KNOW? In the region of Earth, the solar wind travels at between 250 and 750 km/s (155 and 465 miles per second).

Death of the Sun

In around 6 billion years, the Sun will throw out a cloud of hot gas known as a planetary nebula.

Like all stars, the Sun was born and will die. In around 5 billion years, the Sun will run out of the fuel that makes it glow: hydrogen. The Sun will start to die, destroying Earth and the other Solar System planets.

A Slow Death

After the Sun runs out of hydrogen, its outer layers will expand, turning the Sun into a red giant star around 110 million km (70 million miles) across. This will destroy Mercury and Venus—and bake Earth. For around 1 billion years, the red giant Sun will use its helium as fuel. When that runs out, the Sun will shed its outer layers, making a glowing cloud of gas and dust known as a planetary nebula. A dense core of material, known as a white dwarf, will be left behind. Over trillions of years, the white dwarf will probably cool and fade into a black dwarf.

The Sun will eventually fade into a black dwarf, which will emit no heat or light. It takes so long to become a black dwarf that there are none yet in existence in the Universe.

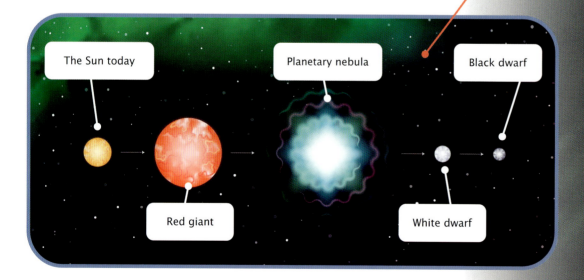

The Sun today → Red giant → Planetary nebula → White dwarf → Black dwarf

DID YOU KNOW? The most massive stars use up their fuel within a few hundreds of millions of years, but the smallest stars could survive hundreds of billions of years.

Although it will no longer be producing energy from its fuel, the dying Sun will still be around 100,000 °C (180,000 °F).

The Solar System's remaining planets will be destroyed, with Neptune boiling away perhaps a few hundred million years after Earth has been obliterated.

A black hole is a region where so much mass is squeezed into so little space that its gravity deforms space. If anything comes too near a black hole, it is pulled inside.

Different Deaths

If stars are between 0.3 and 8 times the Sun's mass, they die in the same manner as our star. Smaller stars shrink straight into white dwarfs when they use up their hydrogen. When a larger star runs out of fuel, its core collapses, throwing out energy in an explosion known as a supernova. A supernova leaves behind a tiny, very dense neutron star or—in the case of stars more than 20 times the mass of the Sun—a black hole.

25

Chapter 2

Earth and the Moon

This photo of Earth and the Moon was taken from the Apollo 11 spacecraft in July 1969, shortly before its astronauts became the first humans to land on the Moon.

The planet we call home is the third planet from the Sun. Earth formed around 4.54 billion years ago in the gas and dust spinning around the young Sun. Earth's companion, the Moon, has been orbiting our planet for around the past 4.51 billion years.

Formation of Earth and the Moon

Earth formed when gas and dust clumped together. As the clump grew, its gravity pulled in more material, making a ball of mixed rock and metal. The ball was so hot the metal melted and—being denser than the rock—sank to the new planet's core. Within the next few million years, astronomers think Earth was hit by a smaller planet. The impact threw out rubble that, pulled both by Earth's gravity and its own, formed a sphere: the Moon. After this impact, the molten Earth released gases, creating an atmosphere.

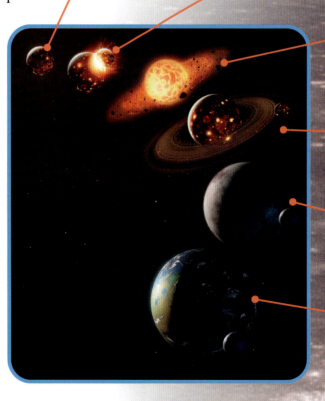

Earth is a molten ball of rock and metal.

Earth is hit by a smaller planet, which astronomers call Theia.

The impact melts Earth and throws out rubble.

The rubble is pulled into a sphere, the Moon.

An atmosphere forms around Earth.

As Earth cools, clouds form in the atmosphere, and—by around 4.4 billion years ago—rain fills the oceans.

DID YOU KNOW? At 27 percent of Earth's size, the Moon is larger compared to its host planet than any other moon in the Solar System.

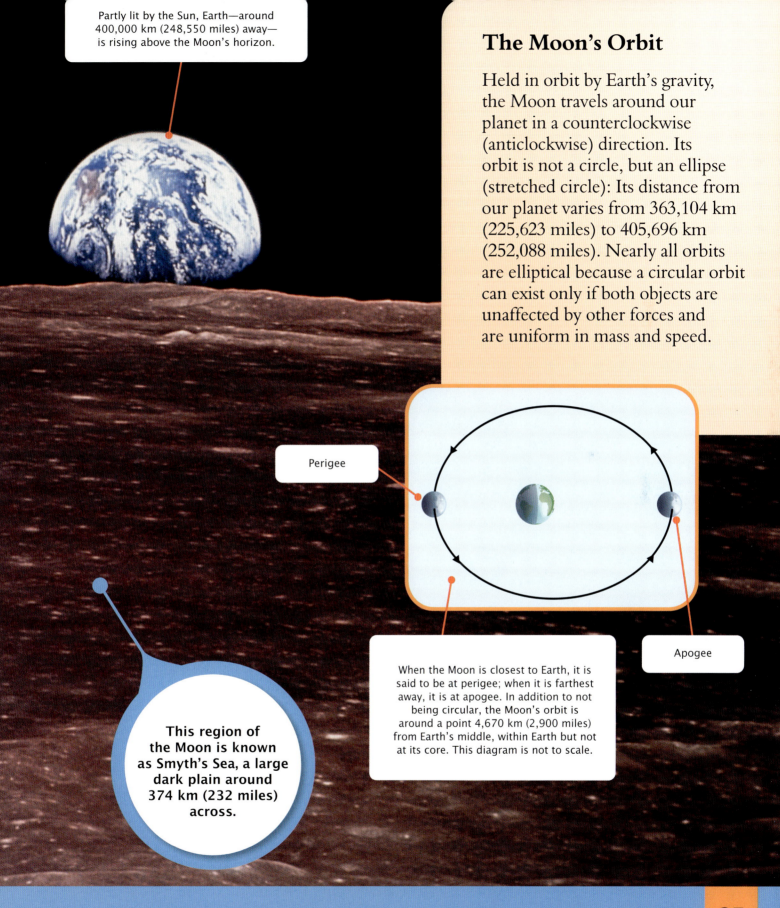

Partly lit by the Sun, Earth—around 400,000 km (248,550 miles) away—is rising above the Moon's horizon.

The Moon's Orbit

Held in orbit by Earth's gravity, the Moon travels around our planet in a counterclockwise (anticlockwise) direction. Its orbit is not a circle, but an ellipse (stretched circle): Its distance from our planet varies from 363,104 km (225,623 miles) to 405,696 km (252,088 miles). Nearly all orbits are elliptical because a circular orbit can exist only if both objects are unaffected by other forces and are uniform in mass and speed.

Perigee

Apogee

When the Moon is closest to Earth, it is said to be at perigee; when it is farthest away, it is at apogee. In addition to not being circular, the Moon's orbit is around a point 4,670 km (2,900 miles) from Earth's middle, within Earth but not at its core. This diagram is not to scale.

This region of the Moon is known as Smyth's Sea, a large dark plain around 374 km (232 miles) across.

Earth's Structure

Earth has four layers: its inner core, outer core, mantle, and crust. The crust, made of rock, is cool enough for animals and plants to live on. The inner core, made of metal, is around 5,400 °C (9,700 °F), which is about as hot as the surface of the Sun.

Under the oceans, Earth's crust—known as the oceanic crust—is only 5 to 10 km (3 to 6 miles) thick.

Earth's Layers

Earth's inner and outer core are made mostly of super-hot iron and nickel. Much of the core's heat is left over from the planet's violent formation. In the outer core, the metal is so hot it is liquid. In the inner core, the metal is squeezed so tightly it is solid. The mantle is made of rock as hot as 3,700 °C (6,690 °F). In places, the rock in the mantle melts, when it is known as magma. The mantle flows very slowly as currents of hot rock rise. Earth's solid rock crust has an average surface temperature of 14 °C (57 °F).

Inner core: Depth of 5,150 to 6,378 km (3,200 to 3,963 miles)

Outer core: Depth of 2,890 to 5,150 km (1,795 to 3,200 miles)

Mantle: Depth of 70 to 2,890 km (45 to 1,795 miles)

Crust: Depth of 0 to 70 km (0 to 45 miles)

EARTH PROFILE

Diameter: 12,756 km (7,926 miles)
Mass: 0.000003 Suns
Average distance from the Sun: 149.6 million km (92.9 million miles)
Orbit: 365.25 days
Rotation: 23.93 hours
Moons: 1

DID YOU KNOW? The distance around Earth's equator (an imaginary line dividing it into northern and southern halves) is 40,075 km (24,901 miles).

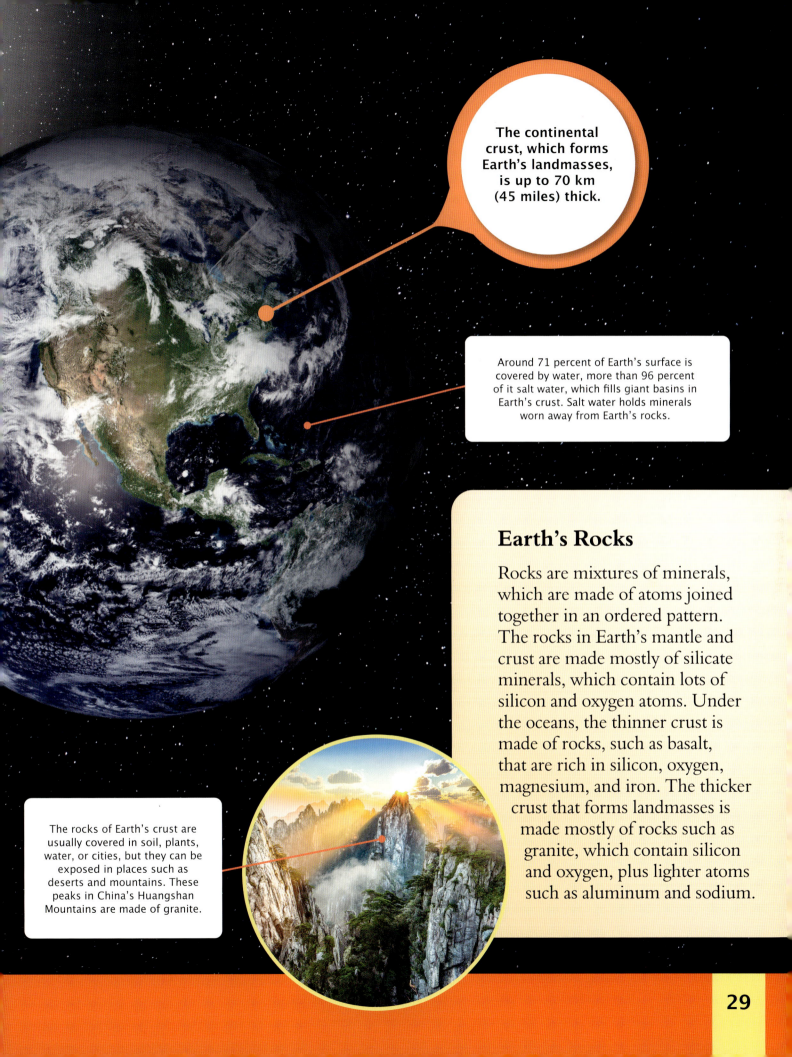

The continental crust, which forms Earth's landmasses, is up to 70 km (45 miles) thick.

Around 71 percent of Earth's surface is covered by water, more than 96 percent of it salt water, which fills giant basins in Earth's crust. Salt water holds minerals worn away from Earth's rocks.

Earth's Rocks

Rocks are mixtures of minerals, which are made of atoms joined together in an ordered pattern. The rocks in Earth's mantle and crust are made mostly of silicate minerals, which contain lots of silicon and oxygen atoms. Under the oceans, the thinner crust is made of rocks, such as basalt, that are rich in silicon, oxygen, magnesium, and iron. The thicker crust that forms landmasses is made mostly of rocks such as granite, which contain silicon and oxygen, plus lighter atoms such as aluminum and sodium.

The rocks of Earth's crust are usually covered in soil, plants, water, or cities, but they can be exposed in places such as deserts and mountains. These peaks in China's Huangshan Mountains are made of granite.

Changing Planet

Earth's crust, along with the top portion of the mantle, is broken into giant plates of rock, known as tectonic plates. These plates float on the slowly moving mantle below, causing changes to our planet's surface both very slowly—and very fast.

Changing Continents

Around 3 to 4 billion years ago, as Earth cooled, the crust and upper mantle cracked into seven large, major plates and many smaller, minor plates. On average, the plates move by 3 to 5 cm (1.2 to 2 in) a year. Yet, over millions and billions of years, plate movement has rearranged the continents, created new oceans, and—where plates are moving toward each other—pushed up mountain ranges as the rock crumpled and folded.

The volcano Tungurahua, in Ecuador, formed where the minor Nazca Plate is moving under the South American Plate.

225 million years ago

150 million years ago

66 million years ago

Around 225 million years ago, the continents were joined as one supercontinent called Pangaea. By 66 million years ago, when the dinosaurs became extinct, the continents were beginning to take the shape they have today.

MAJOR TECTONIC PLATES

Pacific: 103.3 million sq km (39.9 million sq miles)
North American: 75.9 million sq km (29.3 million sq miles)
Eurasian: 67.8 million sq km (26.2 million sq miles)
African: 61.3 million sq km (23.7 million sq miles)
Antarctic: 60.9 million sq km (23.5 million sq miles)
Australian: 47 million sq km (18 million sq miles)
South American: 43.6 million sq km (16.8 million sq miles)

Volcanoes and Earthquakes

Most volcanoes and earthquakes happen near the edges of tectonic plates. A volcano is a hole in the crust through which magma surges to the surface. An earthquake happens when two plates get stuck on each other as they move—then suddenly break free, shaking the ground.

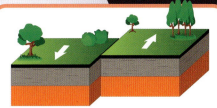

Where plates are moving past each other, known as a transform boundary, earthquakes can happen.

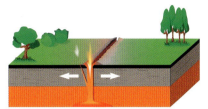

Where plates are moving apart, known as a divergent boundary, earthquakes can happen and magma wells up, forming volcanoes.

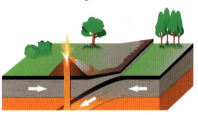

Where plates are moving toward each other, known as a convergent boundary, large earthquakes can happen and magma is forced to the surface, often forming lines of volcanoes.

When magma reaches Earth's surface, it is known as lava.

A volcano can grow into a mountain as lava from eruption after eruption cools and hardens into solid rock.

DID YOU KNOW? Earth's tallest mountain, Mt Everest, currently 8,849 m (29,032 ft), grows by 4 mm (0.16 in) a year due to the collision of the Indian and Eurasian Plates.

Earth's Orbit

Earth's elliptical, counterclockwise orbit round the Sun takes about 365.25 days. Every four years, we add an extra day to the calendar, February 29, so the calendar year—usually 365 days—keeps pace with Earth's orbit. Earth also rotates counterclockwise around its own axis, an imaginary line through its North and South Poles.

Seasons

Earth's axis is not at right angles to the plane of its orbit: It is tilted by 23.4 degrees. It is this axial tilt that causes seasons on Earth. When the northern hemisphere is tilted toward the Sun, it has summer, with hotter weather. At the same time, the southern hemisphere has winter.

In Sweden, in northern Europe, people celebrate the longest day of the year, known as the summer solstice, with traditional music.

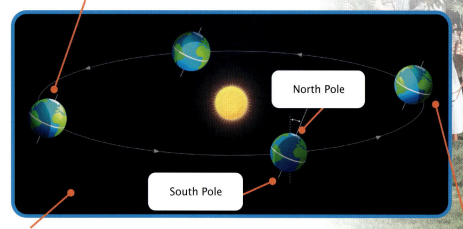

Summer in the northern hemisphere

North Pole

South Pole

Summer in the southern hemisphere

Astronomers think it may have been the collision with Theia (see page 26) that knocked Earth to one side, resulting in seasons.

EARTH'S ORBIT

Distance of one orbit: 942 million km (585 million miles)
Average orbital speed: 107,200 km/h (66,600 miles per hour)
Perihelion (shortest distance to the Sun): Around January 3
Perihelion distance: 147 million km (91.4 million miles)
Aphelion (farthest distance to the Sun): Around July 4
Aphelion distance: 152.1 million km (94.5 million miles)

The northern hemisphere has its summer solstice on June 20 or 21 and its winter solstice (shortest day) on December 21 or 22. In the southern hemisphere, these dates are reversed.

Night and Day

It takes Earth 23 hours and 56 minutes to rotate on its axis, but since Earth is also moving around the Sun, it takes 24 hours for the Sun to appear in the same position in the sky. When one side of Earth faces the Sun, it has day; the other side has night. Due to Earth's axial tilt, nowhere—apart from places near the equator—has 12 hours of day all year. When the northern hemisphere is tilted toward the Sun, it has longer days, while the southern hemisphere has longer nights. The North and South Poles have around 11 weeks of darkness during their winters.

To an observer on Earth, the Sun appears to travel on a curved path through the sky before "setting" below the horizon. In fact, the observer is moving along a curved path as Earth spins on its axis.

DID YOU KNOW? The equinoxes, around March 20 and September 23, are when the Sun is directly overhead at the equator and everywhere has around 12 hours of daylight.

Auroras

Lights, known as auroras, can be seen in the night sky around Earth's poles. They are caused by gases in the atmosphere being given energy by particles from the Sun. The particles are deflected toward Earth's poles by our planet's magnetic field.

A patchy, pulsating aurora is caused by high-energy particles being scattered into the atmosphere.

Earth's Magnetic Field

Magnetism is a force that can be made by the movement of electric current through magnetic metals, such as iron. All materials are made of atoms, which have tiny particles called electrons spinning around their core (see page 170). Electric current is a flow of electrons from atom to atom. As molten iron churns in Earth's outer core, its electrons flow, generating a magnetic field that extends far into space.

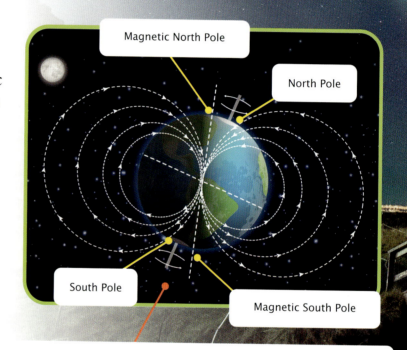

Earth is a giant magnet with—like all magnets—a north pole and a south pole. Magnetic force flows from one pole to the other, due to the coordinated movements of the electrons in Earth's outer core. Earth's magnetic poles are around 500 km (310 miles) from the north and south poles of its axis of rotation.

AURORAS

Green light: Given off by oxygen at heights of 100 to 300 km (60 to 185 miles)
Orange-red light: Given off by very excited oxygen at heights of 300 to 400 km (185 to 250 miles)
Pink, purple, and dark red light: Given off by nitrogen at heights of 80 to 100 km (50 to 60 miles)
Blue and purple light: Given off by hydrogen and helium but usually difficult to see against the night sky

DID YOU KNOW? Mercury is the only Solar System planet that does not experience auroras, as it does not have enough of an atmosphere to be excited by the solar wind.

Green is the most common shade of aurora, but pink to purple shades often fringe the lights' lower edges.

Auroras are best seen on cloudless, dark nights at a distance of between 500 and 2,500 km (300 and 1,550 miles) from the magnetic poles.

There are two main forms of aurora: arc (right) and patchy (above). An arc is caused by a band of high-energy particles entering the atmosphere, trapped between lines of magnetic force.

Making Light

Known as the magnetosphere, the magnetic field shields Earth from having its atmosphere stripped away by the solar wind, a stream of high-energy particles released by the Sun. Yet some of these particles reach Earth's atmosphere around the poles, where the magnetic field is weakest. The particles pass on energy to gases in the upper atmosphere, making them glow.

Lights in the Sky

Earth's atmosphere creates many other light effects that can be seen by day or night. They include rainbow-like haloes around the Sun and Moon and even glowing clouds.

Noctilucent clouds are clouds of ice crystals high in the sky that glow because they catch sunlight shortly after the Sun itself has set.

Icy Glows

In cold weather, ice in Earth's atmosphere can bend light in many different directions, creating circular haloes around the Sun or Moon. The same phenomenon can create bright "sundogs" in clouds to the left or right of the Sun.

Ice crystals in the air create a halo around the Moon.

Sundogs can form when ice crystals in the atmosphere are bending light (just as water drops create a rainbow).

Noctilucent clouds are visible only when the lower atmosphere is in Earth's shadow, but high clouds, in the mesosphere, are still in sunlight.

Noctilucent (meaning "night shining" in Latin) clouds are rare, but can sometimes be seen at twilight in summer.

The Zodiacal Light

One of the most beautiful sky effects is also the most difficult to see. The zodiacal light is a glow caused when dust in the solar system is reflecting sunlight. It stretches through the constellations of the zodiac where the planets are usually seen, but it is very faint and can only be spotted in the darkest, clearest skies.

DID YOU KNOW? Haloes could be seen around the Sun from Mars, Jupiter, Saturn, Uranus, and Neptune, due to water ice, ammonia, or methane crystals in the atmosphere.

The Moon

The Moon is a ball of rock and metal. Like Earth and the other planets, the Moon is not a perfect sphere but an oblate spheroid: a ball that bulges slightly at its equator due to its rotation—a little like a ball of dough flattening into a pizza as it is spun by a chef.

The Moon's Structure

For the Moon's first 100 million years it was molten. As it cooled, metal—mostly iron—sank to the core, while the least dense rocks floated to the surface. Like Earth, the Moon has an inner core of solid metal and an outer core of liquid metal. Since the Moon is much smaller than Earth, it cooled faster: The temperature of its inner core is only around 1,300 °C (2,370 °F). Around the core is a mantle of partly melted rock. The Moon's outer layer is a crust of solid rock.

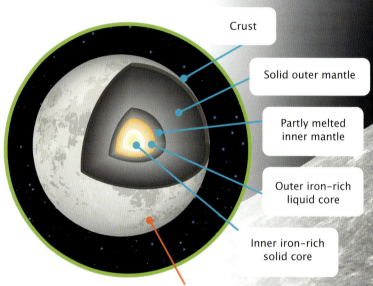

- Crust
- Solid outer mantle
- Partly melted inner mantle
- Outer iron-rich liquid core
- Inner iron-rich solid core

The Moon's outer core of liquid iron is too small and cool to generate more than a weak magnetic field.

Only One Side

From Earth, we can only see one side of the Moon, often called the "near side." This is because the Moon rotates in exactly the same time as it travels around Earth, resulting in it keeping nearly the same face turned toward our planet. This phenomenon is known as tidal locking. All the large moons in the Solar System are tidally locked with their planet. Moons that orbit close to their planet usually become tidally locked within 100 million years of their formation, as their rotation slows to match their orbit due to the pull of the planet's gravity.

The far side of the Moon, seen here in a photo taken by the space probe *Lunar Reconnaissance Orbiter*, has a thicker crust and fewer dark "seas" (see page 42) than the near side.

DID YOU KNOW? Since the Moon's mass is smaller than Earth's, its surface gravity is one-sixth of Earth's—so astronauts can jump much higher on the Moon.

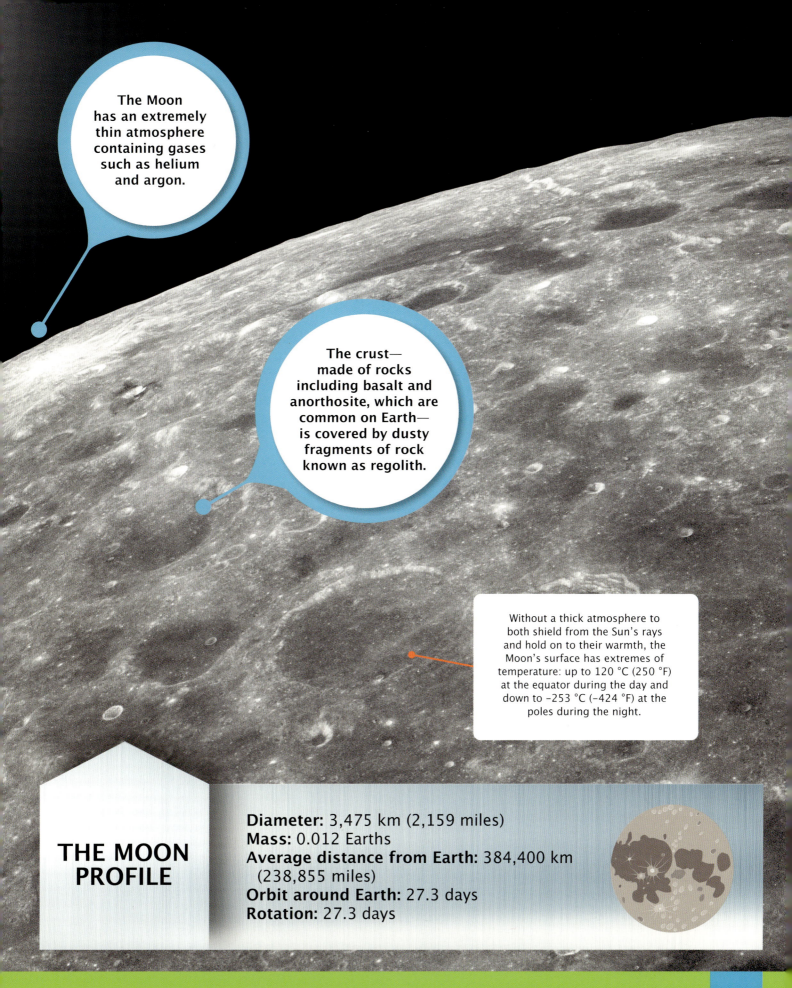

The Moon has an extremely thin atmosphere containing gases such as helium and argon.

The crust—made of rocks including basalt and anorthosite, which are common on Earth—is covered by dusty fragments of rock known as regolith.

Without a thick atmosphere to both shield from the Sun's rays and hold on to their warmth, the Moon's surface has extremes of temperature: up to 120 °C (250 °F) at the equator during the day and down to −253 °C (−424 °F) at the poles during the night.

THE MOON PROFILE

Diameter: 3,475 km (2,159 miles)
Mass: 0.012 Earths
Average distance from Earth: 384,400 km (238,855 miles)
Orbit around Earth: 27.3 days
Rotation: 27.3 days

Craters and Seas

The Moon is marked by thousands of craters, made when asteroids and comets crashed into its surface. The dark patches we can see on the Moon are areas of ancient hardened lava. These were once thought to be filled with water, which is why they are known as "seas."

Impact Craters

The near side of the Moon has around 300,000 craters wider than 1 km (0.6 miles), while the far side is even more heavily cratered. Since the Moon has little atmosphere—which would burn up smaller space rocks before impact—it has been more heavily impacted than Earth. With no water or wind on the Moon to wear away its surface, its craters remain much as they were when they were made, even if that was billions of years ago.

Like most of the Moon's craters, Moltke—around 1.3 km (0.8 miles) deep—has a raised rim created by material thrown outward by the crash. The surrounding area is covered by paler material scattered across the surface.

Lava Seas

Known as maria (plural) and mare (singular) in Latin, seas were made when lava flowed from low volcanoes then cooled into the rock basalt. Huge eruptions filled wide impact craters. Volcanoes on Earth are usually caused by the movement of tectonic plates, but the Moon has no tectonic plates. Its eruptions were caused by super-hot magma welling up from the mantle. Most eruptions took place more than 1 billion years ago, when the Moon's interior was hotter than today.

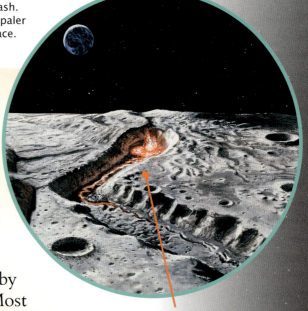

This illustration shows a volcano erupting on the Moon, its lava flowing into a valley known as Schroter's Valley. Such winding valleys, known as rilles, formed when old lava flows collapsed.

DID YOU KNOW? The Moon's largest crater is the far side's South Pole–Aitken Basin, which is 2,500 km (1,600 miles) across and around 4.2 billion years old.

OCEANUS PROCELLARUM PROFILE

Diameter: 2,592 km (1,611 miles)
Area: Around 4 million sq km (1.5 million sq miles)
Age: Around 1 billion years old
Named by: Italian astronomer Giovanni Battista Riccioli in 1651
Visited by: Crewed mission *Apollo 12* (1969) and robotic space probes *Luna 9* (1966), *Luna 13* (1966), *Surveyor 1* (1966), *Surveyor 3* (1967), and *Chang'e 5* (2020)

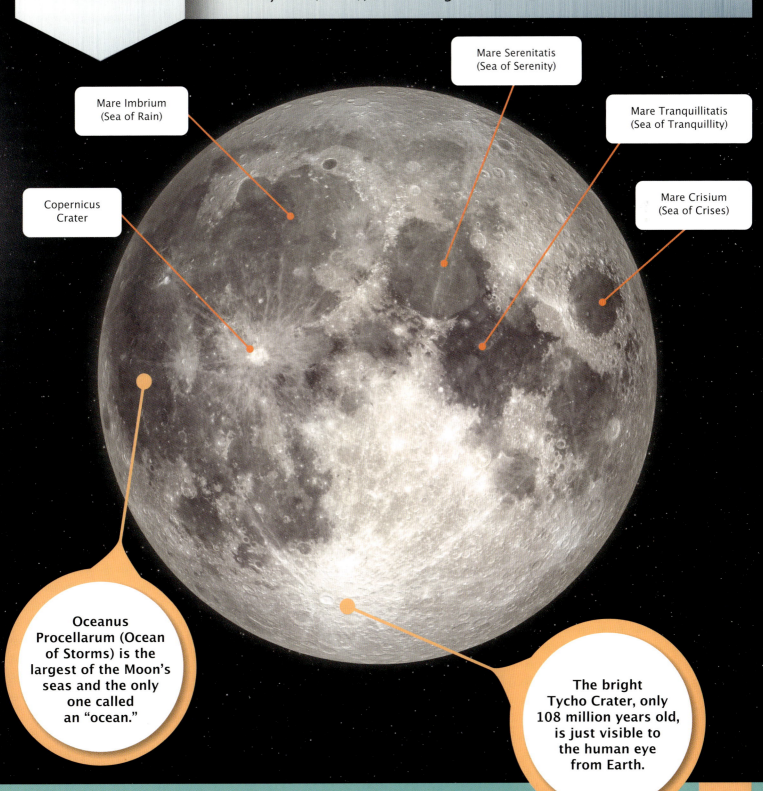

Mare Serenitatis (Sea of Serenity)

Mare Imbrium (Sea of Rain)

Mare Tranquillitatis (Sea of Tranquillity)

Mare Crisium (Sea of Crises)

Copernicus Crater

Oceanus Procellarum (Ocean of Storms) is the largest of the Moon's seas and the only one called an "ocean."

The bright Tycho Crater, only 108 million years old, is just visible to the human eye from Earth.

43

Tides

Tides are the rise and fall of Earth's sea levels, resulting in ocean water moving up and down the shore each day. "High tide" is when the water reaches its highest point on the shore. Tides are caused by the gravitational pulls of the Moon and Sun as Earth rotates.

Pull of the Moon

The Moon's gravity makes the oceans bulge on the side of Earth facing the Moon. On the opposite side of Earth, where the Moon's pull is weakest, ocean water can flow away from Earth, creating another bulge. As Earth rotates, most places pass through both the ocean bulges each day, creating two high tides and two low tides. However, since the Moon does not orbit Earth exactly around the equator (and the continents also get in the way of tidal bulges), some places experience only one high tide each day.

> Low tide leaves behind pools among coastal rocks, where animals such as crabs and prawns take shelter until the ocean returns.

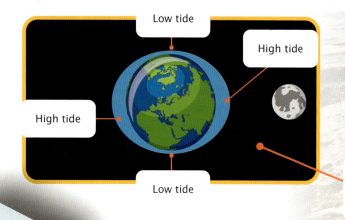

Low tide • High tide • High tide • Low tide

High tides occur on opposite sides of Earth.

GRAVITATIONAL PULLS
As felt on the object's surface

Sun: 28 times Earth's gravitational pull
Jupiter: 2.5 times Earth's gravitational pull
Saturn and Neptune: 1.1 times Earth's gravitational pull
Venus and Uranus: 0.9 times Earth's gravitational pull
Mercury and Mars: 0.38 times Earth's gravitational pull
Moon: 0.17 times Earth's gravitational pull

DID YOU KNOW? The Moon's gravity also creates bulges in Earth's crust, which can be measured using scientific instruments: New York City rises by 35 cm (14 in) at high tide.

The base of this rock has been worn away by waves up to the level of high tide.

The Moon rises above the horizon around 50 minutes later each day than the day before, so the times of high and low tides vary, making it essential to watch out for the rising tide.

Spring tides

Solar tide

Lunar tide

Neap tides

Pull of the Sun

The Sun also pulls on the oceans, but since it is much farther away than the Moon, its effect on tides is smaller. However, when the Sun and Moon are in a line, their combined gravity causes very high tides, known as spring tides. When the Sun and Moon are at right angles, the Sun works against the pull of the Moon, causing lower high tides and higher low tides, known as neap tides.

Spring and neap tides occur twice during each orbit of the Moon around Earth.

Watching the Moon

The side of the Moon facing the Sun is illuminated by sunlight. As the Moon orbits Earth, we can see different amounts of its sunlit side, making it appear to change shape in a cycle that lasts around 29.5 days.

Around 7 days before full moon, the Moon can be seen easily in the afternoon sky. Around 14 days later, it can be seen easily in the morning sky.

Phases of the Moon

When the Moon is on the opposite side of Earth from the Sun, we can see all its sunlit side. This phase is known as the full moon. When the Moon passes between Earth and the Sun, we can see none of its sunlit side. This phase is known as the new moon. Although it takes the Moon 27.3 days to orbit Earth, the Earth's own orbit around the Sun means that it takes around 29.5 days for the Moon to move through its phases.

Our view of the Moon changes as it orbits Earth.

LUNAR ECLIPSES OF 21ST CENTURY

Number: 230 (87 penumbral, 58 partial, and 85 total)
Most eclipses in a year: 4 (in 2009, 2020, 2038, 2085, 2096)
Most total eclipses in a year: 2
Longest duration of a total eclipse: 1 hour 46 minutes
Shortest duration of a total eclipse: 12 minutes

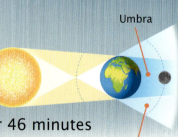

During a total lunar eclipse, the Moon appears red because the only sunlight reaching its face has been bent by Earth's atmosphere. The Sun's blue light has been scattered by Earth's atmosphere, leaving only reddish light.

The Moon rises in the east and sets in the west.

Eclipses of the Moon

An eclipse of the Moon, known as a lunar eclipse, is when the Moon moves into Earth's shadow, which can happen only at full moon. An eclipse does not happen every full moon because the Moon's orbit is tilted 5 degrees away from Earth's orbit around the Sun, so the Moon, Earth, and Sun are not always lined up. A total eclipse is when the Moon moves into the darkest part of Earth's shadow, the umbra. A penumbral eclipse is when it moves into the outer part of Earth's shadow, the penumbra, so its face dims. A partial eclipse is when part of the Moon's face enters Earth's umbra.

The Moon spends around 12 hours out of every 24 hours above the horizon, some of those hours during the daytime. However, near new moon it is too close to the Sun's brightness to be seen during the day. When it is near full moon, it is visible only from the nighttime side of Earth.

DID YOU KNOW? On average, a total eclipse of the Moon happens every 2.5 years and can be seen from the nighttime side of Earth.

Chapter 3

The Inner Planets

From closest to farthest from the Sun, the four inner planets are Mercury, Venus, Earth, and Mars. These planets are also known as terrestrial (from the Latin for "Earthlike") or rocky planets because—like Earth—they are made of rock with a metal core.

Earthlike Planets

The inner planets are made of heavier materials than the outer planets: Silicate rocks (made of minerals containing lots of silicon and oxygen atoms) form their mantles and crusts, while metals such as iron and nickel form their cores. In the heat of the inner solar system, only these materials—which do not melt until they reach a high temperature—can stay solid enough to make planets. However, the small size of the inner planets gives them lower masses (weights) than the outer planets.

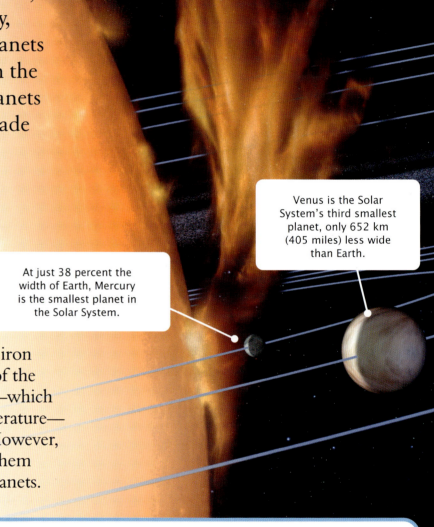

At just 38 percent the width of Earth, Mercury is the smallest planet in the Solar System.

Venus is the Solar System's third smallest planet, only 652 km (405 miles) less wide than Earth.

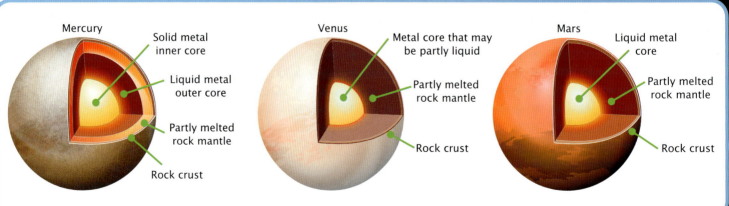

Mercury — Solid metal inner core, Liquid metal outer core, Partly melted rock mantle, Rock crust

Venus — Metal core that may be partly liquid, Partly melted rock mantle, Rock crust

Mars — Liquid metal core, Partly melted rock mantle, Rock crust

Too Small

Unlike the outer planets, the inner planets do not have ring systems. They also have fewer moons or no moons at all. This is largely because the inner planets' smaller masses give them weaker gravity than the outer planets—usually preventing them from capturing passing objects to become moons or holding on to rubble created by collisions.

Due to its immense size, which gives it great mass despite its light materials, Jupiter's gravity is 6.6 times the strength of Mercury's gravity.

The largest inner planet, Earth is the only one with flowing oceans, falling rainwater—and living things.

The second smallest planet, Mars has the most moons of any inner planet: two.

DID YOU KNOW? All the inner planets except Mercury have a thick enough atmosphere to create weather, caused by movements of gas.

Mercury

The Romans named Mercury after their fast-running messenger god, due to the planet's speedy motion. It orbits the Sun in just 88 days, moving at an average speed of 170,496 km/h (105,941 miles per hour), faster than any other planet.

Speedy Planet

Mercury has the fastest orbital speed because it is the closest planet to the Sun. The closer a planet is to the Sun, the faster it has to orbit so it is not pulled into the Sun by the star's immense gravity. The Sun is "trying" to pull all the planets into it, but they are "trying" to travel in a straight path. The balance between these two forces creates a curving path: an orbit.

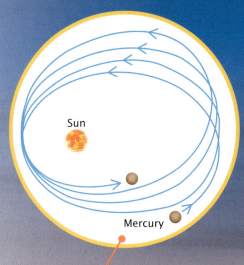

Mercury's orbit is not a circle but an ellipse, ranging from 47 million to 70 million km (29 million to 43 million miles) from the Sun. The ellipse rotates over time.

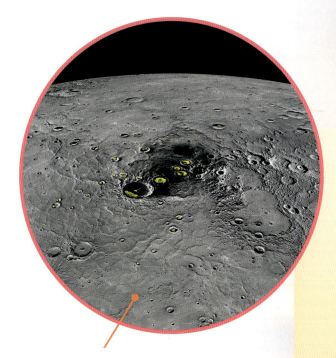

Dark craters at Mercury's poles stay so cold that they may hold water ice. This image captured by the *MESSENGER* space probe shows possible ice in yellow.

Hot and Cold

The surface temperature on Mercury varies more widely than on any other planet. During the daytime, the planet's closeness to the Sun heats it to 430 °C (800 °F). Mercury is too small and too close to the Sun for its gravity to hold on to more than an extremely thin atmosphere. With almost no atmosphere to blanket the planet and retain heat at night, the temperature can fall to -180 °C (-290 °F).

MERCURY PROFILE

Diameter: 4,880 km (3,032 miles)
Mass: 0.055 Earths
Average distance from the Sun: 57.9 million km (36 million miles)
Orbit: 88 days
Rotation: 59 days
Moons: 0

Since Mercury is visible to the naked eye as a bright, starlike object, it has been observed since ancient times.

The largest planet, Jupiter, is just about to set.

Mercury's closeness to the Sun means it can only be seen during twilight, near the western horizon shortly after sunset and near the eastern horizon just before sunrise.

DID YOU KNOW? Mercury rotates exactly three times on its axis for every two orbits it makes around the Sun, due to the Sun's intense gravity slowing its spin.

Mercurian Surface

Mercury has many thousands of impact craters, more than any other Solar System planet. Many craters and lowlands are flooded with dried lava that welled up from the interior when the planet was much hotter than today. The craters are crisscrossed by strange wrinkles called rupes.

> Mercury's surface is composed of dry, brown rock, but this photograph has used brighter shades to show the different materials.

Craters

Mercury is more cratered than the other inner planets because it has little atmosphere to slow down asteroids and comets. Most of Mercury's craters were made within the first billion years after the planet's formation, when there were more stray space rocks than today. The smallest known craters are around 10 km (6 miles) wide, while the largest, the Caloris Basin, is 1,550 km (960 miles) across.

Taken by the *MESSENGER* space probe, this photo shows, at top right, the Brontë Crater (named after English authors Charlotte, Emily, Anne, and Bramwell Brontë) and the adjacent bluish Degas Crater (named after the French painter Edgar Degas).

CALORIS BASIN PROFILE

Diameter: 1,550 km (960 miles)
Area: Around 1.8 million sq km (700,000 sq miles)
Age: Around 3.9 billion years old
Discovered by: The *Mariner 10* space probe in 1974
Named after: The Latin for "heat" because the Sun is almost directly overhead every second time Mercury draws closest to the star

DID YOU KNOW? Mercury's rupes are named after ships used for expeditions on Earth, including Charles Darwin's *Discovery* and Christopher Columbus's *Santa María*.

Around 2 km (1.2 miles) high, Carnegie Rupes runs across the Duccio Crater.

Rupes

Today, Mercury's core is around 2,000 °C (3,600 °F), but when the planet formed it was perhaps five times as hot. As Mercury has cooled over billions of years, its interior has shrunk, making the planet up to 7 km (4.3 miles) less wide. As the interior shrank, it deformed the crust, making tall folds—known as rupes—and deep cracks.

Younger craters, as well as the material that has streaked from them during impacts, are pale blue or white.

Atget Crater

The Caloris Basin is orange, revealing that it is filled with dried lava.

Xiao Zhao Crater

Tolstoy Crater

Neruda Crater

53

Venus

Named after the Roman goddess of love, Venus has been important to many cultures since ancient times, due to its bright appearance in the evening and morning sky. Today, it is often known as Earth's "sister planet" due to its similar size, mass, and composition.

Viewing Venus

Venus can be seen easily with the naked eye as a pale yellow light. It is the brightest object in the night sky apart from the Moon, because its thick clouds reflect much of the sunlight that reaches them. Unlike stars, Venus and the other planets do not appear to twinkle. Since Venus lies closer to the Sun than Earth, it always appears quite near our star. Yet, unlike Mercury, which is so near the Sun that it can be seen only in twilight, Venus can be seen for up to 3 hours before and after sunset and sunrise.

> Like most features on Venus, Llorona Planitia (Llorona Plain) was named after a famous woman or a goddess, in this case a woman from Mexican legends.

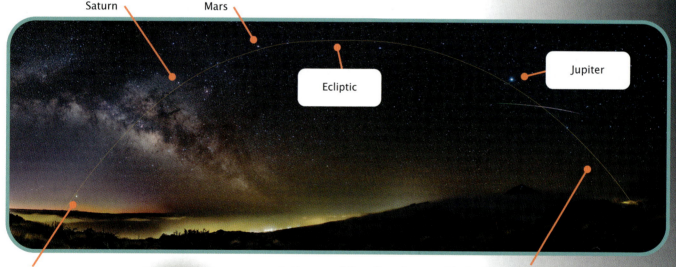

As Venus and the other planets orbit the Sun, they appear to travel slowly backward and forward on an imaginary curving line through the sky, known as the ecliptic. The ecliptic is the plane of the Solar System as seen from Earth, along which the Sun and Moon also appear to travel.

VENUS PROFILE

Diameter: 12,104 km (7,521 miles)
Mass: 0.815 Earths
Average distance from the Sun: 108.2 million km (67.2 million miles)
Orbit: 224.7 days
Rotation: 243 days
Moons: 0

Turning Backward

Apart from Venus and Uranus, all the Solar System planets rotate counterclockwise (anticlockwise) on their axes as viewed from their north pole, the same direction in which they travel around the Sun. Venus rotates the opposite way on its axis, known as retrograde (backward) rotation. Venus must once have rotated the "right" way due to the way it formed in the Sun's spinning disk, but something—such as a crash with another planet—sent it spinning the other way, as was probably also the case with Uranus.

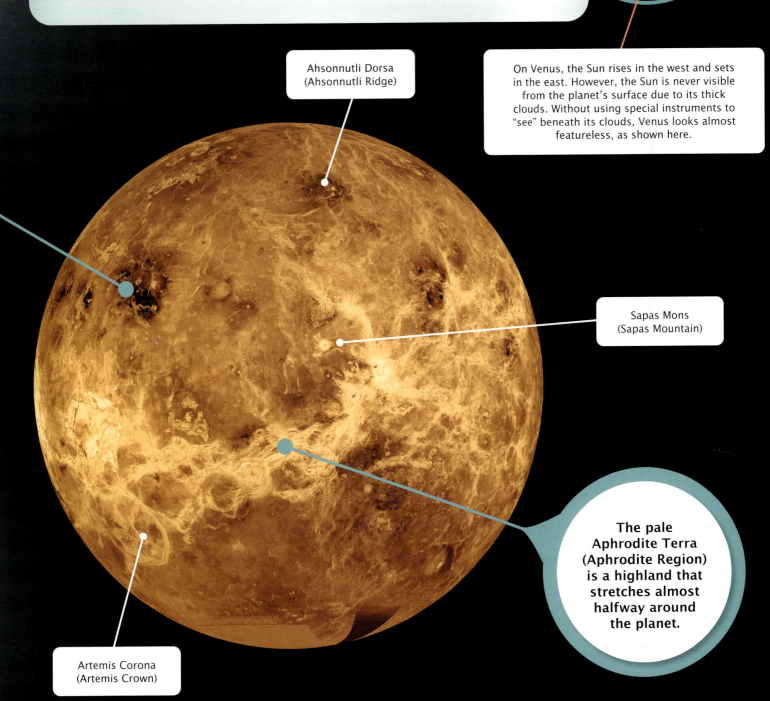

On Venus, the Sun rises in the west and sets in the east. However, the Sun is never visible from the planet's surface due to its thick clouds. Without using special instruments to "see" beneath its clouds, Venus looks almost featureless, as shown here.

Ahsonnutli Dorsa (Ahsonnutli Ridge)

Sapas Mons (Sapas Mountain)

The pale Aphrodite Terra (Aphrodite Region) is a highland that stretches almost halfway around the planet.

Artemis Corona (Artemis Crown)

DID YOU KNOW? Venus rotates more slowly around its axis than any other planet, at 6.5 km/h (4 miles per hour) compared with Earth's 1,674 km/h (1,040 miles per hour).

Venusian Atmosphere

While Earth has an atmosphere that nurtures life, Venus's atmosphere would be deadly to all known life forms. The Venusian atmosphere also makes it the hottest planet in the Solar System, with an average surface temperature of 464 °C (867 °F).

A Deadly Mix

The Venusian atmosphere is extremely thick, with a mass 92 times Earth's atmosphere. If it were possible to stand safely on Venus's surface, the atmosphere would press down with the same weight felt 1 km (0.6 miles) underwater. The atmosphere is largely carbon dioxide, a gas that makes up less than 0.1 percent of Earth's atmosphere and would kill if breathed in such quantities. Venus's thick clouds are composed mainly of sulfuric acid, a dangerous chemical that—on Earth—is used to break down rocks and metals.

This illustration shows the top of Venus's yellowish cloud belt, which is always around 20 km (12.4 miles) thick.

Heating Up

Venus's intense heat is caused by the atmosphere's carbon dioxide, which traps the Sun's heat. Scientists think that, for the first 2 billion years of its life, Venus had less carbon dioxide in its atmosphere and lower temperatures. The carbon dioxide may have been released from the planet's interior. While today the Venusian surface is hot, dry rock, it might once have been cool enough for flowing oceans.

Venus's water boiled away as its temperature rose. Unfortunately, we are seeing a little of the same "global warming" effect on Earth, due to excess carbon dioxide released by cars and factories—but our planet is unlikely to become as hot as Venus.

Venus's clouds may be able to generate lightning, as their droplets of sulfuric acid become electrically charged by rubbing together.

Although Venus's clouds produce sulfuric acid rain, the atmosphere's intense heat makes the drops evaporate (turn to gas) before reaching the surface.

The temperature on the surface would melt metals such as tin and lead.

GASES IN VENUS'S ATMOSPHERE

Carbon dioxide: Around 96.5 percent
Nitrogen: Around 3.5 percent
Sulfur dioxide, argon, water vapor, carbon monoxide, helium, and neon: Traces

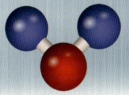

Each molecule of carbon dioxide has one carbon atom joined to two oxygen atoms.

DID YOU KNOW? There is little wind near Venus's surface, but above the clouds, winds can blow at 360 km/h (220 miles per hour).

Venusian Volcanoes

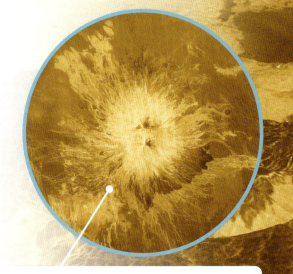

The *Magellan* space probe detected recent ash flows near the summit, suggesting that this volcano is still active.

With more than 1,600 major volcanoes, Venus has more volcanoes than any other Solar System planet. Two-thirds of the Venusian surface is covered by dried lava, which has concealed many impact craters—resulting in Venus having fewer than a thousand visible craters.

Making Volcanoes

On Earth, most volcanoes are caused by the movement of tectonic plates (see page 30), but Venus's crust and upper mantle are not broken into plates. Its volcanoes are caused by super-hot rock, known as magma, rising up from the mantle and through cracks in the crust. Such magma plumes also cause some Earth volcanoes, including those on the islands of Hawaii, in the Pacific Ocean. Although most Venusian volcanoes are probably inactive and we have never witnessed an eruption, astronomers think some are still active.

This overhead image of the volcano Sapas Mons, which is around 400 km (250 miles) wide, shows its twin dark summits. Paler areas are dried lava flows. In 2014, flashes caused by hot gas or lava were detected.

MAAT MONS PROFILE

Diameter: 395 km (245 miles)
Area: Around 122,500 sq km (47,000 sq miles)
Age: Probably less than 500 million years old
Discovered by: The *Pioneer Venus* space probe in 1978
Named after: The ancient Egyptian goddess of truth and justice, Maat, while "Mons" means mountain in Latin

DID YOU KNOW? Venus has 167 volcanoes over 100 km (60 miles) wide, while Earth has only one such volcano complex, on the Island of Hawaii in the Pacific Ocean.

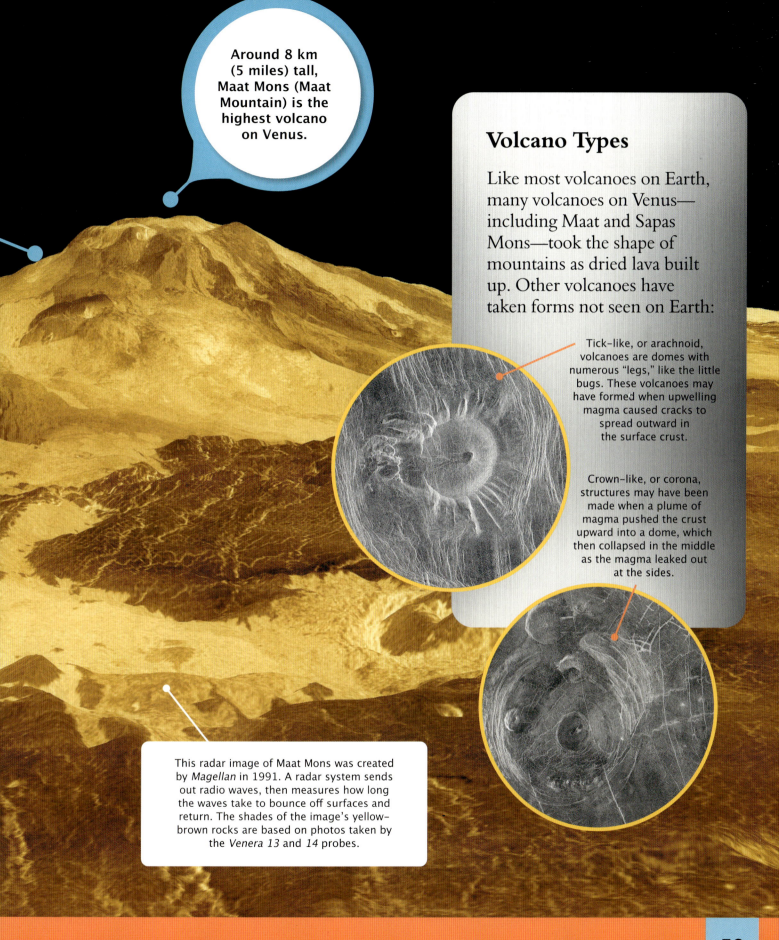

Around 8 km (5 miles) tall, Maat Mons (Maat Mountain) is the highest volcano on Venus.

Volcano Types

Like most volcanoes on Earth, many volcanoes on Venus—including Maat and Sapas Mons—took the shape of mountains as dried lava built up. Other volcanoes have taken forms not seen on Earth:

Tick-like, or arachnoid, volcanoes are domes with numerous "legs," like the little bugs. These volcanoes may have formed when upwelling magma caused cracks to spread outward in the surface crust.

Crown-like, or corona, structures may have been made when a plume of magma pushed the crust upward into a dome, which then collapsed in the middle as the magma leaked out at the sides.

This radar image of Maat Mons was created by *Magellan* in 1991. A radar system sends out radio waves, then measures how long the waves take to bounce off surfaces and return. The shades of the image's yellow-brown rocks are based on photos taken by the *Venera 13* and *14* probes.

Mars

To the naked eye, Mars is a small reddish light, gaining it the nickname "Red Planet." Mars's shade reminded the ancient Romans of blood, so they named the planet after their god of war. Martian features were named after scientists, characters from myths, and Earth towns and rivers.

Red Planet

Mars's reddish shade is caused by the high quantity of iron oxide in its rocks and dust. Iron oxide, also known as rust, usually forms on Earth when iron is in contact with oxygen in the air, resulting in a flaky red coating. In addition to having a core of iron, nickel, and sulfur, Mars's surface rocks also contain large quantities of iron. Mars's atmosphere currently does not contain enough oxygen to rust its rocks, but possibly it once contained more—or perhaps oxygen in ancient water (see page 62) was responsible.

The *Curiosity* rover took this photo of Mars's rocky, sandy, dusty surface, as well as its own tracks.

Not Much of an Atmosphere

Mars has a very thin atmosphere, composed of 95 percent carbon dioxide, 2.8 percent nitrogen, 2 percent argon, and traces of oxygen and water. Earth's atmosphere is 100 times denser than the Martian atmosphere. Astronomers think that the Martian atmosphere was much denser in the past, but was stripped away by the solar wind (see page 22). Due to Mars having little atmosphere to retain heat—as well as its greater distance from the Sun—it is cooler than Earth, with the surface temperature averaging -60 °C (-76 °F).

This side-on view of Mars's atmosphere, photographed by *Viking 1*, shows a reddish haze of dust lifted into the air by wind.

DID YOU KNOW? In 2018, a Mars-wide dust storm destroyed the *Opportunity* rover, probably because dust got inside its equipment or covered its solar panels.

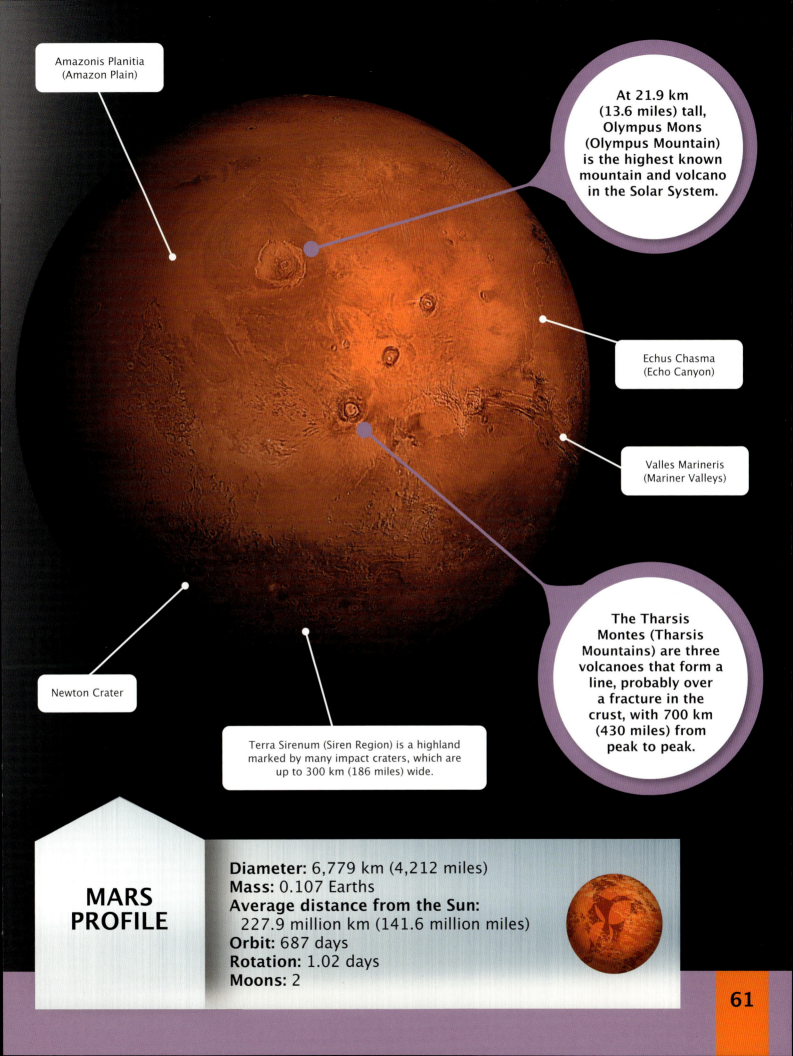

Amazonis Planitia (Amazon Plain)

At 21.9 km (13.6 miles) tall, Olympus Mons (Olympus Mountain) is the highest known mountain and volcano in the Solar System.

Echus Chasma (Echo Canyon)

Valles Marineris (Mariner Valleys)

The Tharsis Montes (Tharsis Mountains) are three volcanoes that form a line, probably over a fracture in the crust, with 700 km (430 miles) from peak to peak.

Newton Crater

Terra Sirenum (Siren Region) is a highland marked by many impact craters, which are up to 300 km (186 miles) wide.

MARS PROFILE

Diameter: 6,779 km (4,212 miles)
Mass: 0.107 Earths
Average distance from the Sun: 227.9 million km (141.6 million miles)
Orbit: 687 days
Rotation: 1.02 days
Moons: 2

61

Water on Mars

Today, Mars is a dry and dusty planet, but astronomers think it may once have had flowing rivers and seas. Since life on Earth began in the oceans, scientists are excited by the idea that Mars could once have been home to life. No evidence of ancient life forms has yet been found.

Ancient Water

Currently, there is plenty of water on Mars, but it is frozen at the cold poles and in the soil. If all this ice melted, it would cover the planet in an ocean 35 m (115 ft) deep. Yet, today, Mars has too thin an atmosphere for liquid surface water. Without a thick atmosphere pressing down, surface water would either turn to gas or freeze into ice. However, astronomers think that, billions of years ago, the Martian atmosphere was thick enough—and warm enough—to allow liquid surface water.

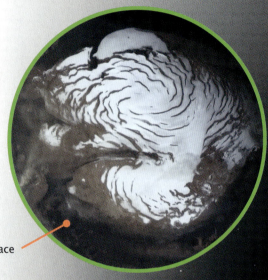

This photo, taken by the *Mars Express* space probe, shows ice at Mars's north pole.

Evidence of Water

Earth's surface has many features created by water erosion: the wearing away of rock by pounding waves and flowing rivers. Some of the same features can be found on Mars, providing possible evidence that the planet was once much wetter than it is now:

This map of the Kasei Valles (Kasei Valleys) uses different shades to show land heights, with yellow highest and blue lowest. The winding valleys, up to 3 km (1.9 miles) deep, may have been carved by rivers flowing toward a lake or sea on the right of the image.

In this photo of the Eberswalde Crater, we can see a delta, a feature that forms on Earth where rivers enter lakes or seas. As the river meets the large body of slower-moving water, it drops the sand, gravel, and mud it is carrying, forming a fan shape.

NORTH POLAR ICE CAP PROFILE

Diameter: Around 1,000 km (620 miles) in summer
Volume of water ice: Around 821,000 cu km (197,000 cubic miles)
Age: Possibly around 1 billion years old
Discovered by: Italian astronomer Giovanni Cassini in 1666, but not identified as ice until 1719, by Giancomo Miraldi
First photographed from orbit by: The *Mariner 9* space probe in 1972

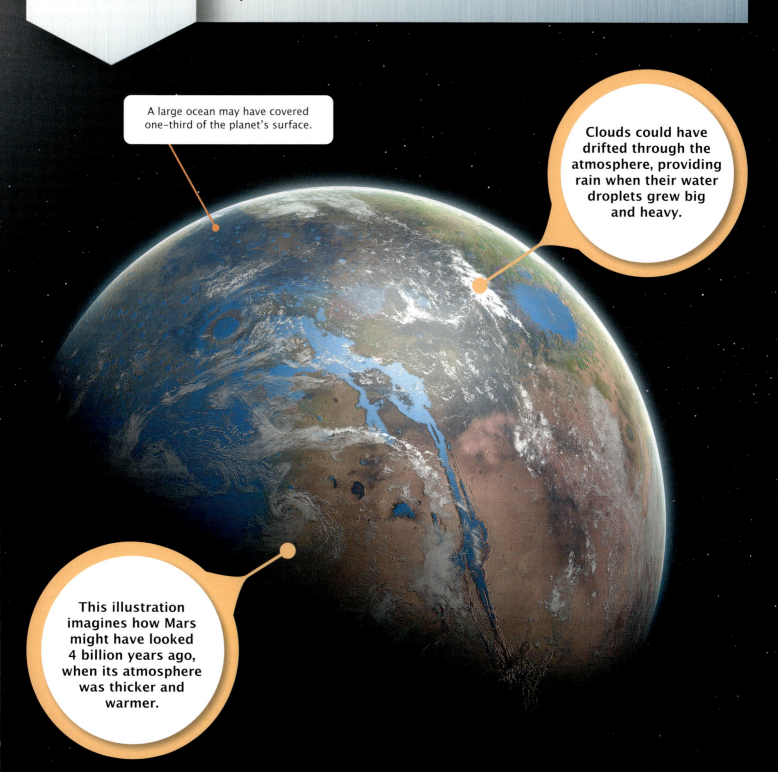

A large ocean may have covered one-third of the planet's surface.

Clouds could have drifted through the atmosphere, providing rain when their water droplets grew big and heavy.

This illustration imagines how Mars might have looked 4 billion years ago, when its atmosphere was thicker and warmer.

DID YOU KNOW? During every 687-day Martian year, each pole has around 300 days of continuous darkness during its winter, due to the planet's tilted axis.

Martian Canyons

Mars is home to one of the largest canyon systems in the Solar System: the Valles Marineris (Mariner Valleys). This series of cracks in the Martian crust was made by the growth of the Tharsis Bulge, a region of high ground that covers a quarter of the Martian surface.

Tharsis Bulge

Tharsis probably formed over an immensely hot region in the planet's mantle. Over billions of years, magma surged upward, pouring over the surface as runny lava—which built up a wide highland, more than 10 km (6.2 miles) higher than the planet's average surface. Three huge volcanoes also formed here, known as the Tharsis Montes (Tharsis Mountains): Ascraeus, Pavonis, and Arsia. The summit of the tallest, Ascraeus, is over 18 km (11 miles) high.

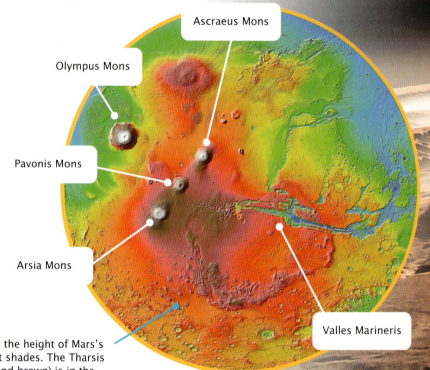

This map shows the height of Mars's crust in different shades. The Tharsis Bulge (in red and brown) is in the middle, while the Valles Marineris (in blue) stretch to the east.

This image of the Valles Marineris was created using information collected by the *Mars Global Surveyor* space probe.

Valles Marineris

The Valles Marineris are a series of parallel canyons up to 8 km (5 miles) deep. In comparison, Earth's Grand Canyon is only 1.8 km (1.1 miles) deep. The cracks began to form around 3.5 billion years ago as Tharsis rose, causing the surrounding crust to stretch and break. As cracks opened, water that had been under the surface escaped, making the ground more unstable. The valleys' steep walls collapsed in landslides that widened the canyons yet more.

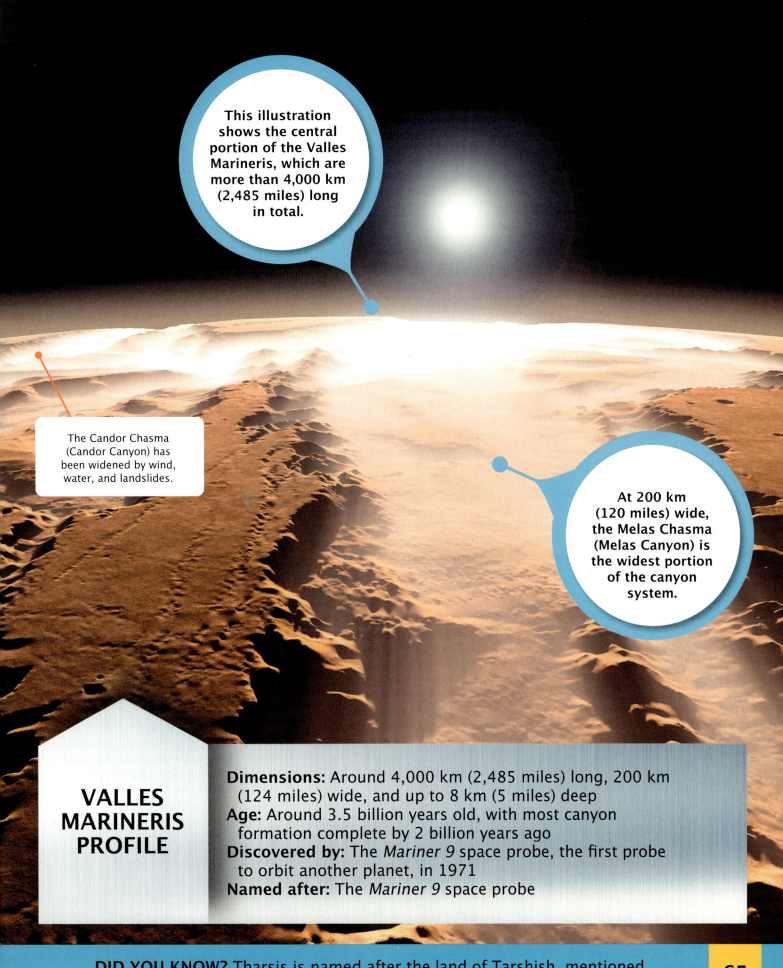

This illustration shows the central portion of the Valles Marineris, which are more than 4,000 km (2,485 miles) long in total.

The Candor Chasma (Candor Canyon) has been widened by wind, water, and landslides.

At 200 km (120 miles) wide, the Melas Chasma (Melas Canyon) is the widest portion of the canyon system.

VALLES MARINERIS PROFILE

Dimensions: Around 4,000 km (2,485 miles) long, 200 km (124 miles) wide, and up to 8 km (5 miles) deep
Age: Around 3.5 billion years old, with most canyon formation complete by 2 billion years ago
Discovered by: The *Mariner 9* space probe, the first probe to orbit another planet, in 1971
Named after: The *Mariner 9* space probe

DID YOU KNOW? Tharsis is named after the land of Tarshish, mentioned in the Bible and other ancient texts as a distant, faraway place.

Phobos and Deimos

Mars has two small moons named Phobos and Deimos. They were named after the twin sons of the Greek god of war, Ares, who was known to the Romans as Mars. Phobos ("fear" in ancient Greek) and Deimos ("dread") always followed their father onto the battlefield.

> Phobos orbits closer to its parent planet than any other moon in the Solar System.

Mysterious Moons

Astronomers are not sure how Phobos and Deimos formed. Some think they were asteroids pulled in from the Asteroid Belt by Mars's gravity. Others think they formed when a larger moon was smashed by a passing object. Both moons are irregularly shaped because their own gravity is not powerful enough to pull them into a sphere.

Phobos orbits faster around Mars than the planet rotates, one of the few moons in the Solar System to do so. This means that, if it were possible to stand on the surface of Mars, Phobos would rise in the west, travel across the sky in 4 hours and 15 minutes or less, then set in the east, repeating this pattern around once every 11 hours and 6 minutes—twice each Martian day.

Deimos orbits slower around Mars than the planet rotates. Although it orbits in the same direction as Phobos—counterclockwise (anticlockwise), the same direction that Mars rotates—its slower motion means it rises in the east and sets in the west, the opposite of Phobos. A simple way to understand why is to imagine you (Mars) are running in a race. One person (Phobos) runs faster than you, so as they pass you their direction of travel appears to be forward. The other person (Deimos) runs slower than you, so as you pass them their direction of travel appears to be backward.

PHOBOS PROFILE

Diameter: 22.2 km (13.8 miles)
Mass: 0.0000000018 Earths
Average distance from Mars: 9,377 km (5,827 miles)
Orbit around Mars: 7.66 hours
Rotation: 7.66 hours

DEIMOS PROFILE

Diameter: 12.6 km (7.8 miles) across
Mass: 0.0000000002 Earths
Average distance from Mars: 23,460 km (14,580 miles)
Orbit around Mars: 30.35 hours
Rotation: 30.35 hours

Viewed from Mars, Deimos would be so far away and so small that it would appear around one-twelfth the size of the Moon as seen from Earth.

Due to the pull of Mars's gravity, Phobos is getting nearer to the planet by 2 m (6.6 ft) every 100 years. In 30 to 50 million years, Phobos will draw so close it will be destroyed.

DID YOU KNOW? Mars's moons were discovered by American astronomer Asaph Hall in 1877, using the telescope at the US Naval Observatory.

Chapter 4

The Outer Planets

From closest to farthest from the Sun, the four outer planets are Jupiter, Saturn, Uranus, and Neptune. Often known as the giant planets, they range in size from Neptune—almost four times the diameter of Earth—to Jupiter, which is eleven times wider than Earth.

Growing Giants

The inner planets are made of rock and metal, but the outer planets are made of materials called volatiles, such as hydrogen and methane. Volatiles turn to gas much more easily than rocks and metals. As the Solar System formed from the materials spinning around the young Sun, the heat in the Inner Solar System turned the volatiles to gas. The Sun's energy expelled the gassy volatiles into the Outer Solar System, where it was cool enough for them to form planets.

Uranus is the third largest Solar System planet, but it has the fourth biggest mass.

Jupiter

During the formation of the Solar System, there were far more volatile materials than rocky and metal materials spinning around the young Sun. This meant that the outer planets grew huge, but the inner planets are small.

Earth

68   **DID YOU KNOW?** The four outer planets make up 99 percent of the mass of all the objects known to orbit the Sun.

Jupiter's mass is 2.5 times the combined mass of all other objects orbiting the Sun.

Like all the outer planets, Neptune has a ring system and many moons.

The Solar System's second largest planet, Saturn is 9.5 times wider than Earth.

Gas or Ice?

Jupiter and Saturn are often known as gas giants, while Uranus and Neptune are called ice giants. These names are misleading, since all four planets are mostly swirling gas and liquid. Jupiter and Saturn are "gas" giants because they are mostly hydrogen and helium, which are gases at room temperature. Uranus and Neptune are "ice" giants because they are mostly water, ammonia, and methane, which freeze into ice at much higher temperatures than hydrogen and helium. For example, water freezes at 0 °C (32 °F), while hydrogen does not freeze until -259 °C (-434 °F).

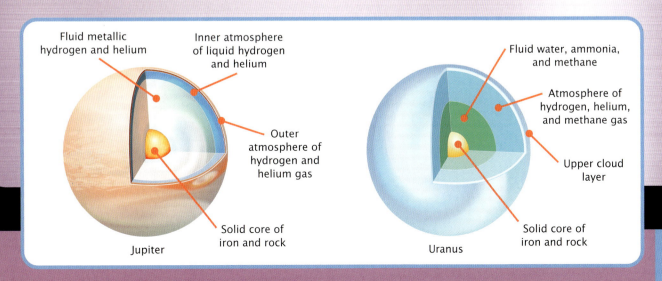

Jupiter

The Solar System's largest planet was named after the Roman king of the gods. At 4.6 billion years old, Jupiter is also the Solar System's oldest planet, perhaps 100 million years older than Earth. The planet has a faint ring system, composed of three rings of orbiting dust.

Jupiter's speedy spin, at nearly 45,000 km/h (28,000 miles per hour), has separated the planet's clouds into bands.

Seeing Jupiter

Humans have observed Jupiter since ancient times as it is big and bright enough to be seen in the night sky without a telescope. It is visible for around eight months, followed by five months when it appears too close to the Sun to be seen from Earth. When visible, Jupiter is usually the third brightest object in the night sky, after the Moon and Venus. Since Jupiter's orbit is outside Earth's, it always appears nearly fully illuminated by the Sun's light.

When two planets appear close when viewed from Earth, it is known as a conjunction. In this photo, a conjunction of Jupiter and Saturn is to the left of the Milky Way Galaxy, which can be seen as a band of gas, dust, and stars.

The Great Red Spot

At the boundaries between Jupiter's belts and zones, where swiftly rising and falling gas meet, circling storms can form. Jupiter's biggest storm, known as the Great Red Spot, has been raging since at least 1831. It forms an orange area south of Jupiter's equator. Winds inside the storm are blowing at around 435 km/h (270 miles per hour) in a counterclockwise direction.

This photo of the Great Red Spot was taken in 1979 by the space probe *Voyager 1*. Since then, the storm has shrunk a little, to around 16,500 km (10,250 miles) across—still wider than Earth.

DID YOU KNOW? Jupiter's core has a temperature of around 19,700 °C (35,500 °F), but its surface is about −108 °C (−163 °F).

The light bands, called zones, are areas of warmer, rising gas that block our view of the orange gas below.

The dark bands, called belts, are regions of cooler, sinking gas containing chemicals stained orange by sunlight.

JUPITER PROFILE

Diameter: 139,822 km (86,881 miles)
Mass: 317.8 Earths
Average distance from the Sun: 778 million km (484 million miles)
Orbit: 11.9 years
Rotation: 9.9 hours
Moons: At least 95 known

Moons of Jupiter

> Ganymede formed from the gas and dust spinning around Jupiter soon after the planet's birth.

The largest of Jupiter's 95 known moons is Ganymede, the biggest moon in the Solar System. Among the smallest of the planet's moons is Valetudo, around 1 km (0.6 miles) across. Jupiter also has several smaller, unnamed moonlets, with perhaps many more still to be discovered.

Four Galilean Moons

Jupiter's four largest moons were the first objects discovered orbiting another planet. In 1609 or 1610, the Italian astronomer Galileo Galilei spotted them through his telescope. From closest to farthest from Jupiter, these moons are Io, Europa, Ganymede, and Callisto. The closer each moon is to the planet, the hotter its interior. This is due to Jupiter's gravity pulling on its rocks, creating heat from friction as they squeeze and bend.

Moon	
Io	Around 421,700 km (262,032 miles) from Jupiter, Io is made of iron and rock with a sulfur surface. It has over 400 active volcanoes due to Jupiter's gravity melting its rock.
Europa	Cooler than Io, Europa has a metal core, a rocky mantle surrounded by an ocean of liquid salt water, and a thin crust of ice.
Ganymede	This moon has a metal core, a rocky mantle surrounded by an ocean of liquid salt water, and a thick crust of ice.
Callisto	Around 1,882,700 km (1,169,856 miles) from Jupiter, Callisto is a mix of rock and ice.

GANYMEDE PROFILE

Diameter: 5,268 km (3,273 miles)
Mass: 0.025 Earths
Average distance from Jupiter: 1,070,400 km (665,116 miles)
Orbit around Jupiter: 7.13 days
Rotation: 7.13 days

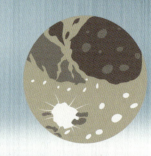

Four Inner Moons

Four small moons orbit closer to Jupiter than the Galilean moons: Metis, Adrastea, Amalthea, and Thebe. The closest, Metis, is around 128,000 km (79,535 miles) from Jupiter. All the inner moons have irregular shapes because they are too small for their own gravity to pull them into a sphere. These moons shed material that keeps Jupiter's ring system supplied with dust.

Ganymede has countless craters, most of them caused by impacts with space rocks between 3.5 and 4 billion years ago.

Astronomers think there could be simple life forms in the ocean that lies beneath Ganymede's icy surface.

Jupiter's fifth largest moon, Amalthea is only 250 km (155 miles) long.

DID YOU KNOW? Jupiter's moons are named after lovers or children of the Roman god Jupiter or his Greek counterpart, Zeus.

Saturn

Like its sister planet Jupiter, Saturn is made mostly of hydrogen and helium. Although Saturn's great size gives it a mass 95 times Earth's, 1 cubic cm of Saturn would weigh only 0.7 g (0.02 oz), while the same quantity of Earth would weigh 5.5 g (0.2 oz).

> Deep inside Saturn, hydrogen and helium gas are squeezed so tightly they become liquid and, deeper still, become metal.

Great White Spots

Around every 30 years, white thunderstorms encircle Saturn's northern hemisphere. They are named Great White Spots after Jupiter's Great Red Spot. The storms happen once every orbit, when Saturn's northern hemisphere is most tilted toward the Sun. They may be caused by rapidly rising hot gas. On Earth, quickly rising, hot, wet air causes thunderstorms.

> On Saturn, clouds are made of ammonia ice and water ice. On Earth, they are made of water ice or water droplets.

The *Hubble Space Telescope* took this photo of an aurora around Saturn's south pole.

Bright Lights

Space telescopes detect lights, known as auroras, around Saturn's poles. These are similar to the auroras seen on Earth (see page 36). Saturn has a magnetic field, possibly caused by electricity flowing inside the planet. A magnetic field is made when electricity is in motion. High-energy particles from the Sun are deflected by the magnetic field but hit near the polar regions where the field is weakest. The particles excite atoms of hydrogen gas, making them give off light.

Saturn's axis is tilted at 26.7 degrees, so we see its rings at different angles as the planet rotates and travels around the Sun.

Saturn's pale yellow shade is caused by ammonia crystals in its upper atmosphere.

SATURN PROFILE

Diameter: 116,460 km (72,365 miles)
Mass: 95 Earths
Average distance from the Sun: 1.43 billion km (890 million miles)
Orbit: 29.5 years
Rotation: 10.7 hours
Moons: At least 146 known

DID YOU KNOW? Astronomers think that it rains diamonds on Saturn after lightning turns the atmosphere's methane into carbon, which hardens into diamonds.

Rings of Saturn

Billions of chunks of almost pure water ice are orbiting Saturn. They form the Solar System's largest and brightest ring system, its brightness due to sunlight reflecting from the ice. The first person to see Saturn's rings was Galileo Galilei as he gazed through his telescope in 1610.

Around 4,800 km (3,000 miles) wide, the Cassini Division is a region between rings A and B where there is little material due to the moon Mimas sweeping it up.

The Encke Gap in the A ring is caused by the moon Pan, which orbits within it.

Ring Structure

The main ring system contains rings named A to D. Rings A and B are the most tightly packed with material. Numerous gaps, where the material is sparser, lie between and among the rings. These gaps are caused by the gravitational pull of Saturn's moons and moonlets. Beyond ring A are several fainter, dustier rings, which extend as far as 13 million km (8 million miles) from Saturn.

This image shows the rings in different shades depending on their particle size. Areas where most particles are larger than 5 cm (2 in) across are in purple, while green areas have lots of smaller particles.

SATURN'S RINGS PROFILE

Distance from Saturn's equator: 7,000 to 13 million km (4,300 to 8 million miles)
Thickness: 10 m to 1 km (33 ft to 0.6 miles)
Size of most particles: 1 cm to 10 m (0.4 in to 33 ft)
Mass: 0.0000026 Earths
Speed of orbit: 60,000 to 84,000 km/h (37,000 to 52,000 miles per hour)

The B ring is the widest of the main rings, stretching for 25,500 km (15,845 miles).

If the rings formed from a shattered moon, the moon was probably 400 to 600 km (250 to 370 miles) across.

Making Rings

Astronomers debate the age of Saturn's rings and how they formed. A common theory is that they formed between 10 million and 100 million years ago when one of the planet's moons was struck by a comet or asteroid. The moon shattered, making a cloud of rubble that was held in place by Saturn's gravity.

At first, the fragments would have been a jumbled cloud, but the gravity of Saturn and its moons produced a disk of fragments with circular orbits.

DID YOU KNOW? The Cassini Division was spotted in 1675 by Italian Giovanni Cassini. The astronomer also had a space probe to Saturn named after him in 1997.

Moons of Saturn

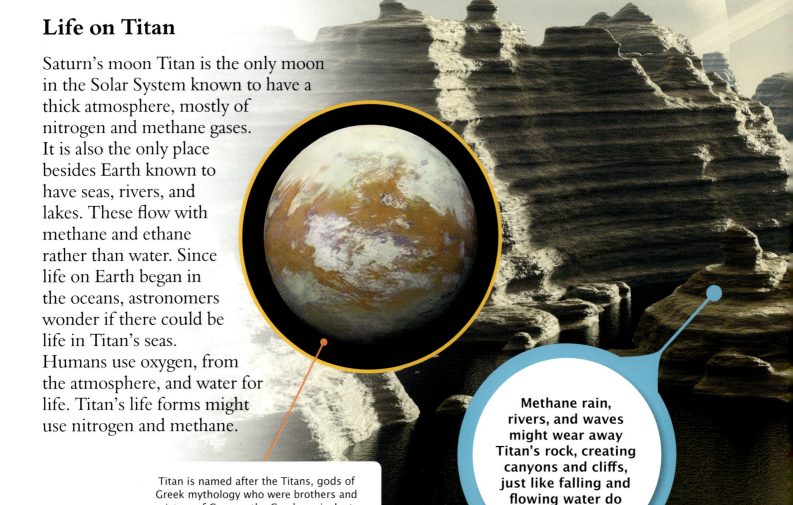

In this illustration, Titan's thick atmosphere makes the view of Saturn hazy.

Saturn has the most known moons of any planet: 146. Like the other giant planets, its great mass gives it immense gravity, so it can hold on to more moons than the inner planets. In addition, millions of unnamed smaller moonlets orbit within Saturn's rings.

Life on Titan

Saturn's moon Titan is the only moon in the Solar System known to have a thick atmosphere, mostly of nitrogen and methane gases. It is also the only place besides Earth known to have seas, rivers, and lakes. These flow with methane and ethane rather than water. Since life on Earth began in the oceans, astronomers wonder if there could be life in Titan's seas. Humans use oxygen, from the atmosphere, and water for life. Titan's life forms might use nitrogen and methane.

Titan is named after the Titans, gods of Greek mythology who were brothers and sisters of Cronus, the Greek equivalent of the Roman god of time, Saturn.

Methane rain, rivers, and waves might wear away Titan's rock, creating canyons and cliffs, just like falling and flowing water do on Earth.

DID YOU KNOW? The Solar System's largest moons are Jupiter's Ganymede, Saturn's Titan, Jupiter's Callisto and Io, Earth's Moon, and Jupiter's Europa.

TITAN PROFILE

Diameter: 5,149 km (3,200 miles)
Mass: 0.023 Earths
Average distance from Saturn: 1,221,870 km (759,235 miles)
Orbit around Saturn: 15.9 days
Rotation: 15.9 days

Titan is Saturn's largest moon. It is slightly bigger than the planet Mercury.

Contrasts on Iapetus

Around 1,469 km (913 miles) in diameter, Iapetus is Saturn's third largest moon, after Titan and Rhea. Iapetus is made of ice and rock. The moon puzzles astronomers by having one side that is light and one dark. The dark side is covered in a thin layer of a material that probably contains carbon, which is found in pencils and coal on Earth. The moon may have been spattered with this material by a nearby moon, such as Phoebe.

Iapetus is named after a Titan from Greek mythology, brother of Cronus, Rhea, and Phoebe.

79

Uranus

Only ever faintly visible to the naked eye, Uranus was believed to be a star until German-British astronomer William Herschel identified it as the Solar System's seventh planet in 1781. The planet's 13 dark, narrow rings were not discovered until 1977.

> Methane in Uranus's atmosphere absorbs red light, making the planet look pale blue.

Turning Sideways

As the planets orbit the Sun, they also rotate around their own axis. Mercury, Venus, and Jupiter have an axis that points roughly "upward," at right angles to their journey around the Sun. Earth, Mars, Saturn, and Neptune have an axis that is tilted a little. Yet Uranus's axis is tilted over by 97.8 degrees, so it rotates on its side, with its ring system pointing upward. Astronomers think this tilt was created 3 to 4 billion years ago, when a planet larger than Earth crashed into Uranus.

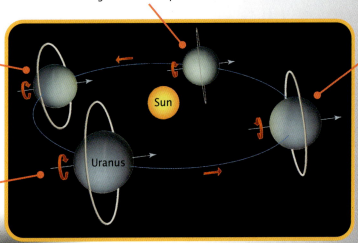

Uranus's North Pole has nearly 42 years of sunlight, while its South Pole is in darkness.

When Uranus's equator faces the Sun, for a brief period the planet has around 8.5 hours of sunlight followed by 8.5 hours of darkness.

Uranus's South Pole has nearly 42 years of sunlight, while its North Pole is in darkness.

Uranus's tilt gives the planet a strange pattern of night and day.

URANUS PROFILE

Diameter: 50,724 km (31,518 miles)
Mass: 14.5 Earths
Average distance from the Sun: 2.87 billion km (1.78 billion miles)
Orbit: 84 years
Rotation: 17.2 hours
Moons: 27 known

Uranus travels around the Sun at a speed of 24,515 km/h (15,233 miles per hour).

The rings may be composed of tiny fragments of a moon or moons shattered by an impact.

Coldest Planet

Although Neptune is farther from the Sun, Uranus is the coldest planet in the Solar System. The temperature of its atmosphere falls to -224 °C (-371 °F). Some astronomers think this is because Uranus's collision (see "Turning Sideways") knocked out much of its heat. Others think Uranus may have a layer of magnesium, which prevents its core from losing heat to its outer layers, like a warm coat.

Taken by the *Hubble Space Telescope*, this photo shows a bright cloud in Uranus's northern hemisphere. Due to its cold atmosphere, Uranus has fewer clouds than the other giant planets, since clouds are caused by warm, rising gas.

DID YOU KNOW? Uranus was the Greek god of the sky, father of the Titans including Cronus, who was known to the Romans as Saturn.

Moons of Uranus

The five largest of Uranus's 27 known moons were discovered between 1787 and 1948. The smaller moons were spotted in photos taken by the space probe *Voyager 2* in 1986, or were identified between 1997 and 2003 using advanced telescopes such as the *Hubble Space Telescope*.

From Titania, Uranus appears around 13 times bigger in the sky than the Moon appears from Earth.

Moon Groups

Orbiting among Uranus's rings are 13 small moons, none bigger than 162 km (100 miles) wide. Made of ice and an unknown dark material, these inner moons probably formed from the same shattered moon as the rings. Beyond the inner moons are five large moons, orbiting 129,390 to 583,520 km (80,400 to 362,580 miles) from Uranus. Far beyond the large moons are another nine small moons, which orbit up to 20.4 million km (12.7 million miles) from Uranus. These outer moons were probably objects captured by Uranus's gravity.

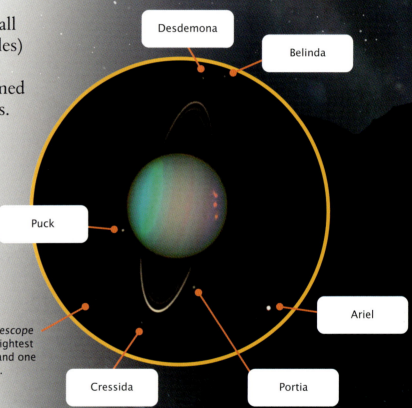

In 2003, the *Hubble Space Telescope* took this photo of Uranus's brightest rings, five of its inner moons, and one of its large moons, Ariel.

TITANIA PROFILE

Diameter: 1,577 km (980 miles)
Mass: 0.00059 Earths
Average distance from Uranus: 435,910 km (270,860 miles)
Orbit around Uranus: 8.7 days
Rotation: 8.7 days

DID YOU KNOW? Uranus's moons are named after characters in the works of English playwright William Shakespeare and English poet Alexander Pope.

The moon Ariel shines as a crescent where it reflects the light of the distant Sun.

Large Moons

From biggest to smallest, Uranus's five large moons are: Titania, Oberon, Umbriel, Ariel, and Miranda. They probably formed from the gas and dust spinning around the young Uranus. Apart from Miranda, which is mostly ice, they are a mix of roughly equal parts rock and ice. Their surfaces are cratered by impacts with space rocks. All five make almost perfect circles around Uranus's dramatically tilted equator.

Miranda — Ariel — Umbriel — Titania — Oberon

Miranda is closest to Uranus's equator, while Oberon is farthest away.

The Solar System's eighth largest moon, Titania's surface has canyons and ridges caused by the moon expanding and cracking during its early life.

Neptune

Invisible to the naked eye, Neptune was the last of the eight planets to be discovered. A deeper blue than Uranus, Neptune gets its hue from methane and an unknown material in its atmosphere. Neptune has five main rings, which are very faint and dusty.

A Team Effort

In the early 19th century, French astronomer Alexis Bouvard realized there must be an undiscovered eighth planet when he noted that Uranus's orbit was affected by the pull of a more distant, large object. The French astronomer and mathematician Urbain Le Verrier then calculated where an eighth planet should be. He sent his findings to German astronomer Johann Galle, who found the new planet, soon named Neptune, through a telescope in 1846.

Urbain Le Verrier used mathematics to locate Neptune, which was the only one of the eight Solar System planets not found by sight alone.

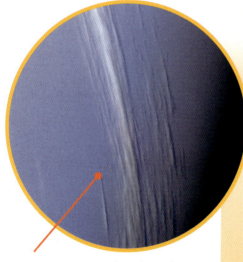

Taken by *Voyager 2*, this photo shows clouds of frozen methane crystals, which are parallel with Neptune's equator.

Windy Planet

Neptune has the fastest winds of any planet in the Solar System, blowing at up to 2,100 km/h (1,300 miles per hour). The super speed of these winds, which usually blow in the opposite direction to Neptune's rotation, is partly caused by Neptune's fast spin of 9,650 km/h (5,995 miles per hour). In addition, the winds are given energy by the planet's internal heat, which reaches 5,100 °C (9,200 °F) at Neptune's core.

DID YOU KNOW? Due to Neptune's great distance, the space probe *Voyager 2* is the only spacecraft that has flown past the planet.

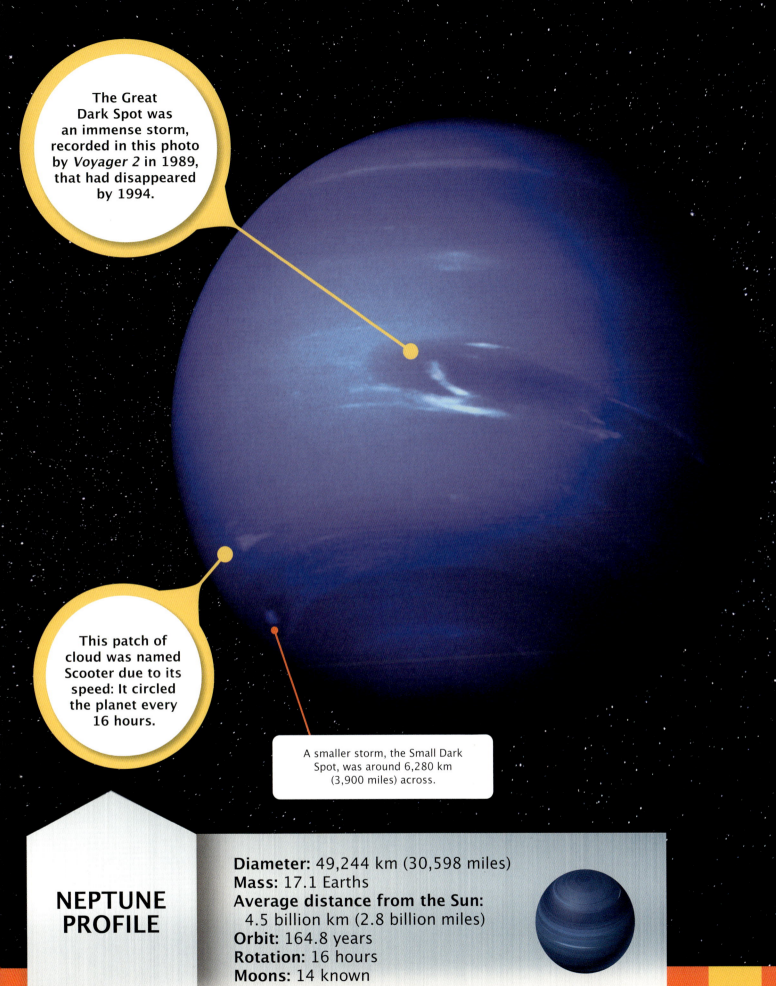

The Great Dark Spot was an immense storm, recorded in this photo by *Voyager 2* in 1989, that had disappeared by 1994.

This patch of cloud was named Scooter due to its speed: It circled the planet every 16 hours.

A smaller storm, the Small Dark Spot, was around 6,280 km (3,900 miles) across.

NEPTUNE PROFILE

Diameter: 49,244 km (30,598 miles)
Mass: 17.1 Earths
Average distance from the Sun: 4.5 billion km (2.8 billion miles)
Orbit: 164.8 years
Rotation: 16 hours
Moons: 14 known

Moons of Neptune

Neptune was the Roman god of the sea, so all the planet's 14 known moons are named after Greek and Roman gods, goddesses, and creatures linked with water. The largest moon, Triton, has a mass more than 500 times greater than the second largest moon, Proteus.

Triton was discovered by English astronomer William Lassell in 1846, 17 days after the discovery of Neptune.

Triton has a core of metal and rock, surrounded by frozen water and covered with frozen nitrogen.

Seven Strange Moons

Neptune's outer moons are Triton, Nereid, Halimede, Sao, Laomedeia, Psamathe, and Neso. These moons have irregular orbits, which means that their path is very elliptical (stretched) and is inclined (tilted) rather than around the planet's equator. Four of them orbit in the opposite direction from the way their planet is turning. All this tells astronomers that the outer moons did not form around Neptune but were objects captured by the planet's gravity.

Orbit of inner moon Proteus

Triton has an irregular orbit and travels in the opposite direction from Neptune's inner moons.

TRITON PROFILE

Diameter: 2,710 km (1,680 miles)
Mass: 0.0036 Earths
Average distance from Neptune: 354,800 km (220,500 miles)
Orbit around Neptune: 5.88 days
Rotation: 5.88 days

Around 420 km (260 miles) across, Proteus was photographed by the space probe *Voyager 2*.

Triton's surface erupts plumes of nitrogen gas and dust 8 km (5 miles) high, probably caused by the Sun heating nitrogen.

Larissa

Galatea

Taken by the *Hubble Space Telescope*, this photo shows Neptune with its four largest inner moons.

Despina

Seven Regular Moons

Neptune's seven inner moons are Naiad, Thalassa, Despina, Galatea, Larissa, Hippocamp, and Proteus. They probably formed when Triton was dragged into orbit, smashing Neptune's existing moons. Neptune's gravity pulled the rubble into orbit around its equator, spinning in the same direction the planet turned. The rubble clumped together, forming seven moons with regular orbits.

DID YOU KNOW? The Solar System's seventh largest moon, Triton was probably a dwarf planet pulled from the Kuiper Belt by Neptune's gravity.

Chapter 5

Other Solar System Objects

In addition to the eight planets and their moons, many trillions of smaller objects—made of rock, metal, dust, or ice—are in orbit around the Sun. The largest are known as dwarf planets, while the smallest are specks of dust in vast clouds.

Types of Objects

Some small Solar System objects, including comets and centaurs (see page 100), travel between different regions of the Solar System. However, most small objects orbit the Sun in distinct regions. Between the orbits of Mars and Jupiter, the Asteroid Belt contains objects known as asteroids, made of rock and metal. Beyond the orbit of Neptune, the Kuiper Belt and Scattered Disk hold objects made mostly of ice and rock. In the farthest regions of the Solar System are "detached objects" and the possible Oort Cloud.

Although most asteroids orbit in the Asteroid Belt, some—known as trojans—share the orbit of a planet or moon. Most trojans share the orbit of Jupiter.

This illustration compares the size of Earth with the three largest widely agreed dwarf planets, Pluto, Eris, and Haumea.

Dwarf Planets

Unlike a moon, a dwarf planet orbits the Sun directly. It has a mass (weight) large enough for its gravity to pull it into a rounded shape, which tends to happen when a rocky object is over 600 km (370 miles) wide. Yet a dwarf planet's gravity is not enough to clear objects out of its orbit, unlike a true planet. Different astronomers count different numbers of dwarf planets, from 5 to over 120. Most agree on 9: Ceres, in the Asteroid Belt; Orcus, Pluto, Haumea, Quaoar, and Makemake in the Kuiper Belt; Gonggong and Eris in the Scattered Disk; and the detached object Sedna.

The Asteroid Belt lies between 2.2 and 3.2 astronomical units (AU) from the Sun, with 1 AU equal to the distance from Earth to the Sun: 150 million km (93 million miles).

The Kuiper Belt extends from 30 to 50 AU from the Sun.

The Oort Cloud is believed to surround the Sun at a distance of 2,000 to 200,000 AU.

DID YOU KNOW? Pluto was called a planet until 2006, when the International Astronomical Union put it in the newly defined category of dwarf planets.

Asteroid Belt

The Asteroid Belt contains up to 1.9 million asteroids larger than 1 km (0.6 miles) across and many millions of smaller ones. Asteroids are rocky and metallic objects left over from the formation of the Inner Solar System.

The combined mass of all the asteroids in the Asteroid Belt is around 4 percent of the mass of Earth's Moon.

Forming the Belt

As the Solar System formed 4.6 billion years ago, the powerful gravity of nearby Jupiter disrupted the material in the Asteroid Belt region, keeping it from clumping together into a true planet. Asteroids are made of similar materials to the inner planets. Most are made of silicate rocks (like Earth's mantle and crust), while others contain large amounts of the metals nickel and iron (like Earth's core). Asteroids are in three main types, based on their composition:

C-type asteroid: Around 50 km (31 miles) across, Mathilde is made mainly of clay (an earthy material that forms in water) and silicate rocks.

S-type asteroid: About 12 km (7.5 miles) wide, Gaspra is made mainly of silicate rocks and nickel–iron.

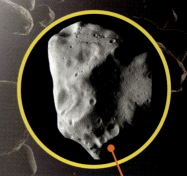

M-type asteroid: Lutetia, around 100 km (62 miles) across, contains high quantities of metal.

ASTEROID BELT PROFILE

Diameter: Around 150 million km (93 million miles)
Mass: 0.0048 Earths
Distance from the Sun: 329 million to 478.7 million km 204.4 million to 297.5 million miles)
Orbit of each asteroid: 3 to 6 years
Rotation of each asteroid: Up to 50 days

DID YOU KNOW? The four largest asteroids—Ceres, Vesta, Pallas, and Hygeia—account for around half the mass of the Asteroid Belt.

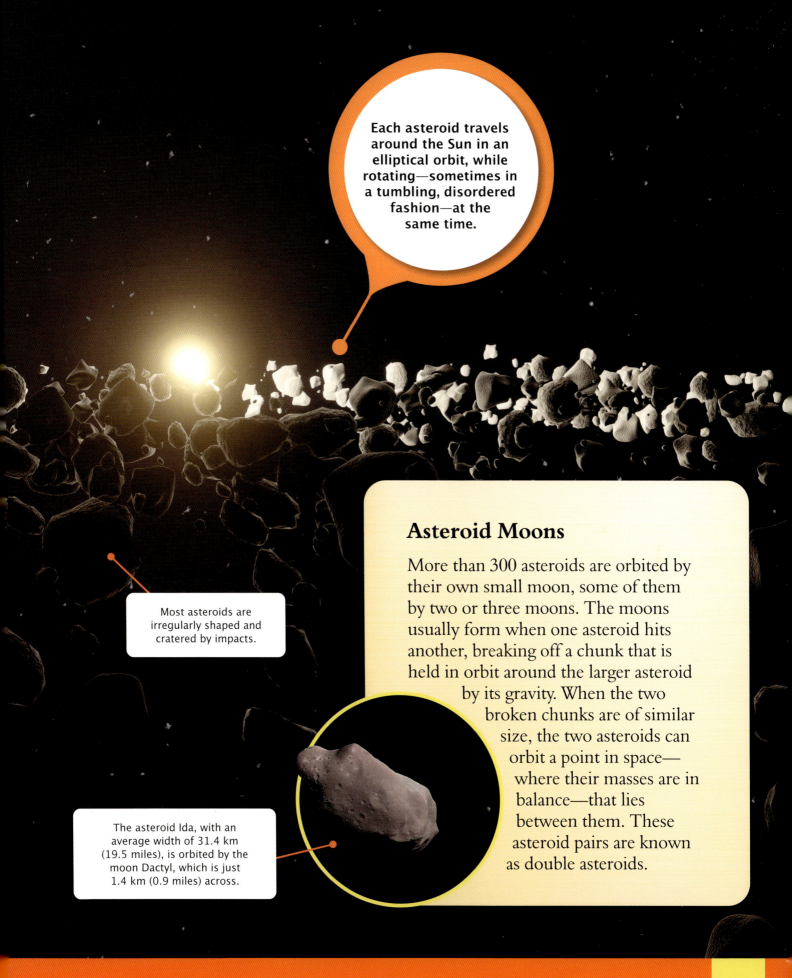

Each asteroid travels around the Sun in an elliptical orbit, while rotating—sometimes in a tumbling, disordered fashion—at the same time.

Most asteroids are irregularly shaped and cratered by impacts.

The asteroid Ida, with an average width of 31.4 km (19.5 miles), is orbited by the moon Dactyl, which is just 1.4 km (0.9 miles) across.

Asteroid Moons

More than 300 asteroids are orbited by their own small moon, some of them by two or three moons. The moons usually form when one asteroid hits another, breaking off a chunk that is held in orbit around the larger asteroid by its gravity. When the two broken chunks are of similar size, the two asteroids can orbit a point in space—where their masses are in balance—that lies between them. These asteroid pairs are known as double asteroids.

Ceres

Orbiting in the middle of the Asteroid Belt, Ceres is the only asteroid large enough to be considered a dwarf planet. It was the first object in the Asteroid Belt to be spotted, in 1801 by Italian astronomer Giuseppe Piazzi, who named it after the Roman goddess of farming.

Watery Rock

Ceres has the most water of any object in the Solar System apart from Earth. Around 25 to 50 percent of Ceres is water, which is mixed with rock, salty minerals, and clay. Since Ceres is cold, the water is almost completely frozen, but pockets of liquid water are believed to lie beneath the surface. Scientists wonder if tiny life forms might be found in this water.

Much of what we know about Ceres was discovered by the *Dawn* space probe, the first probe to orbit a dwarf planet, in 2015.

Ice Volcano

Ceres has one large mountain, Ahuna Mons, which is about 4 km (2.5 miles) high. It is a cryovolcano—an ice volcano. The mountain lies almost exactly on the opposite side of Ceres to the dwarf planet's largest impact crater, the Kerwan Basin, which measures 284 km (176 miles) across. The impact that made the crater may have broken the crust on the opposite side of Ceres, from which icy, muddy water erupted. The muddy water then froze, creating a mountain.

Ahuna Mons probably formed in the last 240 million years but is no longer active.

DID YOU KNOW? With binoculars or a store-bought telescope, Ceres is just bright enough to be seen in the night sky, looking like a dim star.

Far from the Sun, Ceres has a surface temperature between −163 and −38 °C (−261 and −36 °F).

Bright spots in Occator Crater are probably caused by icy salts reflecting the Sun's light.

Ceres has no atmosphere, apart from small amounts of water vapor (water in the form of a gas) that drift from the surface.

CERES PROFILE

Diameter: 939 km (583 miles)
Mass: 0.00016 Earths
Average distance from the Sun: 414 million km (257 million miles)
Orbit: 4.6 years
Rotation: 9 hours
Moons: 0

Kuiper Belt

Beyond Neptune, the Kuiper Belt is a ring of icy objects that orbit the Sun. The Kuiper Belt is 20 times wider than the Asteroid Belt and contains around 20 times more material. There may be 100,000 Kuiper Belt objects (KBOs) more than 100 km (62 miles) wide.

Discovering the Kuiper Belt

The first KBO to be discovered was the largest, Pluto (see page 96), in 1930. Apart from Pluto and its largest moon, there was no proof of other objects beyond Neptune until 1992, when a third object was discovered—named Albion—by David Jewitt and Jane Luu, using a telescope at the Mauna Kea Observatory in Hawaii. Over 2,000 KBOs have been discovered since.

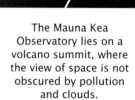

The Mauna Kea Observatory lies on a volcano summit, where the view of space is not obscured by pollution and clouds.

Not a Sphere

The second largest object in the Kuiper Belt is the dwarf planet Haumea, which measures around 2,000 km (1,245 miles) at its longest point. Unlike the other large dwarf planets, Haumea is not a sphere or close to one: It is an ellipsoid (a flattened sphere). Haumea's gravity was powerful enough to pull it into a rounded shape, but its very rapid rotation—of just 4 hours—flattened it, like a spinning ball of dough forms a pizza base.

Named after the Hawaiian goddess of childbirth, Haumea has two moons—Hi'iaka and Namaka, both also named after Hawaiian goddesses—as well as a ring of icy dust.

KBOs are made of rock and materials such as water, methane, and ammonia, which are frozen due to the average temperature of −220 °C (−364 °F).

KUIPER BELT PROFILE

Diameter: Around 3 billion km (1.9 billion miles)
Mass: Around 0.1 Earths
Distance from the Sun: 4.5 billion to 7.5 billion km (2.8 billion to 4.7 billion miles)
Orbit of each KBO: Around 200 to 320 years
Rotation of each KBO: Usually less than 1 day

This illustration imagines the moment when the *New Horizons* space probe flew past the KBO Arrokoth in 2019.

Arrokoth is formed of two KBOs that have joined together, resulting in a peanut-shaped object 36 km (22 miles) long.

DID YOU KNOW? The Kuiper Belt is named after Dutch astronomer Gerard Kuiper, who in 1951 suggested that there might be objects beyond Pluto.

Pluto

Orbiting in the Kuiper Belt, Pluto is the largest dwarf planet by diameter. Pluto was named after the Greek god of the underworld, a suggestion made by 11-year-old English schoolgirl Venetia Burney in 1930.

Pluto's Structure

Pluto has a large core of rock that takes up around two-thirds of its interior. The core is surrounded by a layer of water up to 180 km (112 miles) thick. The water is probably frozen, but some astronomers think Pluto's interior is warm enough for it to be liquid. Pluto's crust is made of frozen nitrogen (a gas that forms the majority of Earth's atmosphere), with traces of frozen water, methane, and carbon monoxide.

This photo of Pluto, taken by the *New Horizons* probe in 2015, has slightly exaggerated the shades of the planet's surface to show its different materials.

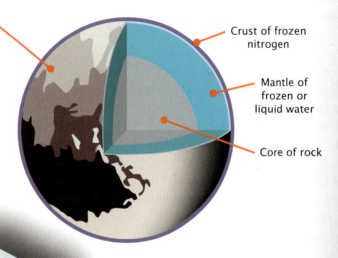

Pluto's core may be around 700 °C (1,292 °F), but its surface temperature is about –229 °C (–380 °F).

Crust of frozen nitrogen

Mantle of frozen or liquid water

Core of rock

Red areas are covered in an unknown material that may be created by sunlight heating the surface's methane and carbon monoxide, turning them red.

PLUTO PROFILE

Diameter: 2,377 km (1,477 miles)
Mass: 0.00218 Earths
Average distance from the Sun: 5.9 billion km (3.7 billion miles)
Orbit: 248 years
Rotation: 6.4 days
Moons: 5 known

DID YOU KNOW? Snow is rare in the Solar System, but when Pluto journeys farthest from the Sun, its thin atmosphere—which is mainly nitrogen gas—freezes and falls as snow.

Monster Moons

Pluto has five moons, all named after monsters or characters and places associated with the underworld in Greek myths. From closest to farthest from Pluto, they are: Charon, Styx, Nix, Kerberos, and Hydra. The largest moon, Charon, is around 1,212 km (753 miles) wide. It is so big compared with Pluto that the two objects orbit around a point in space a little outside Pluto. This has led some astronomers to call the pair a double dwarf planet.

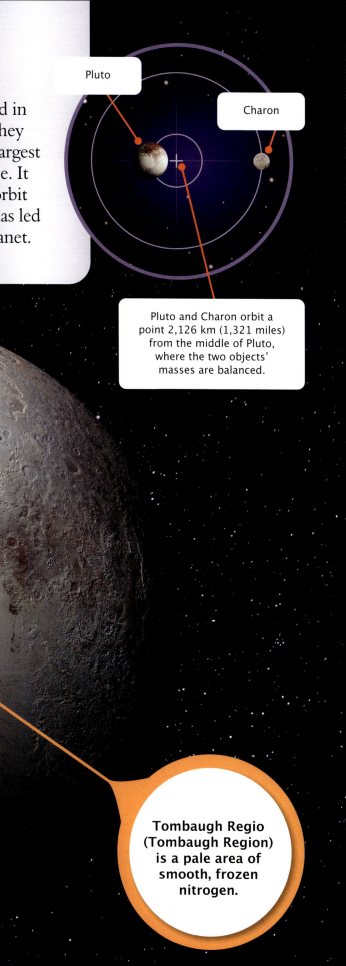

Pluto

Charon

Pluto and Charon orbit a point 2,126 km (1,321 miles) from the middle of Pluto, where the two objects' masses are balanced.

Tombaugh Regio (Tombaugh Region) is a pale area of smooth, frozen nitrogen.

Scattered Disk

Like the Asteroid and Kuiper Belts, the Scattered Disk is a region of small objects that orbit the Sun. Yet Scattered Disk objects (SDOs) have more irregular orbits than the objects in the belts. Although the inner edge of the Scattered Disk overlaps with the Kuiper Belt, its outer edge is twice as far from the Sun.

Eris

The largest object in the Scattered Disk is Eris, which was discovered in 2005 and at first named a "planet" but soon downgraded to "dwarf planet." With a mass of around 0.0028 Earths, Eris is the biggest dwarf planet by mass, but—at 2,326 km (1,445 miles) across—it is slightly smaller than Pluto by diameter. Eris's greater mass is probably due to a larger quantity of rocky materials.

The Sun is an average 10 billion km (6.2 billion miles) from Eris, which rarely passes closer to another SDO (apart from its moon) than a million kilometers.

No space probe has yet taken close-up photos of Eris, but this image of the dwarf planet and its one known moon, Dysnomia, was captured by the *Hubble Space Telescope* in 2007.

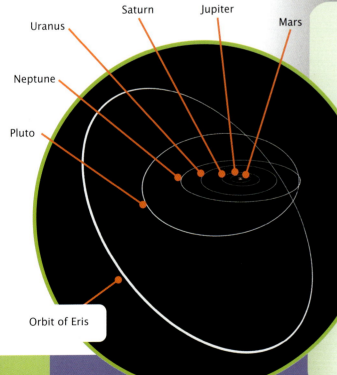

Orbit of Eris

Uranus, Neptune, Pluto, Saturn, Jupiter, Mars

Scattering

Like Kuiper Belt objects (KBOs), SDOs are made of frozen materials such as water and methane, as well as rock. SDOs probably once orbited in the Kuiper Belt, but they have been "scattered" by the gravity of Neptune. This made their orbits much more elliptical (stretched out of a circle). The scattering also tilted the SDOs' orbits away from the plane of the Solar System by up to 40 degrees, so they orbit both far above and below the Sun's equator.

This illustration shows Eris's orbit in comparison with the orbits of the planets and the KBO Pluto. Eris's average distance from the Sun is 68 AUs, but it travels as close as 38 AUs and as far as 97 AUs.

SCATTERED DISK PROFILE

Diameter: Around 10.5 billion km (6.5 billion miles)
Mass: Between 0.01 and 0.1 Earths
Distance from the Sun: 4.5 billion to 15 billion km (2.8 billion to 9.3 billion miles)
Orbit of each SDO: Around 400 to 700 years
Rotation of each SDO: Usually less than 1 day

Eris's moon Dysnomia is about 700 km (435 miles) across, making it the 17th largest known moon in the Solar System.

This illustration imagines Eris with a pale crust, probably made of methane that is frozen due to a surface temperature of around −231 °C (−384 °F).

DID YOU KNOW? Eris was named after the Greek goddess of disagreement, since its discovery started a debate about the difference between a planet and dwarf planet.

Comets

Comets are rocky, dusty, icy objects with elliptical orbits that take them both close to and very far from the Sun. When comets near the Sun, they get so hot they release glowing gas. In most years, a comet can be seen—perhaps faintly—in the night sky without a telescope.

Making a Comet

Comets with orbits less than 200 years, known as short-period comets, probably started life in the Kuiper Belt or Scattered Disk. The gravity of the outer planets disturbed these objects, throwing them into highly elliptical orbits. Long-period comets, which have orbits between 200 and many thousands of years, may have begun in the Oort Cloud when a passing star disrupted their orbit. Centaurs are comet-like objects, probably from the Kuiper Belt, with orbits that cross the paths of the outer planets until they are thrown aside or destroyed.

The orbit of the long-period comet Hale-Bopp takes around 2,400 years. The spectacular comet was visible to the naked eye from Earth between 1996 and 1997.

Two Tails

The core of a comet, known as the nucleus, is made of rock, dust, water ice, and frozen gasses such as carbon monoxide and methane. When a comet passes the orbit of Jupiter, it thaws and starts to release gas. By the time the comet is passing Earth's orbit, it is trailing a tail of gas, which is always blown away from the Sun by the solar wind. As the comet nears the Sun, a second tail—made of dust—develops.

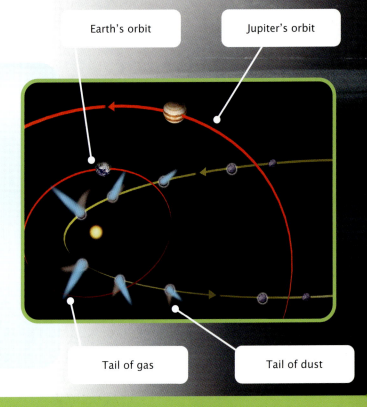

Earth's orbit

Jupiter's orbit

Tail of gas

Tail of dust

DID YOU KNOW? There are more than 4,580 known comets, but there are probably many more long-period comets currently in the far reaches of the Solar System.

The comet's faint, blue gas tail—containing high levels of super-hot carbon monoxide—stretched for hundreds of thousands of kilometers.

This golden tail was made of dust released from the nucleus, the grains reflecting the Sun's light.

The long-period comet Neowise was visible from Earth in 2020.

COMET NEOWISE PROFILE

Diameter of core: 5 km (3 miles)
Closest distance from the Sun: 43 million km (27 million miles)
Farthest distance from the Sun: 106 billion km (66 billion miles)
Orbit: Around 6,792 years
Named for: The *WISE* (Wide-Field Infrared Survey Explorer) telescope, through which astronomers first spotted the comet in 2020

Meteor Showers

Also known as a shooting star, a meteor is a glowing fragment of space rock that is falling through Earth's atmosphere. When many meteors appear from one point in the night sky, it is known as a meteor shower. Showers are caused by dust from a comet's tail or an asteroid.

The Geminids meteor shower appears to come from the direction of the Gemini star constellation.

Burning Up

Every day, millions of fragments from comets and asteroids enter Earth's atmosphere. These fragments crash into air molecules again and again, which makes them very hot—and creates a streak of light. Meteors become visible between 75 to 120 km (47 to 75 miles) above Earth's surface. Since most fragments are smaller than a grain of sand, they burn up completely before reaching Earth's surface, the majority of them without being noticed.

During its journey through the atmosphere, a space rock's surface can heat up to 1,800 °C (3,270 °F).

GEMINIDS SHOWER PROFILE

Source of dust: Near-Earth asteroid Phaethon
Time of year: December
Seen from: Best viewed from the northern hemisphere, but also visible from the southern hemisphere close to the horizon
Number of meteors per hour at peak: 120 to 160
First observed: 1862

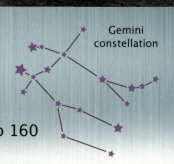

Gemini constellation

DID YOU KNOW? The first written record of the Perseids meteor shower dates from the year 36, when it was observed over China.

This photo was taken with a long camera exposure, so it shows the night sky over several minutes.

Geminid meteors travel at 35 km/s (22 miles per second) and disintegrate at heights above 39 km (24 miles) from Earth's surface.

Yearly Events

Earth's year-long orbit takes it through the dust from several comet tails and disintegrating asteroids. This results in a series of meteor showers that take place at particular times of year, including the Lyrids in April, Leonids in November, and Ursids in December. Showers are named after the star constellation that lies in the direction from which they fall.

The Perseids meteor shower is caused by dust from the comet Swift-Tuttle and appears from the direction of the Perseus constellation in August. At the shower's peak, one meteor can be seen per minute, shown here in a long camera exposure.

Meteorite Impacts

Space rocks that are large enough to make it all the way to Earth's surface are called meteorites. They can cause damage when they hit the ground. Large meteorites smash craters into Earth's surface, scatter debris across a wide area, and can even change the weather.

Fragments (small pieces) of meteorite found around the Meteor Crater site show that the incoming space rock was rich in iron.

The Moon records impacts (crashes) from up to 4 billion years ago (see page 42).

DID YOU KNOW? Much of the world's nickel is mined at the site of a large comet impact crater in Ontario, Canada.

Meteorite Hunting

Scientists find meteorites interesting because they are often made of material that has not changed since the early days of the Solar System. But unless you see it fall, how do you tell a meteorite from a normal Earth rock? The trick is to look for them where no natural rocks should be—in deserts or on top of the ice in polar regions.

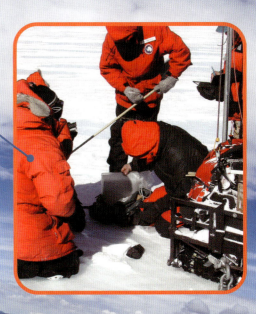

Scientists in Antarctica collect a meteorite lying on top of the ice.

In 1908, a meteorite exploded over Russia, flattening 80 million trees.

Meteor Crater in Arizona is about 1,200 m (3,900 ft) wide. It was created when a 50-m (165-ft) meteorite landed about 50,000 years ago.

Dangers from Space

The largest meteorites can cause damage far beyond where they land. They fling fiery debris very far and throw huge amounts of dust into the air, blocking out sunlight. Around 66 million years ago, a huge asteroid impact in the Gulf of Mexico blocked sunlight, killing many plants and wiping out the dinosaurs.

Farthest Regions

Beyond the Scattered Disk may lie two other groups of cold, distant, and mysterious objects: the detached objects and the even more distant Oort Cloud. Despite their vast distances from our star, these objects are still held in orbit by the Sun's immense gravity.

Detached Objects

These objects are too far away to be affected by the outer planets' gravity—making them appear "detached" from the rest of the Solar System. The few detached objects discovered so far have extremely elliptical orbits, which may have been affected by the pull of a passing star. The largest known detached object is the dwarf planet Sedna. When closest to the Sun (as it is now), Sedna is within the Scattered Disk, but at its most distant it is 140 billion km (87 billion miles) away.

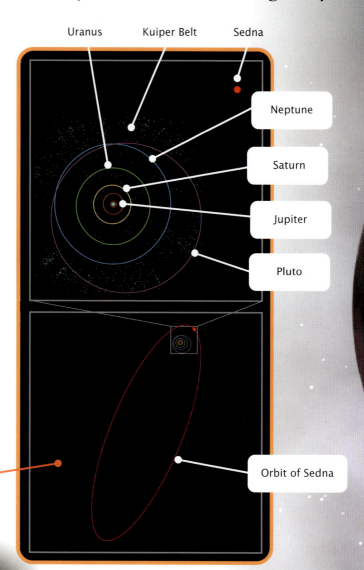

This diagram shows the orbit of Sedna compared with the orbits of the outer planets and Pluto.

SEDNA PROFILE

Diameter: Around 1,000 km (620 miles)
Mass: Not known
Average distance from the Sun: 75.7 billion km (47 billion miles)
Orbit: Around 11,390 years
Rotation: Around 10 hours
Moons: None yet found

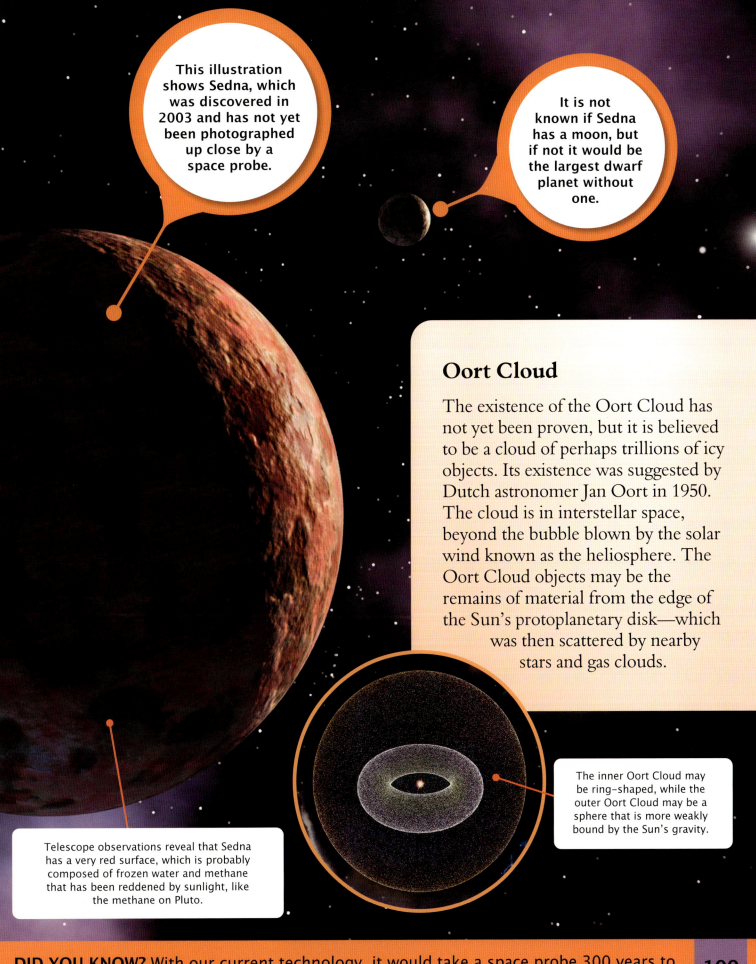

This illustration shows Sedna, which was discovered in 2003 and has not yet been photographed up close by a space probe.

It is not known if Sedna has a moon, but if not it would be the largest dwarf planet without one.

Oort Cloud

The existence of the Oort Cloud has not yet been proven, but it is believed to be a cloud of perhaps trillions of icy objects. Its existence was suggested by Dutch astronomer Jan Oort in 1950. The cloud is in interstellar space, beyond the bubble blown by the solar wind known as the heliosphere. The Oort Cloud objects may be the remains of material from the edge of the Sun's protoplanetary disk—which was then scattered by nearby stars and gas clouds.

The inner Oort Cloud may be ring-shaped, while the outer Oort Cloud may be a sphere that is more weakly bound by the Sun's gravity.

Telescope observations reveal that Sedna has a very red surface, which is probably composed of frozen water and methane that has been reddened by sunlight, like the methane on Pluto.

DID YOU KNOW? With our current technology, it would take a space probe 300 years to reach the inner edge of the Oort Cloud, perhaps 300 billion km (186 billion miles) away.

Chapter 6

Astronomy

> A typical person can see about 3,000 stars in the night sky with just their normal eyesight.

Seeing the wonders of space for yourself could not be easier. On a clear, dark night, anyone can stargaze. Special tools such as binoculars or telescopes can help you, but you can also see a lot with nothing more than your eyes.

Ready to Stargaze

To see as much as possible in the night sky, allow your eyes to get used to the dark. If you can, get out into the countryside, away from the glow of nearby cities. Be away from streetlights and phone screens, and do not shine flashlights. After about ten minutes you will find your eyes are much better at seeing faint stars.

Binoculars

If you want to explore more of the night sky, see if you can borrow a pair of binoculars. They are a lot easier to use than a telescope, and you will see thousands more stars than with the naked eye because they pick up more light. They also make everything you view appear larger, so you can see objects such as the Moon in more detail.

Binoculars are an ideal way to get a deeper look at the night sky.

How far can you see without a telescope? All the way to the Andromeda Galaxy, some 2.5 million light-years from Earth!

Many areas of the world are lit up at night. This makes it harder and harder to find really dark skies.

ANDROMEDA GALAXY PROFILE

Diameter: 200,000 light years
Mass: Around 1 trillion Suns
Catalogue number: Messier 31
Constellation: Andromeda
Distance from Earth: 2.5 million light-years
Description: This large spiral galaxy appears as a fuzzy blob of light in dark skies. Binoculars show its oval shape.

DID YOU KNOW? If you need to use a flashlight while stargazing, cover it with red film—your eyes are less sensitive to red light so you will not ruin your night vision.

Early Ideas

People have looked up at the stars and planets, and tried to explain them, since before written history. Many believed that these strange lights in the sky could control events on Earth, and they tried to foresee their movements. This was the birth of astronomy.

Greek Astronomers

The ancient Greeks were the first people to come up with complete models of the Universe, in the last few centuries BCE. Believing that Earth was the biggest and most important object, they decided it was in the middle of space, with everything else moving around it.

The peoples of Central and South America built huge stone temples in arrangements that lined them up with the stars and planets in the night sky.

The Greek astronomer Hipparchus realized that the Earth was tilted on its axis.

DID YOU KNOW? A Greek astronomer called Aristarchus suggested the Earth moves round the Sun as early as 250 BCE.

Before the invention of telescopes, astronomers used instruments such as this armillary sphere.

An armillary sphere helps to measure where objects are in the sky.

A Solar System

The idea of Earth in the middle of everything lasted almost 2,000 years, even though astronomers found it did not help them work out the movement of planets. In 1514, Polish priest Nicolaus Copernicus suggested that the Sun was actually at the heart of our Solar System, and Earth was just one of many planets moving around it.

Copernicus's ideas were not proven until the early 1600s.

Signs of the Zodiac

Ancient astronomers made pictures out of the stars in the sky—the patterns that we call constellations. They soon noticed that the Sun and planets followed paths around the sky that moved through just 12 of these constellations, so they gave these special importance. They became the signs of the zodiac.

Most of the zodiac constellations are animals.

Telescopes

Telescopes are the most important tools astronomers use to look at objects in space. They gather up much more light than our human eyes so that we can see fainter objects, and they create a magnified (enlarged) image so that we can see much smaller details.

Two Designs

Telescopes come in two types. Refractors use two or more lenses at either end of a long tube to create a magnified image. Reflectors use a mirror to reflect light to a lens, and can have a more compact design. The job of the first lens or mirror is to collect light from a large area and bend or reflect it so that it passes through the smaller eyepiece lens.

The Yerkes Observatory refractor is the world's largest lens-based telescope.

Birth of the Telescope

The first telescopes were made by Dutch lensmakers around 1608, but the invention was made famous by Italian astronomer Galileo Galilei, who built his own telescope a few months later. He used it to make important discoveries, studying moons around Jupiter, craters on the Moon, and star clouds in the Milky Way.

Galileo's studies made him believe that the planets move around the Sun, as Copernicus had suggested.

DID YOU KNOW? Galileo's first telescope could magnify by only 3 times, but even today's amateur telescopes can magnify by up to 500 times.

YERKES TELESCOPE PROFILE

Telescope type: Refracting
Built: 1897
Lens diameter: 102 cm (40 in)
Length: 19.2 m (63 ft)
Mass: 23.5 tonnes (26 US tons)
Location: Williams Bay, Wisconsin, United States

An observatory dome protects the telescope from the weather.

A shutter opens to allow the telescope to see out into space.

A refracting telescope uses a big lens to bend light to a focus, and a smaller eyepiece to make a magnified image.

A reflecting telescope uses two curved mirrors to collect and focus light, before passing it to a magnifying eyepiece.

A stand holds the telescope's weight so that it can swivel with a gentle push.

Giant Telescopes

Today's largest telescopes are all reflectors. They use huge mirrors to collect enormous amounts of light, but astronomers do not look through them directly—instead of an eyepiece, the telescopes direct their light into electronic detectors that can reveal any hidden details.

Many Mirrors

Instead of using a single mirror, many professional telescopes use many hexagonal (six-sided) mirror pieces, set together in a honeycomb pattern. Their position and shape can be changed by computer-controlled motors as the telescope swings to look in different directions. A single mirror might bend out of shape under its own weight.

The Canada-France-Hawaii Telescope (CFHT) has a single 3.6-m (11.8-ft) mirror. Its camera takes some of the largest pictures of the sky.

Today's large telescopes are built on high mountains that put them above most of Earth's clouds.

The back of the Keck Telescope shows its many mirrors.

GEMINI TELESCOPES PROFILE

Telescope types: Reflecting
Built: 1999 and 2000
Mirror diameters: 8.1 m (26.6 ft)
Mirror masses: 20 tonnes (22 US tons)
Locations: Mauna Kea, Hawaii and Cerro Pachón, Chile

116

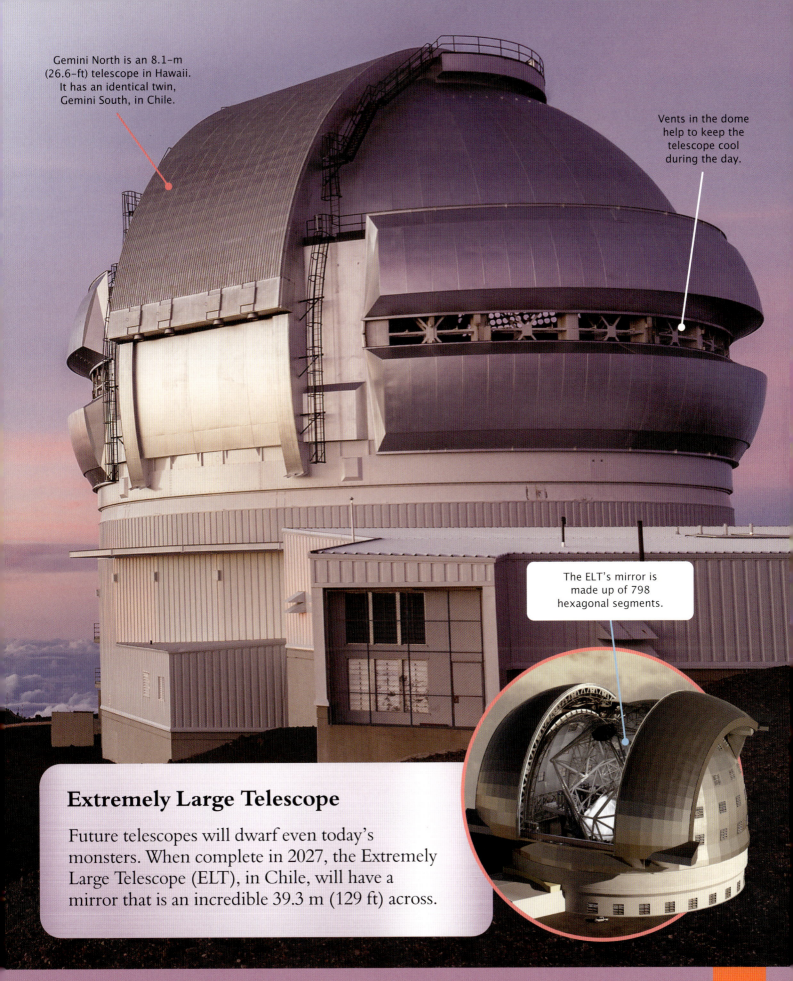

Gemini North is an 8.1-m (26.6-ft) telescope in Hawaii. It has an identical twin, Gemini South, in Chile.

Vents in the dome help to keep the telescope cool during the day.

The ELT's mirror is made up of 798 hexagonal segments.

Extremely Large Telescope

Future telescopes will dwarf even today's monsters. When complete in 2027, the Extremely Large Telescope (ELT), in Chile, will have a mirror that is an incredible 39.3 m (129 ft) across.

DID YOU KNOW? The summit of the volcano Mauna Kea, on the Island of Hawaii, is home to 13 giant telescopes.

The Electromagnetic Spectrum

Scientists call the light we see with our eyes a form of electromagnetic radiation—a pattern of electric and magnetic waves moving through space at the speed of light. Light is just one small part of a much wider electromagnetic spectrum, and different objects release different kinds of radiation.

This image of spiral galaxy M81 was captured by the *GALEX* space telescope in ultraviolet light.

Wavelength and Frequency

All kinds of electromagnetic radiation move at the speed of light—the differences between them are because of their wavelength (the distance between the peaks of the waves) and frequency (the number of waves that pass a fixed point every second). The shorter the wavelength and higher the frequency, the more energy a wave can carry.

WAVELENGTHS

FREQUENCY

Astronomers split the spectrum into regions depending on the amount of energy carried in different waves.

VISIBLE LIGHT

GAMMA RAYS | X-RAYS | ULTRAVIOLET | VISIBLE LIGHT | INFRARED | MICROWAVES | RADIO WAVES

High-energy gamma rays are released only by violent cosmic events, such as exploding stars.

X-rays are high-energy rays that are released by superhot gas at million-degree temperatures.

Infrared radiation carries less energy than visible light, and is released by cool space objects.

Infrared Telescopes

Objects that are too cold to shine in visible light can still send out a lot of infrared radiation, which humans can feel as heat. Almost everything on Earth glows in the infrared, but so do other planets, and the clouds of gas and dust from which stars are born.

Finding Infrared

In order to find the faint infrared radiation from distant space objects, astronomers need to try to block out all the radiation from Earth and even from the telescope itself. This is why infrared telescopes are built on high, cold mountaintops or—even better—launched into space as satellites.

Discovery by Accident

Infrared was the first invisible radiation to be discovered, in 1800. It was found by chance by astronomer William Herschel, during an experiment to measure the temperatures of blue, yellow, and red sunlight. Herschel split light through a prism into a rainbow-like spectrum, but discovered that the temperature was hottest just beyond the red end of this spectrum, where no light can be seen.

As well as infrared, William Herschel is famous for discovering the planet Uranus in 1781.

Winds from newborn stars blow the gas around.

DID YOU KNOW? The *Spitzer Space Telescope* was chilled using liquid helium, one of the coldest substances known, so its own heat did not affect its observations.

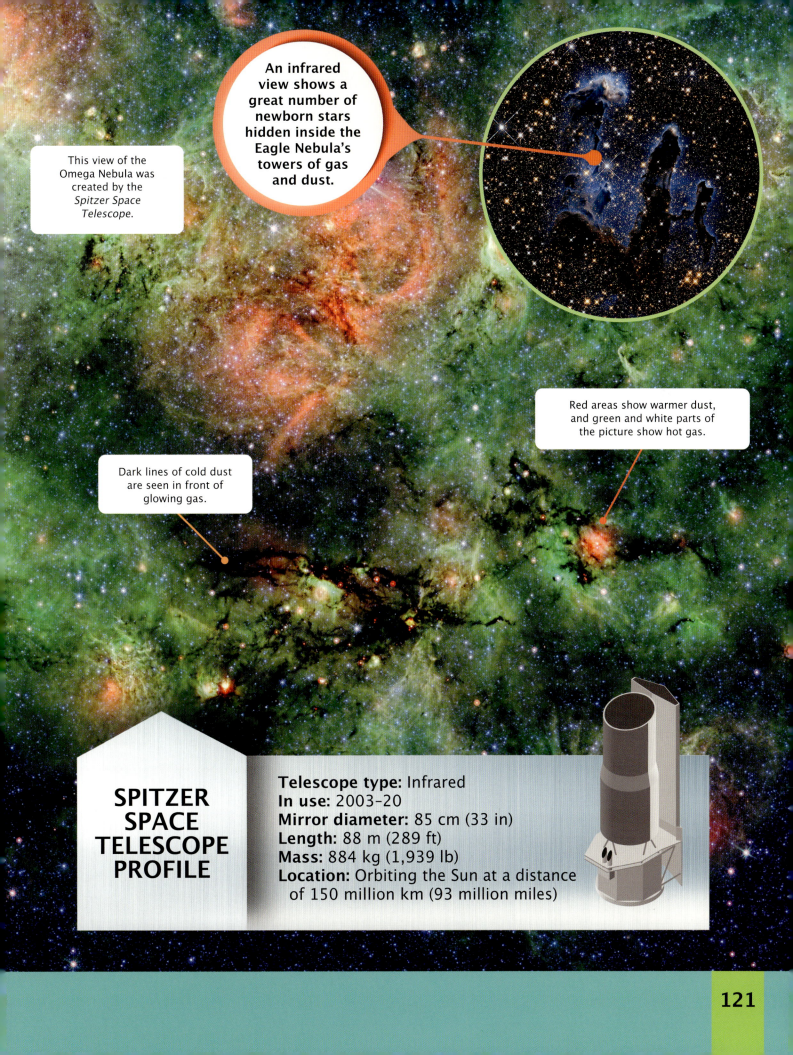

This view of the Omega Nebula was created by the *Spitzer Space Telescope*.

An infrared view shows a great number of newborn stars hidden inside the Eagle Nebula's towers of gas and dust.

Red areas show warmer dust, and green and white parts of the picture show hot gas.

Dark lines of cold dust are seen in front of glowing gas.

SPITZER SPACE TELESCOPE PROFILE

Telescope type: Infrared
In use: 2003–20
Mirror diameter: 85 cm (33 in)
Length: 88 m (289 ft)
Mass: 884 kg (1,939 lb)
Location: Orbiting the Sun at a distance of 150 million km (93 million miles)

Radio Astronomy

Radio waves are the longest, lowest-energy type of electromagnetic radiation, released by some of the coldest objects in the Universe. They help astronomers to find clouds of hydrogen that shape our galaxy and others.

Giant Dishes

Radio wavelengths are millions of times longer than visible light—so spread out that it is hard to work out where they are coming from. So astronomers build giant radio telescopes—metal dishes that collect waves across a huge surface before measuring them with sensitive electronics.

The Very Large Array in New Mexico combines the signals from 27 dishes to create radio pictures of the sky.

Biggest Dishes

The largest single-dish radio telescope used to be an enormous 300-m (1,000-ft) instrument at Arecibo in Puerto Rico. This huge "detector horn" was hung from cables high above the dish. In 2016, Arecibo was overtaken by FAST, an even larger telescope at Dawodang in southern China. It is an amazing 500 m (1,600 ft) across.

The Arecibo Telescope, in Puerto Rico, was in use between 1963 and 2020.

VERY LARGE ARRAY PROFILE

Telescope types: Radio
Built: 1973–80
Number of dishes: 27
Dish diameter: 25 m (82 ft) each
Mass: 209,000 kg (460,000 lb) each
Track length: 3 x 21 km (13 miles)
Location: Socorro, New Mexico, United States

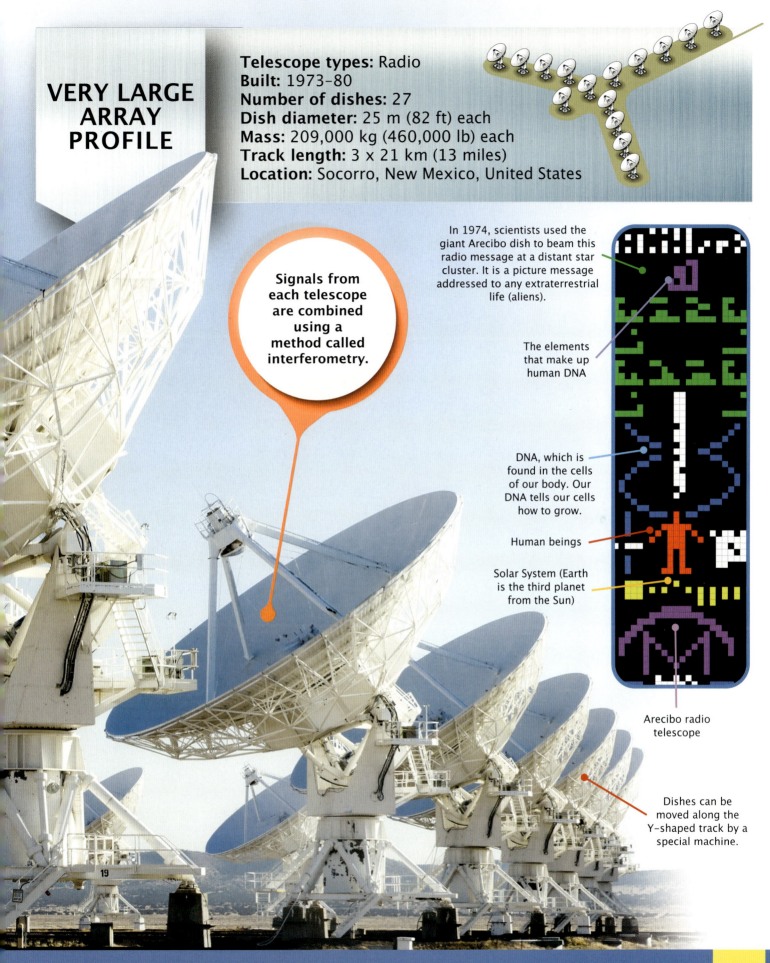

Signals from each telescope are combined using a method called interferometry.

In 1974, scientists used the giant Arecibo dish to beam this radio message at a distant star cluster. It is a picture message addressed to any extraterrestrial life (aliens).

The elements that make up human DNA

DNA, which is found in the cells of our body. Our DNA tells our cells how to grow.

Human beings

Solar System (Earth is the third planet from the Sun)

Arecibo radio telescope

Dishes can be moved along the Y-shaped track by a special machine.

DID YOU KNOW? The Arecibo message is on its way to a star cluster some 25,000 light-years away, so it could be 50,000 years until we get a reply!

Special Rays

Electromagnetic waves with more energy than visible light are mostly stopped by Earth's atmosphere. This is good for life on Earth, because these rays can be dangerous to humans and animals. But it is a problem for astronomers.

Sunrise is a telescope with a 1-m (40-in) mirror, made to study the Sun's ultraviolet rays.

Types of Ray

There are three types of high-energy rays. Those closest to visible light are called ultraviolet (UV) rays, and are released by many objects including the Sun. Those with higher energy are called X-rays and gamma rays. These are created only by the hottest objects and most violent events in the Universe.

Gamma-Ray Bursts

The strongest gamma rays from space come in sudden bursts, and astronomers are still trying to work out where they come from. One kind of gamma-ray burst may come from huge supernova explosions that happen during the death of massive stars. Other, much shorter bursts could be created when superdense neutron stars or black holes come together.

Some supernova explosions may shoot out thin beams of gamma rays.

A helium-filled weather balloon lifted *Sunrise* more than 30 km (19 miles) high, where a lot of UV has not been stopped by Earth's atmosphere yet.

The *Sunrise* UV telescope is strapped to a balloon. It carried out two missions, in June 2009 and June 2013.

Solar panels make energy to power the telescope.

X-rays from the Sun are reflected off the Moon.

Both *Sunrise* missions were launched from the Esrange Space Center in northern Sweden. It is in the Arctic Circle where, during summertime, the Sun never sets.

DID YOU KNOW? Some scientists believe a gamma-ray burst close by meant that a lot of life on Earth got destroyed about 450 million years ago.

Hubble Space Telescope

The most successful telescope ever built, the *Hubble Space Telescope* (*HST*) was the first large visible-light telescope ever put into space. From where it is above Earth's atmosphere, it has clear, sharp views of the Universe.

HST has four bays for carrying many different cameras and other measuring instruments.

Radio antennae connect *HST* with its controllers on Earth using other satellites.

A special tube keeps the mirror safe from direct sunlight and extreme temperature changes.

Hubble has been repaired and upgraded by five Space Shuttle missions during its lifetime. The last time was in 2009.

DID YOU KNOW? The first successful space telescope—*Orbiting Astronomical Observatory 2*—was launched in 1968 and operated until 1973.

HUBBLE SPACE TELESCOPE PROFILE

Telescope type: Reflecting, infrared, and ultraviolet
Launch: 1990
Mirror diameter: 2.4 m (7.9 ft)
Length: 13.2 m (43.5 ft)
Mass: 11,110 kg (24,500 lb)
Location: Orbiting Earth at a distance of 540 km (336 miles)

Clever Design

Sent into space in 1990, the *Hubble Space Telescope* is still working with up-to-date technology more than 30 years later. This is because it has a flexible design, with instrument units that can be replaced and upgraded. The telescope was named after the American astronomer Edwin Hubble (see page 222).

An astronaut replaces one of the *HST*'s instruments.

Solar panels make 1,200 watts of electricity to power the telescope and its instruments.

Discoveries

The *Hubble Space Telescope* has made many important discoveries. It has shown how stars are born in close-up for the first time, helped to discover some of the biggest stars and most distant galaxies in the Universe, and measured the speed at which our Universe is expanding (growing larger). Above all, it has taken amazing images that have forever changed the way we see space.

This *Hubble* image shows the Arches, a giant star cluster near the middle of the Milky Way.

Space Observatories

The *HST* is the most famous space telescope, but there are many others. Earth's atmosphere blocks out almost all radiation apart from visible light and radio waves, so if astronomers want to study the Universe at these other wavelengths, they need to do it from orbit.

Benefits and Problems

Nearly all kinds of radiation can be measured better from outside Earth's atmosphere. Space telescopes can collect huge amounts of information. However, being so far from Earth is also a problem. When space telescopes break down, they are usually just left. The *HST* is the only telescope in orbit that has been repaired with the help of a service mission.

Staring at the Stars

Another good thing about having telescopes in orbit is that they do not have to stop observing during daytime. This was useful for *Kepler*, a NASA satellite launched in 2009 to search for planets around other stars. *Kepler*'s camera was designed to watch stars in the Cygnus constellation non-stop for many years. It was looking for the dips in starlight that happen if a planet passes in front of its star. This mission could only be carried out in space.

In use between 2009 and 2018, *Kepler* orbited the Sun rather than the Earth.

A sun shield protects the mirror from getting hot so it can detect distant sources of infrared (heat) energy without being disturbed.

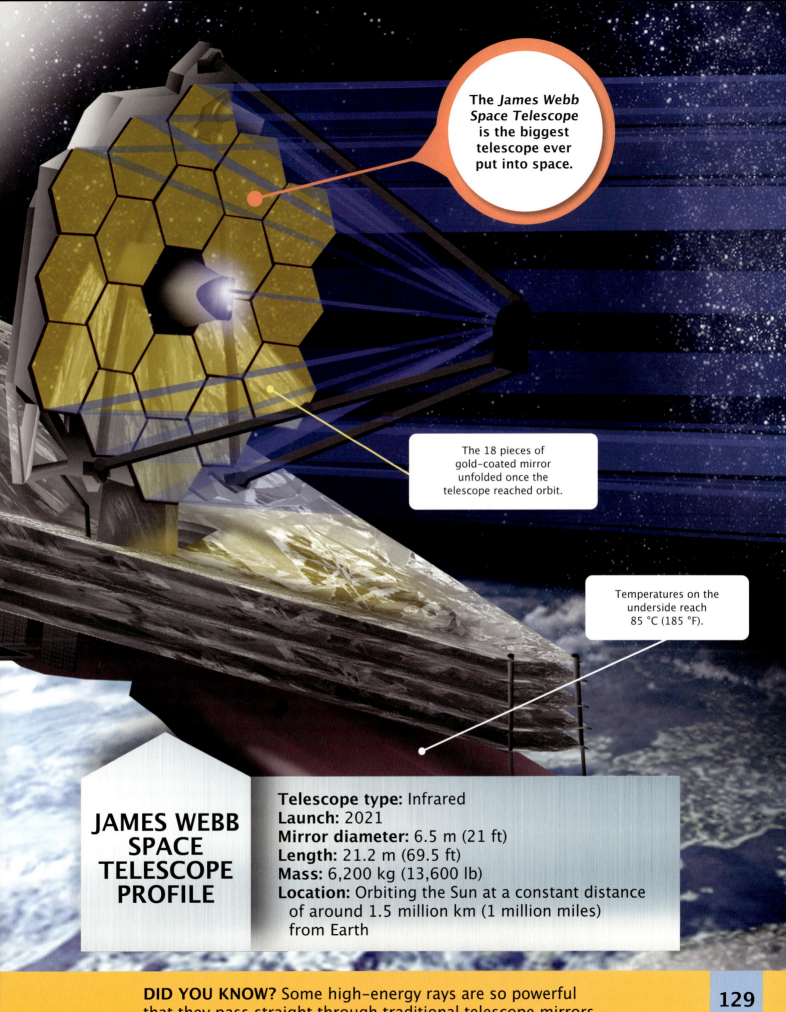

The *James Webb Space Telescope* is the biggest telescope ever put into space.

The 18 pieces of gold-coated mirror unfolded once the telescope reached orbit.

Temperatures on the underside reach 85 °C (185 °F).

JAMES WEBB SPACE TELESCOPE PROFILE

Telescope type: Infrared
Launch: 2021
Mirror diameter: 6.5 m (21 ft)
Length: 21.2 m (69.5 ft)
Mass: 6,200 kg (13,600 lb)
Location: Orbiting the Sun at a constant distance of around 1.5 million km (1 million miles) from Earth

DID YOU KNOW? Some high-energy rays are so powerful that they pass straight through traditional telescope mirrors.

The Northern Night Sky

> In the course of a night, Earth's rotation makes the northern night sky slowly spin around the central pole star, Polaris.

Astronomers split Earth's sky into two hemispheres, or halves, but most people on Earth can see more than half of the sky in a year. People living north of the equator can see all of the northern sky and, depending on where they are, a good amount of the southern sky.

From Earth's north pole, all of the northern sky can be seen.

Northern Stars

The northern sky surrounds Polaris, the pole star, which lies directly above Earth's own north pole. Its most famous constellations include Ursa Major (the Great Bear), Leo (the Lion), and Taurus (the Bull). The Milky Way (see page 7) is most visible in the constellation of Cygnus (the Swan). Virgo (the Maiden) is home to a dense cluster of galaxies.

This old star map shows many of Ptolemy's constellations.

Ancient Constellations

Astronomers split the sky into 88 constellations—areas of the sky marked by a pattern of stars. Forty-eight of these (including most of the northern ones) date back almost 2,000 years to the work of Greek-Egyptian astronomer Ptolemy. His constellations include the even more ancient star patterns of the zodiac, as well as figures from Greek myths such as King Cepheus, Queen Cassiopeia, the hero Perseus, the princess Andromeda, and the winged horse Pegasus.

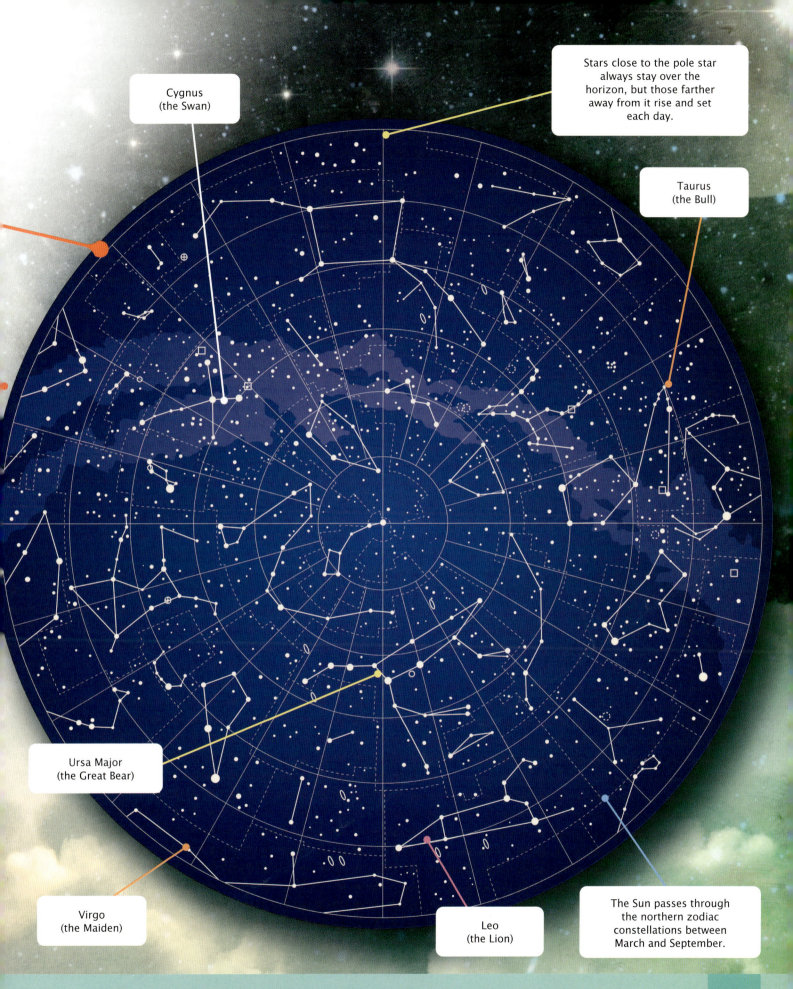

Cygnus (the Swan)

Stars close to the pole star always stay over the horizon, but those farther away from it rise and set each day.

Taurus (the Bull)

Ursa Major (the Great Bear)

Virgo (the Maiden)

Leo (the Lion)

The Sun passes through the northern zodiac constellations between March and September.

DID YOU KNOW? The farther north you live, the higher Polaris—which lies in the constellation of Ursa Minor (the Lesser Bear)—sits in your sky.

The Southern Night Sky

People living south of the equator can see all of the southern sky and, depending where they are, a good amount of the northern sky. Confusingly, these northern constellations look like they are "upside down" compared to how they are often drawn.

The southern hemisphere is home to the brightest stars in the sky—Sirius in Canis Major (the Great Dog) and Canopus in Carina (the Keel).

Southern Stars

The southern hemisphere is home to the densest parts of the Milky Way, around the constellations of Sagittarius (the Archer), Centaurus (the Centaur), Carina (the Ship's Keel), and Crux (the Southern Cross). Other famous southern constellations include Scorpius (the Scorpion) and Cetus (the Sea Monster).

The famous constellation Orion sits on the boundary between northern and southern skies.

This map includes the "southern birds," but was drawn before Lacaille added his constellations.

Later Names

Some of the names for southern constellations come from Ptolemy's lists, but most are newer. One group, named after birds—including Grus (the Crane) and Pavo (the Peacock)—was described in the late 1500s by Dutch sailors. These were the first Europeans to see them, although peoples of the southern hemisphere had their own names for the stars. Other names were decided by French astronomer Nicolas-Louis de Lacaille, who worked in South Africa in the 1700s. Most of Lacaille's constellations are named after scientific tools.

DID YOU KNOW? The easiest way to find the pole of the southern sky is to look down the long arm of the Southern Cross.

Chapter 7

Exploring the Universe

Space is not far away—in fact, it starts just 100 km (60 miles) above your head. That is where scientists and pilots place the "edge of space"—the region where Earth's air starts to fade away to nothing, and where people need spacesuits and spacecraft to survive.

Weightless in Orbit

Most spacecraft and astronauts work in a region called Low Earth Orbit (LEO), where they fly around our planet at a fast enough speed to balance out the downward pull of Earth's gravity. This means that astronauts on board an orbiting spacecraft float around in "weightless" conditions, appearing to be unaffected by gravity.

Solar panels on the service module make electricity in space to power the craft's life-support systems and computers.

Like most spacecraft that have reached Earth orbit, Orion is a wingless space capsule, designed to fall back through Earth's atmosphere, slowed by parachutes and downward-blasting engines.

The service module houses the engines and machines that supply oxygen and water for the crew.

Astronaut Chris Hadfield relaxes on board the *International Space Station*, which is in LEO.

ORION PROFILE

Spacecraft type: Space capsule
Crewed launch: 2024
Height: 3.3 m (11 ft)
Diameter: 5 m (16 ft)
Mass: 25,800 kg (57,000 lb)
Crew size: 6 people
Launch vehicle: Space Launch System

Orion flew on its first uncrewed test launch in 2014.

The crew module houses the astronauts and is the only part of the craft that returns to Earth.

Lost in Space

Early spacecraft did not get far enough away from Earth to see our whole planet afloat in space. The first people to do this were the crew of Apollo 8, who flew all the way to the Moon and back in December 1968. The pictures they took showed for the first time how tiny and fragile our planet is, and moved people to start taking better care of it.

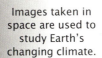

Images taken in space are used to study Earth's changing climate.

NASA's Orion spacecraft is designed to carry astronauts into Earth orbit and to nearby space objects.

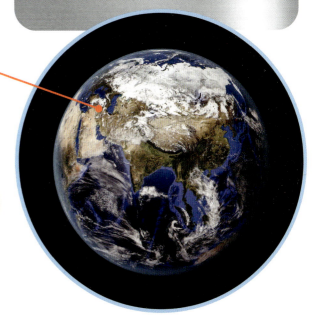

DID YOU KNOW? The Orion spacecraft may one day form part of the first mission to put people on Mars.

Rockets

Pushed into space by a jet of super-hot gas, rockets need an explosive chemical reaction to push them through Earth's atmosphere. They are noisy, wasteful, and expensive, but they are still the best way of reaching orbit around Earth.

> A rocket stage is mostly made of fuel tanks and engines. Only a small cargo on the top of the rocket reaches space.

Stage by Stage

Most rockets are made up of several sections called "stages," each with their own fuel tanks and rocket engines. These stages may be stacked on top of each other, or sit side by side. Only the top stage reaches orbit with its cargo—the burnt-out lower stages fall back to Earth and are usually destroyed.

> One by one, a rocket's stages fire their engines, use up their fuel, then fall back to Earth.

NASA's Space Launch System carries the Orion spacecraft (see pages 134-135) into orbit.

The V-2 was a rocket with explosive cargo, used as a weapon during World War II. Most modern rockets are based on the V-2.

SATURN V PROFILE

Spacecraft type: Three-stage rocket
In use: 1967-73
Total launches: 13
Height: 110.6 m (363 ft)
Diameter: 10.1 m (33 ft)
Mass: 2.29 million kg (5.04 million lb)

DID YOU KNOW? The Saturn V rocket that took astronauts to the Moon in 1969 is still the biggest rocket ever built.

Action and Reaction

Rockets rely on a rule that the English scientist Isaac Newton worked out in 1686: "For every action, there is an equal and opposite reaction." This means that the force of exploding gases coming from a rocket engine is matched by a reaction: a force pushing the engine itself in the opposite direction. This action and reaction can work even in space, where there is no air.

Isaac Newton discovered the principle of the rocket.

Space Race

The first satellites and astronauts were launched during the Space Race, a time of competition between the United States and Soviet Union. Both sides made huge breakthroughs while they tried to beat the other country and complete many space "firsts."

Gagarin reached space in a Vostok 3KA space capsule, on the first crewed flight of the capsule design.

Russian astronaut Yuri Gagarin became the first human in space during the Vostok 1 mission on April 12, 1961.

DID YOU KNOW? In 2008, a statue of Laika, standing on a rocket, was erected in the capital of Russia, Moscow.

Race to the Moon

The Soviet Union (a group of countries including Russia) put the first satellite in space in 1957, and the first human in space four years later. The United States found it hard to catch up, but it ended up winning the Space Race thanks to its Apollo missions, which landed the first astronauts on the Moon in July 1969.

Americans James Lovell, William Anders, and Frank Borman were the first humans to orbit the Moon (without landing on it), on the Apollo 8 mission in December 1968.

Laika's Story

After the successful launch of the *Sputnik 1* satellite in October 1957, Soviet politicians ordered their engineers to work on a new "spectacular." The answer was *Sputnik 2*, a much larger satellite that carried a living passenger—Laika. This small dog had been picked up as a stray and specially trained. Sadly, Laika died from stress shortly after launch in November 1957.

Laika was the first animal to orbit the Earth.

VOSTOK 1 MISSION PROFILE

Date: April 12, 1961
Spacecraft: Vostok 3KA
Rocket: Vostok-K 8K72K
Flight duration: 108 minutes
Orbits of Earth: 1
Launch site: Baikonur, now in Kazakhstan
Crew: Yuri Gagarin

Space Shuttles

After the end of the Space Race, the US space agency NASA built a new kind of spacecraft: spaceplanes that—unlike space capsules—were reusable. Although they completed some amazing missions, the Space Shuttles were not as safe as hoped. They were retired in 2011.

Shuttle Launch

The Space Shuttle system was made up of a plane-like "orbiter" vehicle with a large cargo hold and rocket engines on its tail. It launched into orbit fuelled by a huge external (outside) tank, and helped out by two strap-on booster rockets. These boosters fell away during takeoff but could be found and reused.

The shuttle blasts off from Launch Complex 39 at NASA's Kennedy Space Center.

Gliding back to Earth

After finishing its mission, a Shuttle orbiter dropped back into Earth's atmosphere in a fiery process called re-entry. When it was back in the atmosphere, the Shuttle moved like a giant high-speed glider, heading for a landing strip in either California or Florida, USA. When it touched down at a speed of about 343 km/h (213 mph), the tail part released parachutes that helped the wheel brakes to stop the Shuttle.

Black tiles on the underside of a Shuttle were designed to shield it from the heat of re-entry. They did not work during *Columbia*'s 2003 re-entry, which meant that the Shuttle broke up.

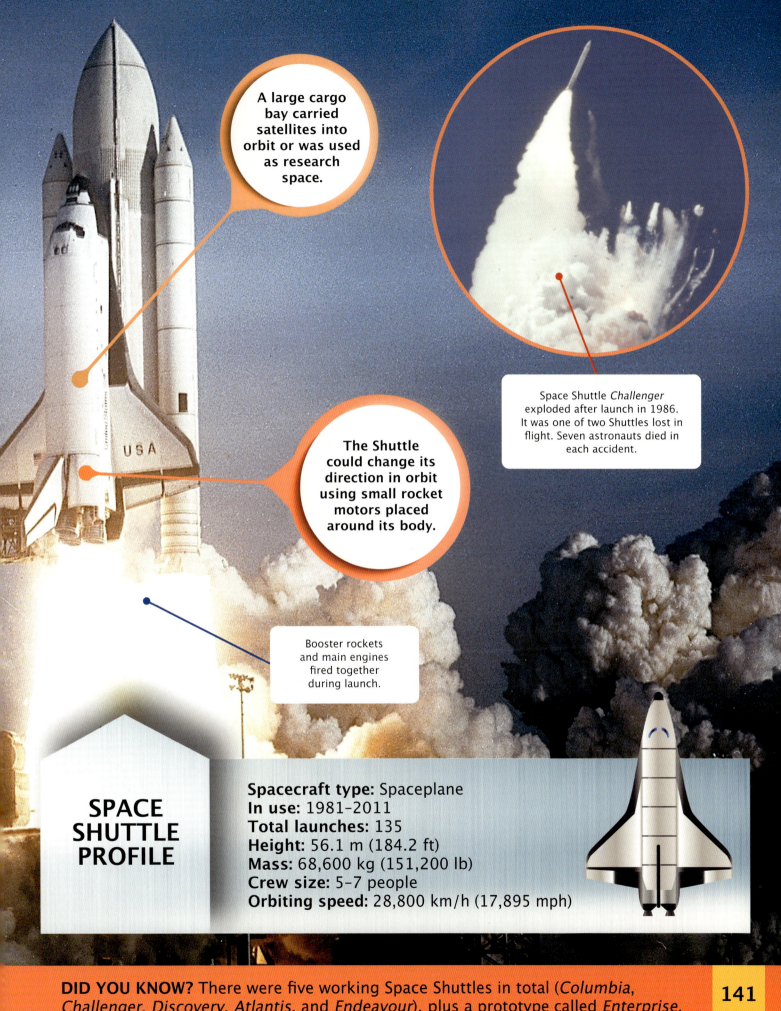

A large cargo bay carried satellites into orbit or was used as research space.

Space Shuttle *Challenger* exploded after launch in 1986. It was one of two Shuttles lost in flight. Seven astronauts died in each accident.

The Shuttle could change its direction in orbit using small rocket motors placed around its body.

Booster rockets and main engines fired together during launch.

SPACE SHUTTLE PROFILE

Spacecraft type: Spaceplane
In use: 1981–2011
Total launches: 135
Height: 56.1 m (184.2 ft)
Mass: 68,600 kg (151,200 lb)
Crew size: 5–7 people
Orbiting speed: 28,800 km/h (17,895 mph)

DID YOU KNOW? There were five working Space Shuttles in total (*Columbia, Challenger, Discovery, Atlantis,* and *Endeavour*), plus a prototype called *Enterprise*.

Launchpads

Sending rockets and their cargo into space is a dangerous and noisy business. Space agencies build large, specialized launch areas that are a long way from where people live.

Fuel is not pumped into the tanks until the rocket is in position on the launchpad.

At Baikonur, in Kazakhstan, rockets are moved around on huge trains. They are only stood upright when they reach the launchpad.

Russia has used the *Soyuz* rocket since the 1960s.

Launch towers lock into place around the rocket and release during takeoff.

DID YOU KNOW? Soyuz rockets at Baikonur are still launched from the same pad that launched Yuri Gagarin's Vostok 1 mission in 1961.

Escape rocket system pulls crew capsule away from the main rocket in an emergency.

Mission Controllers

Rocket launches are watched from a control room inside the launch area. Not long after the rocket has safely left the pad, control passes to a separate mission control room that may be far away. For example, NASA's mission control at Houston, Texas, is more than a thousand miles from its launchpads at Cape Canaveral, Florida.

Experts check different parts of the spacecraft's systems from their desks.

Floating Launchpad

Since 1999, some satellite-carrying rockets haves been launched from a floating platform called *Ocean Odyssey*. By placing the platform close to the equator in the Pacific Ocean, rockets can use the speed boost from the Earth's rotation. Missions are cheaper because they use less fuel and can carry heavier cargo. Launching at sea also means there is a smaller risk of rockets falling back on areas where there are people.

The command ship is moored beside the launch platform.

SOYUZ ROCKET FAMILY PROFILE

Spacecraft type: Three-stage rockets
In use: 1966–present
Total launches: 1,900+
Height: 46.3 m (152 ft) for current Soyuz-2 model
Mass: 312,000 kg (688,000 lb)

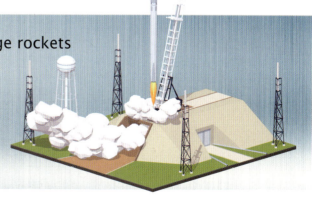

Astronaut Training

Over 600 people have journeyed into space. Most of them had years of training before their launch. Some astronauts are specialist pilots, but many are scientists or engineers.

In the Tank

Sometimes an astronaut will need to do difficult work while he or she is weightless and wearing a bulky spacesuit. The best way to train for this on Earth is in a special water tank. Astronauts wear a suit designed for training and use dummy tools for practice. Divers watch over them.

Space Tourists

Not all astronauts are professionals (trained experts). Since the 1990s, Russia has given wealthy space fans the chance to make short trips into orbit—if they can pay a few million dollars toward the costs of the Soyuz rocket. These space tourists still go through many months of training, however—if only to make sure they do not get in the way of the professionals!

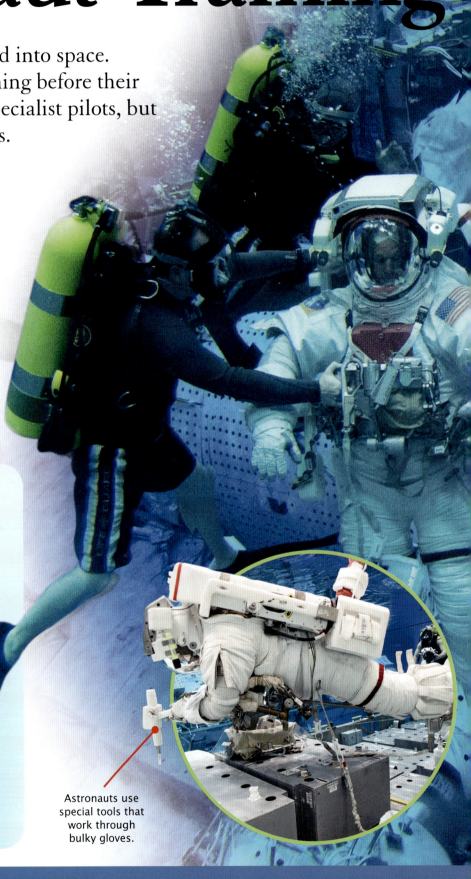

Astronauts use special tools that work through bulky gloves.

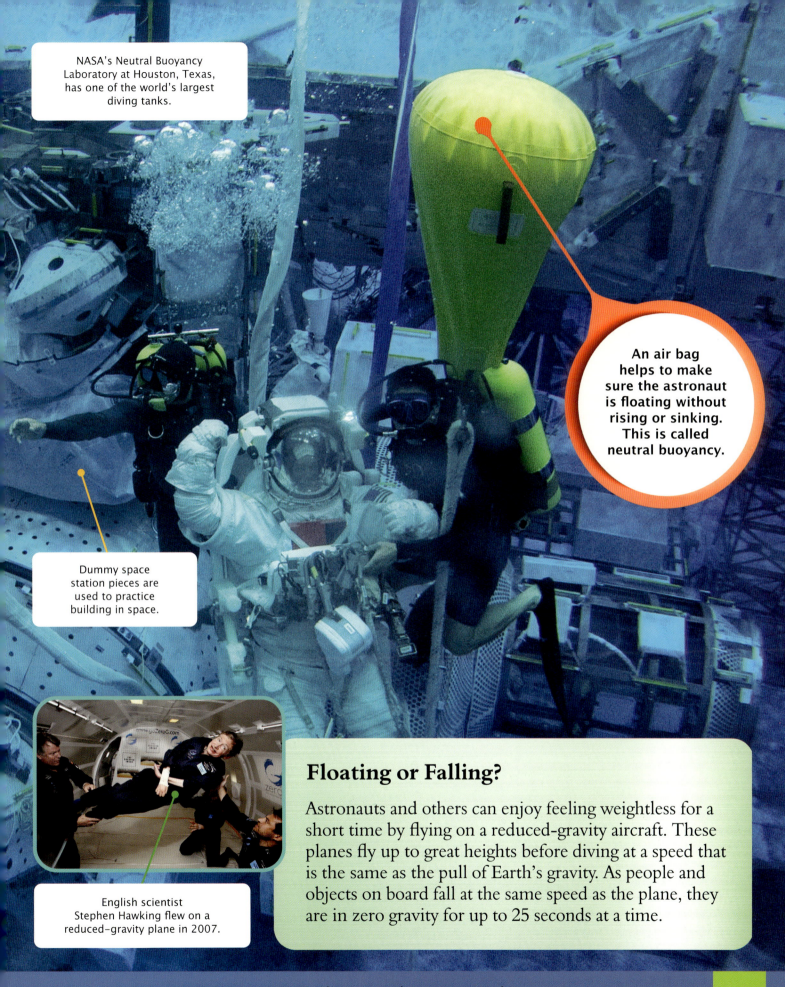

NASA's Neutral Buoyancy Laboratory at Houston, Texas, has one of the world's largest diving tanks.

An air bag helps to make sure the astronaut is floating without rising or sinking. This is called neutral buoyancy.

Dummy space station pieces are used to practice building in space.

English scientist Stephen Hawking flew on a reduced-gravity plane in 2007.

Floating or Falling?

Astronauts and others can enjoy feeling weightless for a short time by flying on a reduced-gravity aircraft. These planes fly up to great heights before diving at a speed that is the same as the pull of Earth's gravity. As people and objects on board fall at the same speed as the plane, they are in zero gravity for up to 25 seconds at a time.

DID YOU KNOW? The Neutral Buoyancy Laboratory pool holds 23 million l (6.2 million gallons) of water.

Early Space Stations

The inside of *Mir* became cluttered and messy over the years.

A space station is a base that is in orbit around the Earth, where astronauts can live and work for weeks or even months. The first stations were launched by Russia and the United States in the 1970s, and Russia carried on building them and improving their designs for the next 20 years.

Record-Breakers

From 1971, Russia launched a series of seven stations called *Salyut*. NASA, meanwhile, launched a single station called *Skylab*, which was visited by three crews in 1973–74. From 1986, Russia built *Mir*, an orbiting laboratory with a few different modules (units) for living and working. Russian astronauts working on *Mir* set a number of records including the first person to spend a year in space.

A Russian Soyuz space capsule attached to *Mir* was used as a lifeboat by the crew in emergencies.

SKYLAB PROFILE

Spacecraft type: Space station
In use: May 1973–February 1974
Width: 17 m (55.8 ft)
Length: 25.1 m (82.4 ft)
Completed missions: 3
Crew size: 3 people per mission
Re-entry: July 1979 (burnt up and crashed in Western Australia)

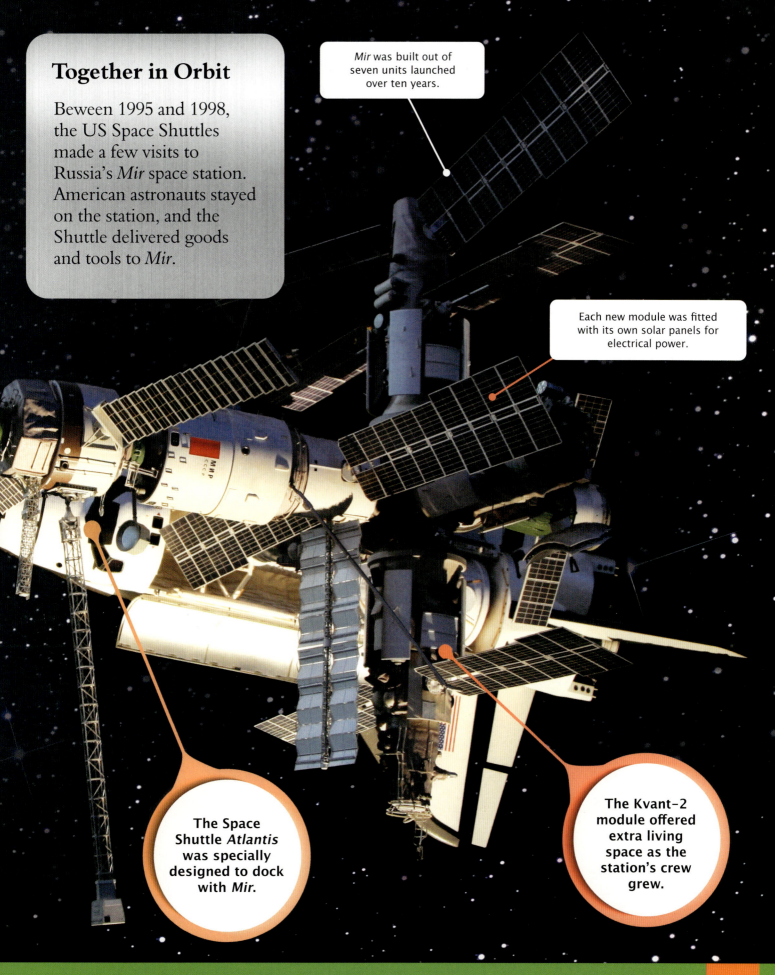

Together in Orbit

Beween 1995 and 1998, the US Space Shuttles made a few visits to Russia's *Mir* space station. American astronauts stayed on the station, and the Shuttle delivered goods and tools to *Mir*.

Mir was built out of seven units launched over ten years.

Each new module was fitted with its own solar panels for electrical power.

The Space Shuttle *Atlantis* was specially designed to dock with *Mir*.

The Kvant-2 module offered extra living space as the station's crew grew.

DID YOU KNOW? In 1997, supply spacecraft without crew on board crashed into *Mir*, creating damage that almost forced the crew to leave the station.

International Space Station

The ISS's solar panels can produce (make) up to 110 kW of power.

The *International Space Station* (*ISS*) is the ninth space station that humans have built in space. It is the first one where agencies from different countries have worked together—16 nations are part of the project. The *ISS* is the largest and most expensive spacecraft ever built.

Panel Power

The *ISS* has eight main pairs of solar panels. Solar cells in the panels change energy from the Sun into electricity. A system of trusses (joining corridors) connects the different modules. The trusses hold electrical lines, cooling lines for machines, and mobile transporter rails. The solar panels and robotic arms fix to the trusses, too.

Zvezda docking port

Solar panel

Each solar panel measures more than the wingspan of a Boeing 777.

DID YOU KNOW? Canadarm2, the *ISS*'s main robotic arm, is 16.7 m (55 ft) long and can lift weights up to 116 tonnes (127.8 US tons).

Life on the Station

The *ISS* has four main laboratories: Europe's Columbus, Japan's Kibo, the USA's Destiny, and Russia's Nauka. *ISS* crew carry out science experiments in the labs, and scientists on Earth also take part. There are research projects into making new materials and growing special crystals.

- Kibo laboratory
- Destiny laboratory
- Columbus laboratory
- Canadarm2

NASA astronaut Karen Nyberg works in the Destiny laboratory.

The first *ISS* module launched into orbit was the Russian-built Zarya, in 1998.

INTERNATIONAL SPACE STATION PROFILE

Spacecraft type: Space station
Launch: 1998
Width: 109 m (358 ft)
Length: 73 m (239 ft)
Mass: 450 tonnes (496 US tons)
Orbiting speed: 8 km/s (17,895 mph)
Crew size: 7 people

Satellites

Satellites are robot spacecraft put in orbit around Earth to do many different jobs. Some watch the weather, or photograph our planet to learn more about it. Others help us communicate or find our way around the world.

Different Orbits

Satellites are put into an orbit that is best for the job they have to do. Some sit happily in a Low Earth Orbit (LEO) that puts them just beyond the atmosphere. Others enter much higher geostationary (fixed) orbit above the equator, where they stay above a single point on Earth's surface. Satellites that try to study the whole of Earth's surface are put in tilted orbits that loop above and below Earth's poles as the planet rotates beneath them.

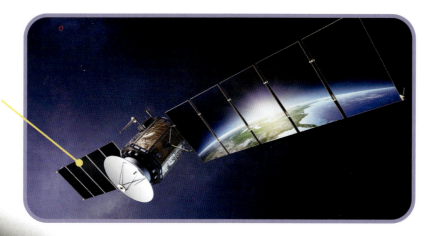

Communications satellites often use geostationary orbits.

Cameras take images of Europe and Africa every 15 minutes.

METEOSAT 10 PROFILE

Spacecraft type: Weather satellite
Launch: 2012
Diameter: 3.2 m (10.5 ft)
Height: 2.4 m (7.9 ft)
Orbit: 35,786 km (22,236 miles) above Earth
Orbital period: 23 hours 56 minutes (matching Earth's rotation)

DID YOU KNOW? The higher a satellite orbits, the longer it takes to go around Earth but the slower it needs to travel to balance the pull of Earth's gravity.

The drum-shaped satellite spins 100 times per second.

Space Helpers

The curved shape of the Earth makes it impossible to send radio signals (which travel in straight lines) very far. Communication satellites solve this problem. Orbiting high above Earth, they can be seen from places on Earth that are far away from each other. This means signals can be bounced from one place to another along two straight-line paths.

NASA's Tracking and Data Relay satellites are designed for communication with orbiting spacecraft.

The European-built Meteosat satellites are designed to watch weather on Earth from an orbit high above the equator.

Sputnik 1 was the first satellite, launched in October 1957. Its 84-kg (185-lb) metal ball held a simple radio beacon that could send and receive signals.

Landing on the Moon

The greatest breakthrough in space exploration came on July 21, 1969, when the first humans walked on the Moon: Neil Armstrong and Edwin "Buzz" Aldrin. Since then, only 10 other people have walked there, the last in 1972.

Apollo 11

The mission that landed the first humans on the Moon was the United States' Apollo 11. The Apollo spacecraft had three parts: a command module (with living quarters) and service module (with engines and supplies), which were together known as *Columbia*; and a lunar module, known as *Eagle*.

Since there is no wind on the Moon, the US flag was fitted with a horizontal bar so it would not hang limp in photos of the Moon landing.

The Apollo spacecraft was launched by a Saturn V rocket on July 16, 1969.

After entering Moon orbit, Armstrong and Aldrin flew *Eagle* (pictured) down to the Moon's surface, while pilot Michael Collins remained alone aboard *Columbia*, from where he took this photo.

The command module holding the astronauts was the only spacecraft portion intended to return to Earth, which it did on July 24, in the Pacific Ocean.

Robot Visitors

A rover is a robotic space probe that travels across the surface of a space object. The first lunar rover—and the first successful rover on any space object—was the Soviet Union's *Lunokhod 1* in 1970. The first rover to operate on the Moon's far side was China's *Yutu-2*, in 2019. *Yutu-2* has solar panels to supply power, as well as a heater that uses radioactivity (the decay of unstable atoms) to warm it during the long, cold nights.

This photo of *Yutu-2* was taken by its lander *Chang'e 4*, which extended a ramp for the rover to roll onto the surface. *Yutu-2* uses radio waves to send information back to Earth.

During the Apollo 11 mission, Armstrong and Aldrin loaded 21.5 kg (47.5 lb) of lunar rocks and dust onto *Eagle*.

This is one of the few photos of Neil Armstrong on the Moon, since he took most of the photos, showing Aldrin. Armstrong was the first to step out of *Eagle*, saying: "That's one small step for [a] man, one giant leap for mankind."

COLUMBIA PROFILE

Spacecraft type: Space capsule
Size: 11 m (36.2 ft) long and up to 3.9 m (12.8 ft) wide
Mass at launch: 28,000 kg (62,000 lb)
Volume: 6.2 cu m (218 cu ft)
Engines: 1 AJ10 rocket engine
Design in use: 1966 to 1975
Crew: 3

DID YOU KNOW? There was no toilet on the Apollo 11 spacecraft, so the astronauts peed and pooped in bags that were taken back to Earth.

Studying the Sun

Satellites with special cameras and equipment, known as solar observatories, are monitoring the Sun. Due to the Sun's temperature and lack of a solid surface, it is not possible for a probe to land—but in 2021, a probe "touched" the Sun for the first time.

Touching the Sun

In April 2021, the *Parker Solar Probe* was the first probe to orbit through the Sun's corona, touching its upper atmosphere, around 13 million km (8.1 million miles) above the "surface." The probe sampled solar wind particles and magnetic fields. On *Parker*'s even closer approaches to the surface, of around 6.16 million km (3.83 million miles), the Sun's gravity accelerated the probe's speed to 690,000 km/h (430,000 miles per hour), making it the fastest object ever built.

The *Parker Solar Probe* has a solar shield—made of the engineered material "carbon reinforced with carbon"—that can withstand temperatures of 1,370 °C (2,500 °F), keeping its instruments at around 30 °C (85 °F).

The *Solar and Heliospheric Observatory* (*SOHO*) studies the Sun's interior by observing vibrations on its surface, a technique known as helioseismology.

Orbiting the Sun

Launched in 2021, *Solar Orbiter* (*SolO*) is currently the closest probe to the Sun with a camera, 42 million km (26 million miles) away at its nearest. It orbits the Sun rather than Earth, having reached that orbit with help from the Sun's pull and through gravity assists from Earth and Venus. A gravity assist, also known as a slingshot, is when a spacecraft uses the movement and gravity of a planet or moon to alter its path and speed, in order to save fuel on its long journey.

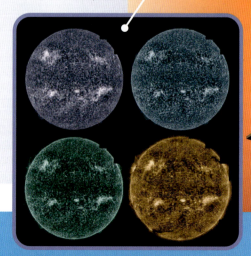

These images of the Sun's surface materials were taken by *SolO* using different wavelengths of ultraviolet light. Clockwise from top left, they show: hydrogen, carbon, neon, and oxygen.

SOHO PROFILE

Spacecraft type: Probe
Size: 4.3 m (14 ft) long and 3.7 m (12 ft) wide
Mass: 610 kg (1,340 lb)
Average distance from Earth: 1.5 million km (932,000 miles)
Average distance from the Sun: 148 million km (92 million miles)
Orbit: 6 months around Lagrange point; 1 year around the Sun
Launched: 1995

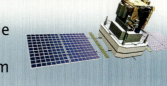

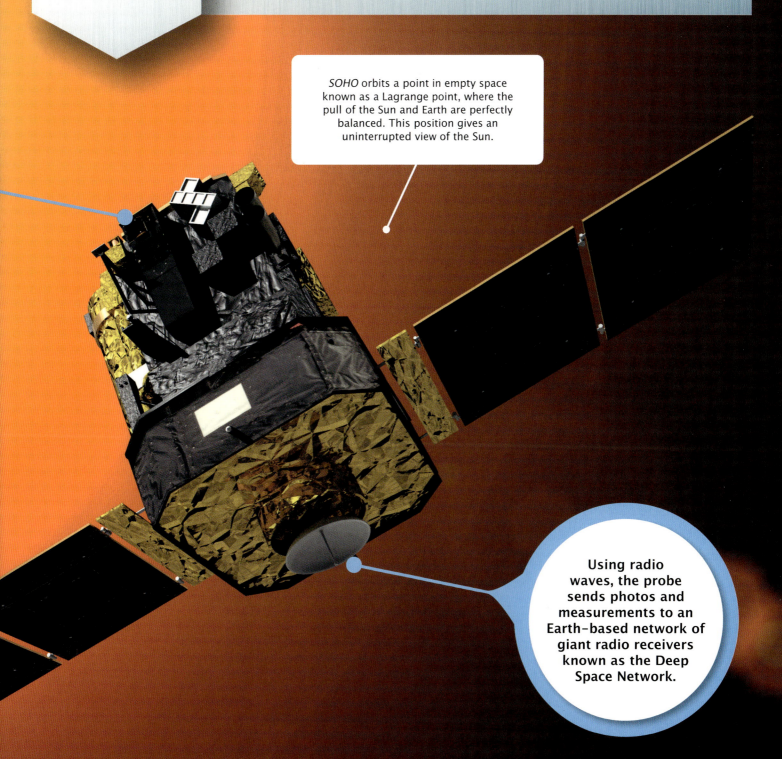

SOHO orbits a point in empty space known as a Lagrange point, where the pull of the Sun and Earth are perfectly balanced. This position gives an uninterrupted view of the Sun.

Using radio waves, the probe sends photos and measurements to an Earth-based network of giant radio receivers known as the Deep Space Network.

DID YOU KNOW? The first probe to orbit the Sun was *Luna 1*, which in 1959 missed its target of the Moon and sailed into an orbit between Earth and Mars.

Missions to Mars

Apart from Earth and the Moon, Mars is the most explored object in the Solar System. Mars has been successfully visited by 6 rovers, more than 10 landers (which land on the surface and survey one spot), and 18 orbiters (which monitor the planet and atmosphere from orbit).

Researching Rovers

Mars is the only planet to which we have sent rovers. The Mars rover *Sojourner* was the first wheeled vehicle to travel on a planet other than Earth, in 1997. Rovers use drills, lasers, and testing equipment such as X-ray tubes to study the chemicals in Martian rocks, searching particularly for signs of water or life. Rovers contain computers that are programmed to perform some tasks independently, but other instructions are received from Earth by radio waves.

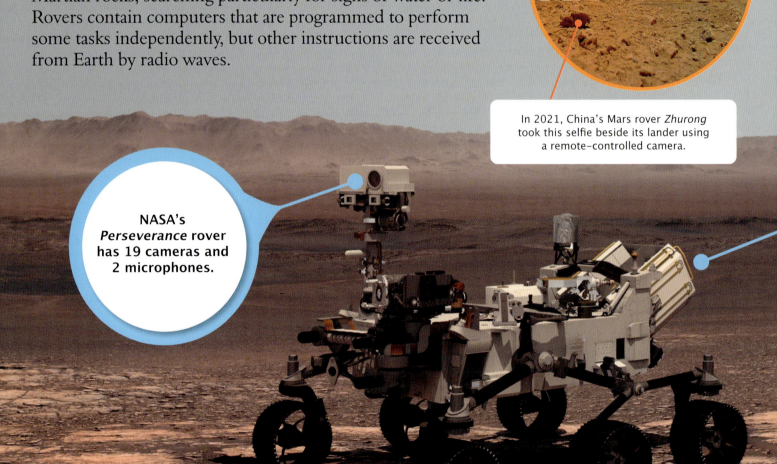

In 2021, China's Mars rover *Zhurong* took this selfie beside its lander using a remote-controlled camera.

NASA's *Perseverance* rover has 19 cameras and 2 microphones.

DID YOU KNOW? In April 2021, *Perseverance* became the first spacecraft to record the noise of another spacecraft, *Ingenuity*, on another planet.

Perseverance is supported by the helicopter *Ingenuity*, which looks for areas of possible interest for the rover to explore.

Humans on Mars

Several national space agencies, including the United States' NASA and Russia's Roscosmos, have plans to send humans to Mars within 30 years, possibly to set up a base on the planet or in orbit. With current spacecraft technology, and taking advantage of the best positions of the planets in their orbits, the shortest trip would be a 9-month journey from Earth to Mars, about 16 months on Mars to wait for the right moment to return, then a 9-month journey home.

NASA is developing a spacecraft, Deep Space Transport, large enough for a crew of six as they rest and exercise on a journey to Mars. It is based on NASA's Orion space capsule (see pages 134-135) attached to a Deep Space Habitat.

No lander has yet taken off from Mars, but *Perseverance* is collecting tubes of samples that will be picked up by a future lander–rover mission.

Deep Space Habitat

Orion

PERSEVERANCE PROFILE

Spacecraft type: Rover
Size: 2.9 m (9.5 ft) long and 2.2 m (7.2 ft) wide
Mass: 1,025 kg (2,260 lb)
Location: Jezero Crater, Mars
Landed on Mars: 2021
Carried to Mars by: *Mars 2020* spacecraft
Launched from Earth by: Atlas V rocket

Mars 2020 spacecraft

- Cruise stage
- Protective backshell
- Descent stage
- *Perseverance* and *Ingenuity*
- Heat shield

157

Mapping the Inferior Planets

Mercury and Venus are known as the inferior planets because they are closer to the Sun than Earth. Due to the intense heat of these planets, no rover has journeyed on either, but probes have sent us images and information that let us map their cratered surfaces.

> Two square solar panels, 2.5 m (8.2 ft) across, made electricity from sunlight and charged batteries that were used for power when *Magellan* was in shadow.

Meeting Mercury

Mercury is the least explored inner planet because of its closeness to the Sun. Mercury orbits the Sun so quickly that a spacecraft must travel very fast to meet it. The intense gravity of the nearby Sun means that a spacecraft then has to brake very hard to enter orbit around Mercury. The first probe to orbit Mercury was *MESSENGER*, from 2011 to 2015. It was the second mission to near the planet, after *Mariner 10*, which flew past Mercury three times in 1974–75, passing 327 km (203 miles) away while orbiting the Sun.

MESSENGER became the first human-made object on the surface of Mercury when it was allowed to crash into the planet at the end of its mission.

MAGELLAN PROFILE

Spacecraft type: Probe
Size: 6.4 m (21 ft) long and 4.6 m (15 ft) wide
Mass: 1,035 kg (2,282 lb)
Average distance from Venus: 10,470 km (6,510 miles)
In orbit around Venus: 1990–94
Named after: Portuguese sailor Ferdinand Magellan, who led the first circumnavigation (journey around) Earth in 1519–22

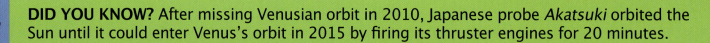

DID YOU KNOW? After missing Venusian orbit in 2010, Japanese probe *Akatsuki* orbited the Sun until it could enter Venus's orbit in 2015 by firing its thruster engines for 20 minutes.

Venus's clouds are opaque to visible light, but radio waves can pass through them, bounce off Venus's surface, then return to a probe.

As *Magellan* orbited Venus, the probe used a large antenna to send out radio waves that mapped 95 percent of the planet's surface.

Visiting Venus

Due to Venus's closeness to Earth, many probes have carried out flybys, orbits, and landings. The first successful interplanetary probe, *Mariner 2*, flew past Venus in 1962. The probe that spent longest in Venusian orbit was *Pioneer Venus*, which studied Venus's atmosphere from 1978 to 1992. Due to Venus's heat and the pressure of its atmosphere, the longest any lander has transmitted from Venus's surface is 127 minutes, the record held by *Venera 13*, in 1982.

The Soviet Union's *Venera 13* lander recorded sounds and took photos, which were transmitted to its orbiter, which relayed them to Earth.

Watching the Giant Planets

No probe can land on the giant planets due to their lack of a solid surface, but nine probes have orbited or flown past at least one of them. All nine of these probes visited Jupiter, four also passed or orbited Saturn—and just one went on to fly past Uranus and Neptune.

Three Orbiters

Only three probes have orbited one of the giant planets. From 1995 to 2003, *Galileo* orbited Jupiter, discovering the planet's rings are made of dust from the inner moons. Having performed a gravity assist (see page 154) around Jupiter, the *Cassini* probe orbited Saturn from 2004 to 2017, capturing photos of immense storms. *Juno* entered orbit around Jupiter in 2016.

In 1995, *Galileo* (right) dropped a probe (left) into Jupiter's atmosphere. The probe transmitted information—revealing thunderstorms larger than Earth—for 58 minutes, until it was crushed by Jupiter's pressure.

JUNO PROFILE

Spacecraft type: Probe
Size: 4.6 m (15 ft) long and 20.1 m (66 ft) wide
Mass: 1,593 kg (3,512 lb)
Average distance from Jupiter: 4 million km (2.5 million miles)
Entered orbit around Jupiter: 2016
Named after: Roman goddess Juno, wife of the god Jupiter, who alone was able to see Jupiter's true nature

Lonely Voyager

The only probe that has flown past Uranus and Neptune is *Voyager 2*. Launched by NASA in 1977, it passed Uranus in 1986 and Neptune in 1989. As it flew 81,500 km (50,600 miles) from Uranus, it discovered 11 new moons and 2 new rings. While passing only 4,951 km (3,076 miles) from Neptune, it measured the planet's mass, the length of its day, and the strength of its winds.

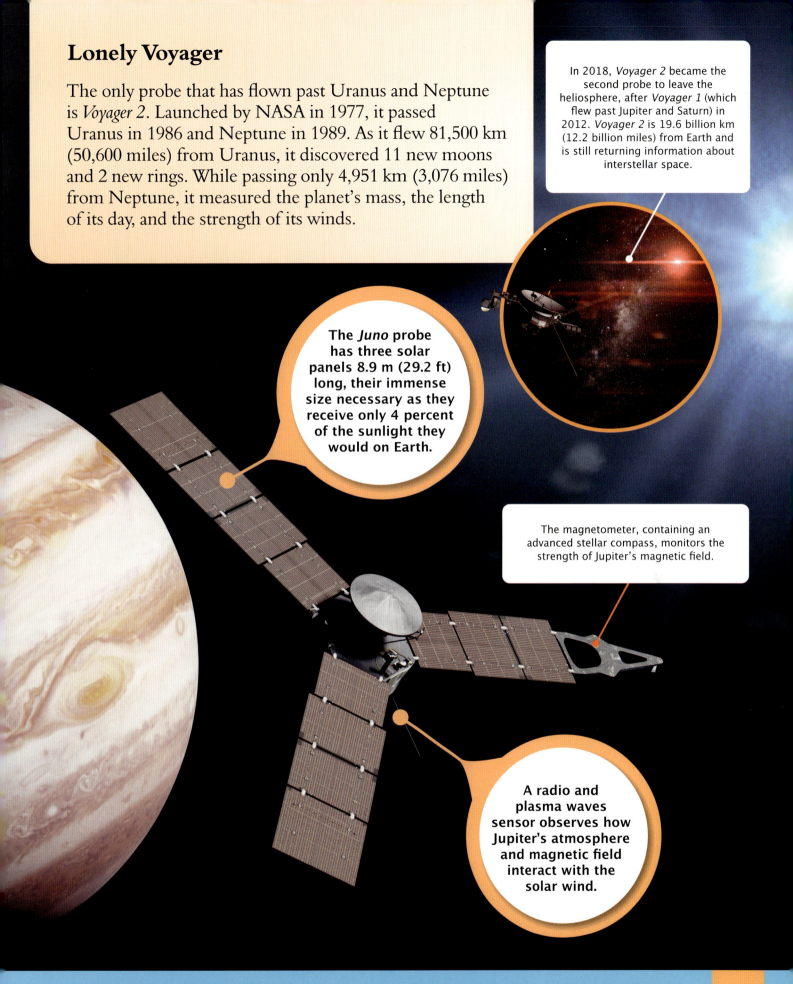

In 2018, *Voyager 2* became the second probe to leave the heliosphere, after *Voyager 1* (which flew past Jupiter and Saturn) in 2012. *Voyager 2* is 19.6 billion km (12.2 billion miles) from Earth and is still returning information about interstellar space.

The *Juno* probe has three solar panels 8.9 m (29.2 ft) long, their immense size necessary as they receive only 4 percent of the sunlight they would on Earth.

The magnetometer, containing an advanced stellar compass, monitors the strength of Jupiter's magnetic field.

A radio and plasma waves sensor observes how Jupiter's atmosphere and magnetic field interact with the solar wind.

DID YOU KNOW? Probes that have visited the giant planets are *Pioneers 10* and *11*, *Voyagers 1* and *2*, *Galileo*, *Ulysses*, *Cassini*, *New Horizons*, and *Juno*.

Distant Moons

Only one moon apart from our own has been landed on: Titan, the largest moon of Saturn. However, other moons—belonging to Mars, Jupiter, and Saturn—have been flown past by probes that have taken photos and studied their motion, surface, and atmosphere.

This illustration shows *Huygens'* descent to Titan, at first protected by its heat shield, which reached 1,800 °C (3,270 °F) due to friction with the moon's atmosphere.

Touching Titan

Due to its nitrogen atmosphere a little like Earth's, Titan attracted astronomers hoping for signs of tiny life forms. During its orbits of Saturn, the *Cassini* probe flew close by Titan several times, on one occasion releasing a lander named *Huygens*, which touched down on the Moon in 2005. Although no signs of life were found, the *Cassini-Huygens* mission revealed that Titan has seas of methane and ethane, as well as a possible underground ocean of water and ammonia.

Huygens transmitted information and photos, including this one, for 90 minutes after touchdown. The rocks and pebbles are made of water ice.

HUYGENS PROFILE

Spacecraft type: Probe
Size: 1.3 m (4.3 ft) across
Mass: 320 kg (710 lb)
Location: Adiri region, Titan
Landed on Titan: 2005
Named after: Dutch astronomer Christiaan Huygens, who discovered Titan in 1655

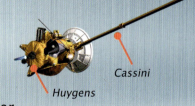

DID YOU KNOW? The European, Japanese, Russian, and US space agencies have plans to take rock samples from the Martian moon Phobos, then return them to Earth.

About 180 km (112 miles) above Titan's surface, *Huygens* opened a parachute to slow its descent.

Galileo Gains

During its orbits of Jupiter, *Galileo* flew close to Jupiter's four largest moons: Ganymede, Callisto, Io, and Europa. The probe's camera and nine other instruments sent home information that revealed Ganymede as the first moon known to have its own magnetic field, as well as evidence of subsurface oceans on Ganymede, Callisto, and Europa. On its way to Jupiter, *Galileo* also discovered the first moon around an asteroid: Dactyl, which orbits the asteroid Ida.

Huygens made the most distant landing from Earth ever achieved by a spacecraft.

Photos taken by *Galileo* and *Voyager 1* were combined to make this image of Io. It shows the moon's volcano Pele surrounded by a red ring made by a huge plume of erupted gas and dust.

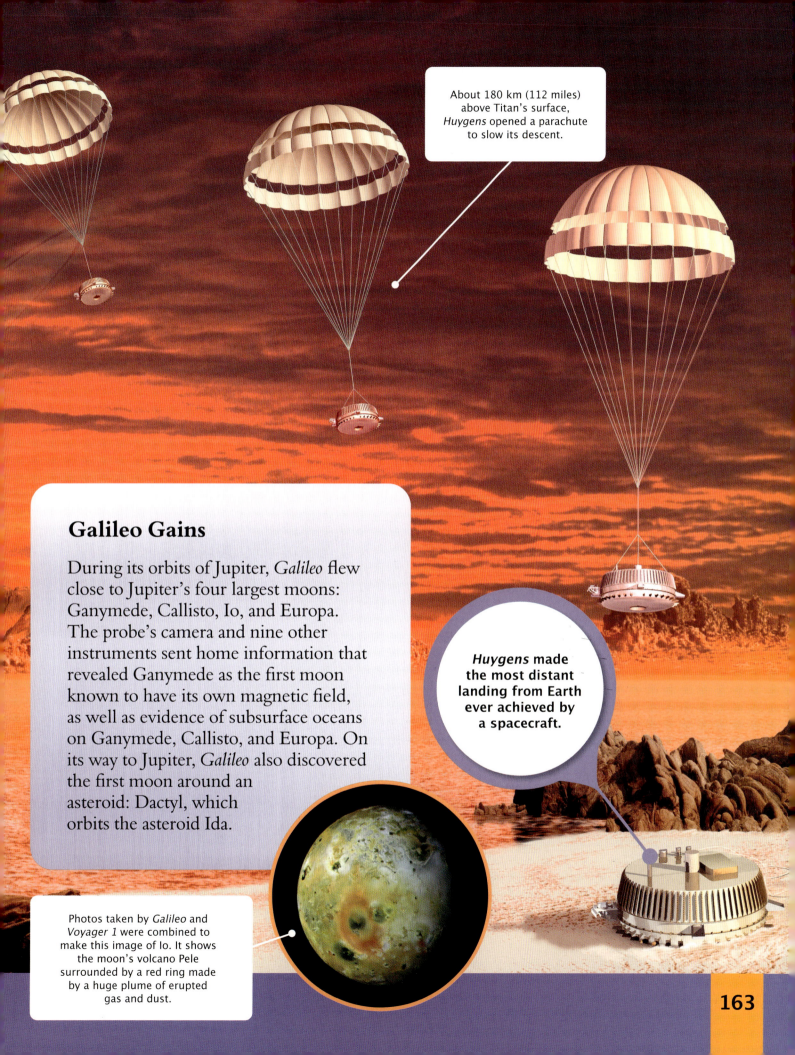

Small Objects

More than 25 asteroids, comets, and Kuiper Belt objects have been visited by space probes. The largest of these objects was the biggest dwarf planet in the Kuiper Belt, Pluto, which was flown past by *New Horizons* in 2015. Among the smallest was the asteroid Itokawa, around 330 m (1,080 ft) across.

> In 2005, the NASA probe *Deep Impact* released an impactor to study the interior of comet Tempel 1.

Catching Comets

A mission to the comet Wild 2 was the first to return a sample of material from a space object other than Earth's Moon. In 2004, the *Stardust* probe passed within 237 km (147 miles) of Wild 2 to collect dust flying from its nucleus. The dust landed on Earth in 2006 aboard *Stardust*'s sample-return capsule. Comets were not believed to get warm enough to melt their icy nucleus fully, but—unexpectedly—the particles showed signs of liquid water.

As Wild 2 overtook *Stardust* in their orbits round the Sun, dust flying from the comet's nucleus was collected in a grille filled with aerogel, a human-made, sponge-like material.

The impactor, a probe designed to dent a space object, made a crater on the comet around 100 m (328 ft) wide and 30 m (98 ft) deep.

DEEP IMPACT PROFILE

Spacecraft type: Probe
Size: 3.3 m (10.8 ft) long and 2.3 m (7.5 ft) wide
Mass of main probe: 601 kg (1,325 lb)
Mass of impactor: 372 kg (820 lb)
Meeting with Tempel 1: Around 230 million km (143 million miles) from the Sun
Distance from Tempel 1 of main probe: 575 km (357 miles)
Launched: 2005

DID YOU KNOW? In 2002, *Stardust* tested its flyby technique on the asteroid Annefrank, named after the Jewish teenage diary writer who died in the Holocaust in 1945.

Approaching Asteroids

Missions to asteroids are trying to learn more about the motions and materials of asteroids, since these leftovers offer clues about the formation of the Solar System. The first orbit of an asteroid, as well as the first landing, was made by *NEAR (Near Earth Asteroid Rendezvous) Shoemaker* on the near-Earth asteroid Eros, in 2000–2001. The first probe to collect dust from an asteroid was Japan's *Hayabusa*, which took material from Itokawa in 2005.

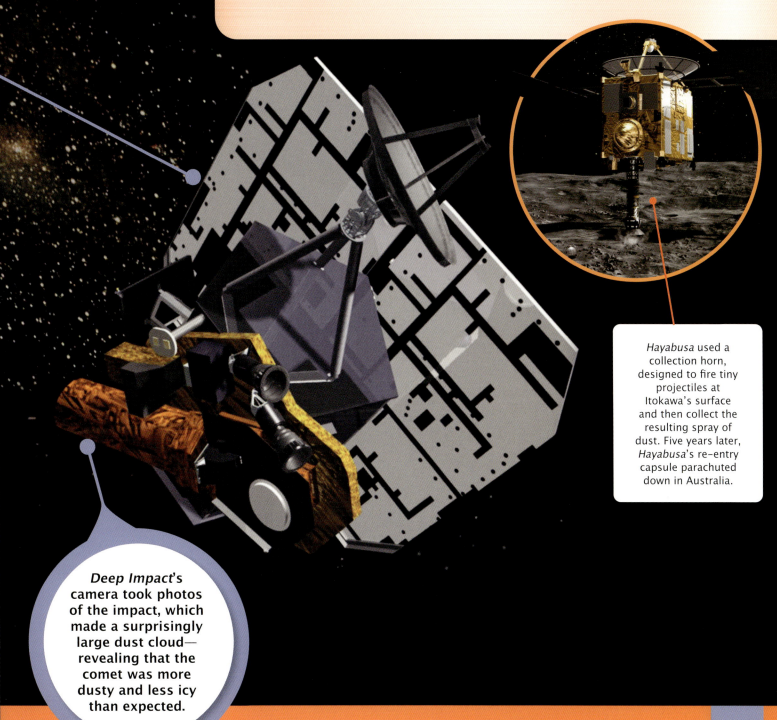

Hayabusa used a collection horn, designed to fire tiny projectiles at Itokawa's surface and then collect the resulting spray of dust. Five years later, *Hayabusa*'s re-entry capsule parachuted down in Australia.

Deep Impact's camera took photos of the impact, which made a surprisingly large dust cloud—revealing that the comet was more dusty and less icy than expected.

The Future

Although astronauts have not journeyed farther than Earth orbit since the early 1970s, the United States plans to send humans back to the Moon soon, on its Artemis missions. This will be the first step in a new age of space missions, which may eventually see humans land—and even live—on Mars.

Terraforming Mars

Mars has a lot more to offer than the Moon when it comes to creating new living spaces for humans on another world. The main problem is that it is a lot farther away. In the future, though, some scientists think we might be able to change the planet's climate and "terraform" it into a world much more like Earth.

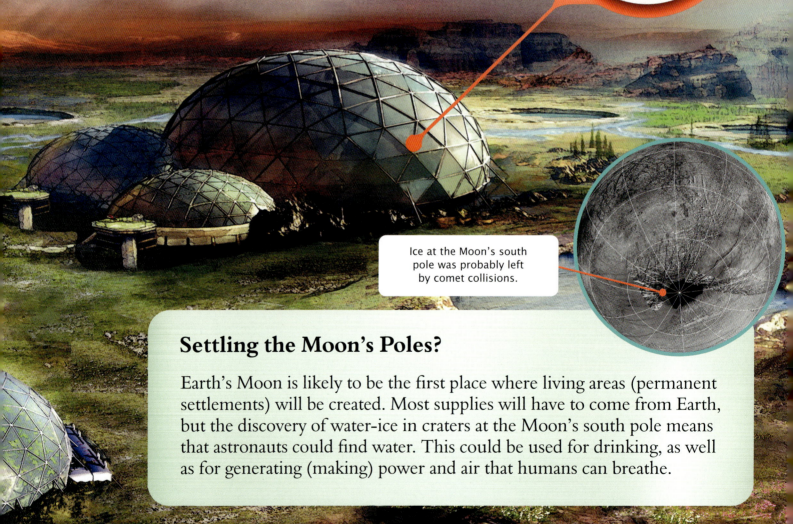

Living domes keep Earth-like air inside, protecting those inside from the thin, toxic Martian atmosphere.

Ice at the Moon's south pole was probably left by comet collisions.

Settling the Moon's Poles?

Earth's Moon is likely to be the first place where living areas (permanent settlements) will be created. Most supplies will have to come from Earth, but the discovery of water-ice in craters at the Moon's south pole means that astronauts could find water. This could be used for drinking, as well as for generating (making) power and air that humans can breathe.

STARSHIP PROFILE

Spacecraft type: Rocket and space capsule
Company: SpaceX
Test launch: 2023
Height: 120 m (394 ft)
Mass: 5 million kg (11 million lb)
Payload: 450,000 kg (990,000 lb) to Mars with refueling in Earth orbit

Immense spacecraft could land a hundred people, or a huge amount of equipment, on Mars, helping to build up the first cities.

As the air thickens, small aircraft can be used for transport.

Part of terraforming is creating a way to trap heat from the Sun, so the planet never gets too cold.

Over the centuries, water would melt out of the Martian surface. Plants could spread long before humans and animals could step outside without protection.

Hardy Earth micro-animals such as this tardigrade can survive in lots of environments. They might be able to live on Mars even today.

DID YOU KNOW? Gravity on Mars is just 40 percent of Earth's, so the muscles of people who move to Mars may be too weak to cope back on their home planet.

Chapter 8
The Universe

Our Universe is a massive area of space that stretches farther than we can see in every direction. It has more galaxies, stars, and planets than we could ever hope to count, and huge amounts of other material, most of which is invisible to even our most powerful telescopes.

Looking back in Time

We can only see objects in other parts of the Universe thanks to the light and other radiation we see in our telescopes. Light is the fastest thing in the Universe, so we measure huge distances in space in light-years (the distance light travels in a year, which is 9.5 trillion km or 5.9 trillion miles). The farther an object is in the Universe, the longer its light has taken to reach Earth, and the farther back in time we are seeing.

We see far-away parts of space as they were thousands or even millions of years ago, when their light set out toward us.

Curved Space

It might be hard to imagine, but space can be curved in different directions by objects with mass (weight and density). This is the basis of the force of gravity. An easier way to think about this is to imagine space as a flat rubber sheet. Heavy objects create a dent within the sheet, and this will change the paths of any other objects passing nearby.

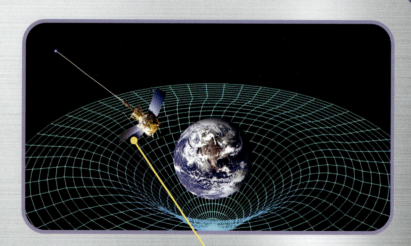

A satellite's orbit around a planet such as Earth stops it from "falling" into the curved space created by Earth's mass.

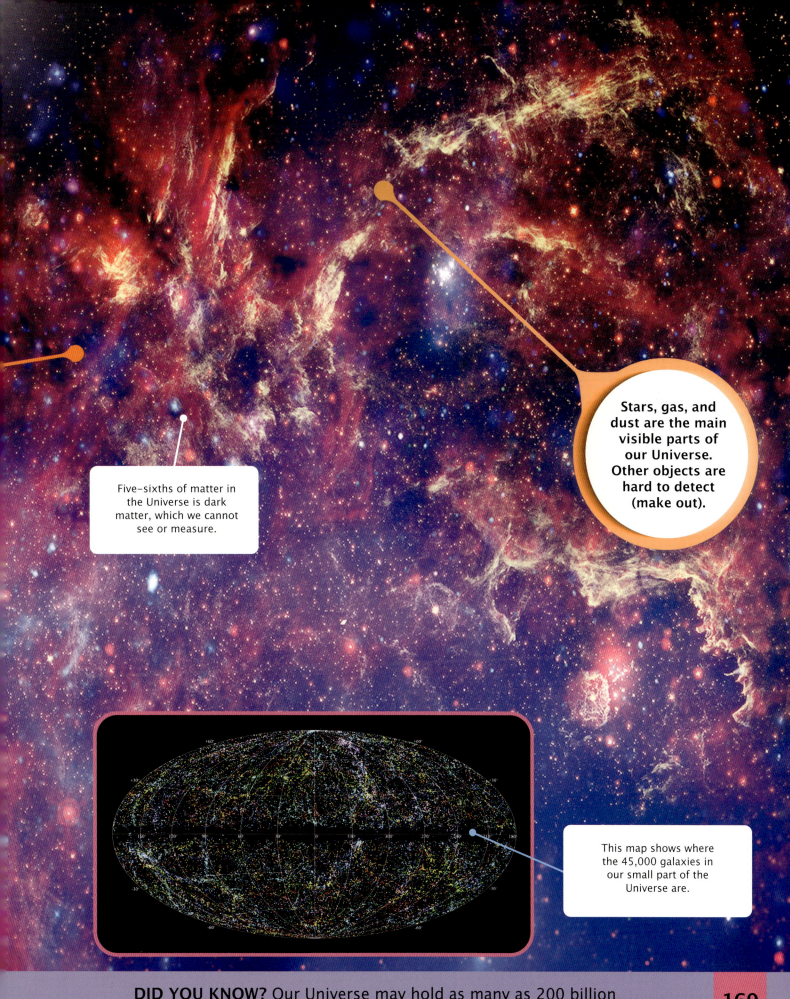

Five-sixths of matter in the Universe is dark matter, which we cannot see or measure.

Stars, gas, and dust are the main visible parts of our Universe. Other objects are hard to detect (make out).

This map shows where the 45,000 galaxies in our small part of the Universe are.

DID YOU KNOW? Our Universe may hold as many as 200 billion galaxies, each holding perhaps 100 billion stars!

Big Bang

Our Universe was born 13.8 billion years ago in a huge explosion called the Big Bang. The event not only created all the matter in the Universe, but also space and time, so it is meaningless to ask what happened before it took place.

Discovery

The Russian scientist Alexander Friedmann was the first person to suggest that the Universe might be expanding (growing), in 1924. The American Edwin Hubble proved this in 1929. The Belgian Georges Lemaître followed the expansion backward and stated that the Universe began in a hot, dense ball of matter.

Alexander Friedmann was the first scientist to work on the idea of an expanding Universe.

Atoms have a central region, called a nucleus, made up of particles called protons and neutrons. Spinning around the nucleus are particles called electrons.

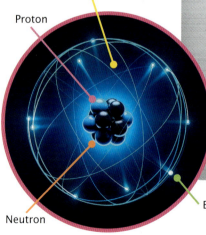

Proton

Neutron

Electron

The Beginning

The Big Bang released huge amounts of energy, but as the Universe expanded, it cooled quickly and the energy was locked up within the tiniest of particles. Over the first few minutes, these particles joined together until they formed the building blocks of atoms. Atoms are the smallest particles that make up any matter, from people to planets and stars.

13.8 BILLION YEARS AGO	+1 SECOND	+20 MINUTES	+380,000 YEARS	+100 MILLION YEARS
The Big Bang creates all matter and energy in the Universe.	Energy changes into the tiniest of particles.	Heavy particles group together to form the cores (nuclei) of atoms. Small particles called electrons stay loose. Light waves are trapped in the fog of particles.	Electrons combine with nuclei to form the first atoms. The earliest atoms are the simplest and lightest: hydrogen and helium. The fog clears and the Universe becomes transparent.	The first stars and galaxies begin to form in clouds of hydrogen and helium gas.

One second after the Big Bang, the Universe was—and is still today—a huge expanding bubble. There is no way of getting outside the bubble.

During the first moments after the Big Bang, energy could change into mass and back, creating the building blocks of matter.

DID YOU KNOW? Some astronomers think the Big Bang that started our Universe was just one of many, and that we are a tiny part of an endless "multiverse."

Expanding Universe

The farther away we look in space, the faster things are rushing away from us in all directions. It is a sign that the Universe is expanding, just as we would expect if it started as the explosion of the Big Bang.

Galaxies are pulled away from each other like raisins in a rising sponge cake—the farther apart they are, the faster they move away from each other.

13.8 billion years ago, the Big Bang created the Universe.

Matter formed from energy in a foggy early Universe.

The first stars and galaxies were packed quite close together.

Hubble's Law

In the mid-1920s, Edwin Hubble measured the distance to other galaxies. Then, in 1929, he compared these distances to measurements of the way the galaxies moved, and found an amazing pattern—the farther away a galaxy is, the faster it is moving away from us.

Edwin Hubble discovered the expanding Universe.

172   **DID YOU KNOW?** Some astronomers think that if the Universe goes on expanding, it could tear itself apart in a Big Rip.

Cosmic Background

Short radio waves called microwaves, coming from every part of the Universe, are called cosmic background radiation. Discovered in 1964, they are left over from the Big Bang itself, and hold important information about the growing Universe.

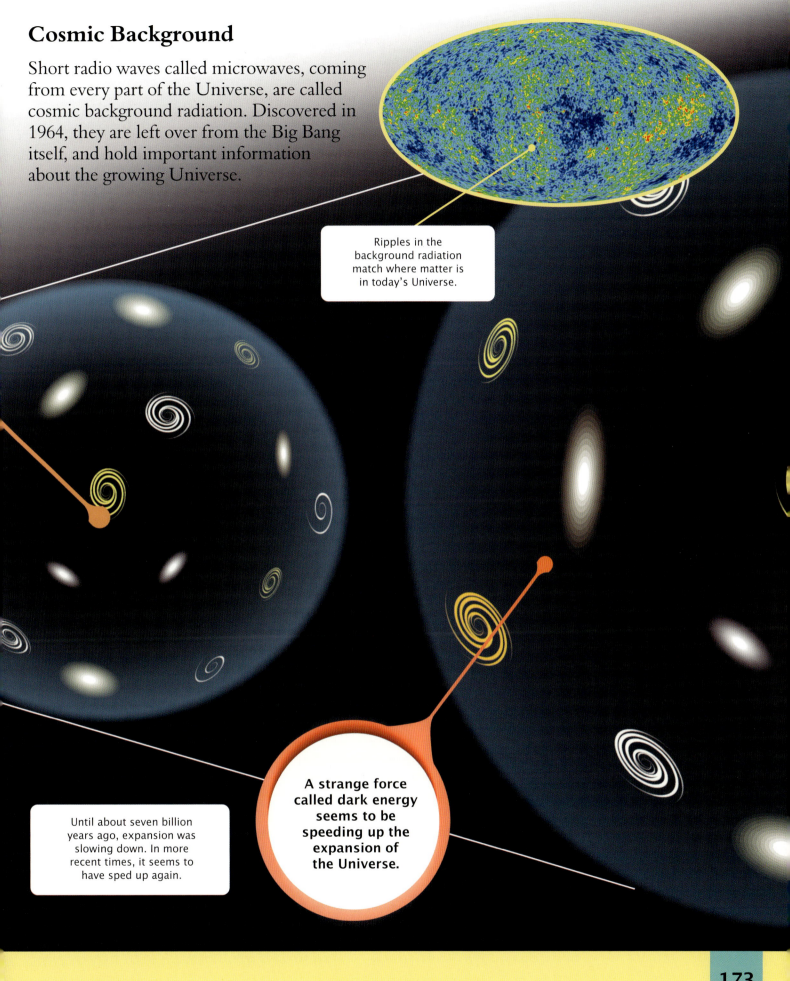

Ripples in the background radiation match where matter is in today's Universe.

Until about seven billion years ago, expansion was slowing down. In more recent times, it seems to have sped up again.

A strange force called dark energy seems to be speeding up the expansion of the Universe.

Galaxies

Galaxies are groups of stars, gas, and dust. Some are huge balls of trillions of stars and others are small clouds of just a few million. Pulled together by the force of gravity, these clouds become factories for making new stars.

Crowded Universe

Galaxies are huge objects—tens or even hundreds of thousands of light-years across, and with powerful gravity that has an effect on the galaxies nearest to them. This means that they tend to crowd together in some places, forming clusters of anything from tens to thousands of galaxies. On the largest scales, clusters join together to form superclusters that are hundreds of millions of light-years wide.

Every dot or blob you can see in this photo is a galaxy. The photo covers an area with 5,500 galaxies.

Galaxy Types

Astronomers group galaxies into different shapes. The most common are spirals (disks with spiral arms where the brightest stars are close together) and ellipticals (balls of red and yellow stars that look like the cores of spirals). There are also irregulars (shapeless clouds, often made up of many bright stars).

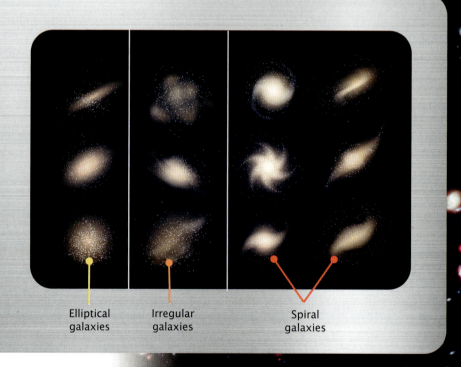

Elliptical galaxies

Irregular galaxies

Spiral galaxies

The oldest galaxies in this image look like they did 13.2 billion years ago.

This image was created when the *Hubble Space Telescope* focused on what looked like an empty area of space for 23 days.

The most distant galaxies are shapeless blobs. They are still being formed.

DID YOU KNOW? Astronomers believe there are also dark galaxies, with very few stars but lots of gas and dark matter (see page 184).

Crashing Galaxies

All the different types of galaxy are related to each other by how they developed. Over billions of years, galaxies join together and change type, then slowly change back—or change into something else entirely.

Galactic Chaos

Unlike planets or stars, galaxies collide (crash into) each other quite often. Most galaxies have one large collision in their lifetime. When galaxies hit each other, gravity can change the orbits of stars, creating a chaotic cloud of stars that takes a long time to settle back down.

Longer-lived red and yellow stars join together in an elliptical (oval) ball.

In a spiral galaxy, bright stars form in the spiral arms.

A huge "starburst" blows away gas and stops more stars forming.

Galaxy collisions can stop stars being created.

New Stars, Old Stars

Galaxies can only form new stars if they have enough of the raw materials—gas and dust clouds. When galaxies crash again and again, the gas heats up until it is too fast-moving to form new stars. This is why old ball-shaped elliptical (oval) galaxies have very little gas and no new or young stars—they mostly have long-lived, red and yellow stars.

The Antennae Galaxies are a pair of spiral galaxies that are joining together—and will be fully joined in 400 million years.

A band of dust blocks light from the bright core.

Crashing gas clouds are heated and pushed together, which leads to lots of star births.

ANTENNAE GALAXIES PROFILE

Diameter: 500,000 light-years
Catalogue numbers: NGC 4038 and NGC 4039
Constellation: Corvus
Distance from Earth: 45 million light-years
Description: A pair of colliding spiral galaxies with unwound spiral arms in the shape of an insect's antennae.

DID YOU KNOW? The Antennae Galaxies were first spotted by astronomer William Herschel through his telescope in 1785.

Milky Way

Our home galaxy, the Milky Way, is a large spiral with a bar of stars across its middle. Our Solar System orbits in the flattened disk, between two of the major spiral arms and about 26,000 light-years from the star clouds that form the heart of the galaxy.

Binoculars or a telescope show that the Milky Way is made up of countless faint stars that seem close together in the sky.

Band across the Sky

From Earth, we see the Milky Way as a band of light that wraps around the night sky. Because of its disk shape, we see more stars when we look across the disk, and many fewer when we look "up" or "down" out of the disk. The band is brightest where we look toward the middle of the galaxy.

The middle of the Milky Way lies in the constellation Sagittarius, hidden behind dense clouds of stars and dust.

Dark Secret

The orbits of stars close to the middle of the Milky Way show they are moving very fast around an object with the mass of millions of Suns. This object is a huge black hole—known as a supermassive black hole—that formed early in the Milky Way's history (see page 230). Most galaxies have a supermassive black hole at their core.

MILKY WAY PROFILE

Diameter: 120,000 light-years
Mass: Approx 1.2 trillion Suns
Number of stars: Around 200 billion
Distance to core: 26,000 light-years
Description: A spiral galaxy with four main spiral arms and a central bar of stars.

This image shows a flash of X-rays from the area around the Milky Way's central black hole, called Sagittarius A*. It could mark the last moments of an asteroid that moved too close and was pulled in.

The Milky Way is about 120,000 light-years across, but just 2,000 light-years thick.

Dark patches in the Milky Way are created by dust clouds that are blocking out more distant stars.

DID YOU KNOW? The word "galaxy" comes from the ancient Greek word for "milky" due to the Milky Way's pale appearance in the night sky.

Nearby Galaxies

The Milky Way is one of about 50 galaxies in a small, loose cluster that astronomers call the Local Group. The cluster is about 10 million light-years across. Most of its mass is made up by three large galaxies—the Milky Way, and the Andromeda and Triangulum spirals.

The Tarantula Nebula is a huge cloud of star-forming gas and dust in the Large Magellanic Cloud.

Ruled by Gravity

The Local Group is an area of space where the gravity of these three galaxies is slowly pulling everything together. For example, the Milky Way and Andromeda galaxies are being drawn toward an unavoidable crash that will mean they join together in about 4.5 billion years.

This infrared image shows the Large Magellanic Cloud as a place where a lot of stars are born.

Satellite Galaxies

In the night sky, the brightest galaxies of the Local Group are two irregular galaxies called the Large and Small Magellanic Clouds. Visible from Earth's southern hemisphere, they look like separate clumps of the Milky Way, but are actually in orbit around it at distances of 160,000 and 200,000 light-years. The shapes of both are changed by our galaxy's huge gravity.

LARGE MAGELLANIC CLOUD PROFILE

Diameter: 15,000 light-years
Mass: Around 100 billion Suns
Constellation: Dorado and Mensa
Distance from Earth: 160,000 light-years
Description: A galaxy with some signs of a spiral structure, including a central bar.

Andromeda is our closest large galaxy. It is a spiral galaxy, about the same size as the Milky Way.

This central star cluster is home to immense newborn stars.

Wind from newborn stars has blown away gas from around them.

DID YOU KNOW? The Tarantula Nebula's central star cluster is home to one of the most massive stars so far discovered, R136a1, with a mass of about 196 Suns.

Active Galaxies

Quite a lot of galaxies seem to release more radiation—both light and other types—than their stars alone can account for. Astronomers call these "active galaxies," and they think their activity comes from a hungry, young supermassive black hole.

Different Kinds of Activity

When astronomers first found active galaxies, they thought they were looking at many different objects. Some active galaxies have huge clouds of radio waves around them; others seem quite normal except for a slightly brighter core. The most impressive are quasars, where the core shines so brightly that the light of the galaxy around it cannot be seen.

The core of galaxy M106 appears bright because of its active nucleus.

A quasar has a brightly shining disk at its core.

Centaurus A is a nearby "radio galaxy."

Water heated up around the central black hole causes the galaxy to release large amounts of microwave radiation.

Heart of the Matter

The black holes at the middle of most galaxies are usually quiet and inactive, but some younger galaxies are "active": They have an active galactic nucleus, a central area where stars, gas, and dust are being pulled into a supermassive black hole. As they are, they form a superhot spinning disk that releases light and other energy. Jets of energy "spat out" from above and below the disk billow out into huge clouds of radio waves.

This is the view down the jet of an active galactic nucleus.

GALAXY M106 PROFILE

Diameter: 135,000 light-years
Mass of supermassive black hole: 39 million Suns
Constellation: Canes Venatici
Distance from Earth: 23.5 million light-years
Description: A distorted spiral "Seyfert" galaxy. Seyfert galaxies have very bright nuclei, but are less bright than quasars.

DID YOU KNOW? Collisions between galaxies often seem to "wake up" their central black holes and turn them into active galactic nuclei.

Dark Matter

One of the strangest things about our Universe is that everything we see and measure is just a tiny part of everything there is. The visible Universe of stars and galaxies is dwarfed by five times as much dark matter, a strange substance that does not release or take in radiation of any kind. This makes it totally invisible.

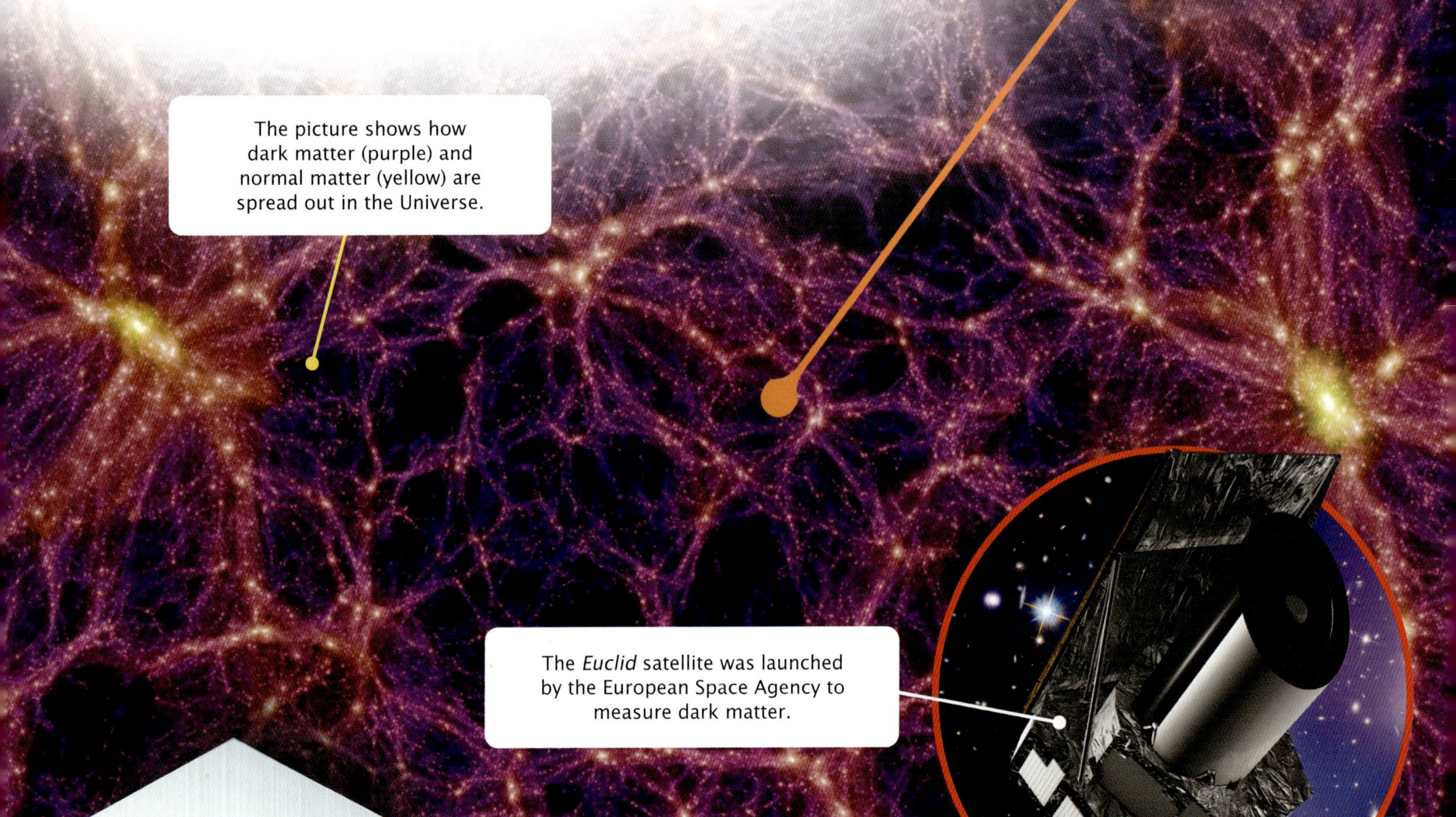

Pictures like this one, created on a computer, help scientists to work out where dark matter is compared to visible objects.

The picture shows how dark matter (purple) and normal matter (yellow) are spread out in the Universe.

The *Euclid* satellite was launched by the European Space Agency to measure dark matter.

EUCLID PROFILE

Telescope type: Infrared and visible light
Launch: 2023
Mirror diameter: 1.2 m (4 ft)
Mass: 2,160 kg (4,760 lb)
Description: The *Euclid* mission is mapping how dark matter deflects light.

DID YOU KNOW? Astronomers call the undiscovered forms of dark matter WIMPs, short for Weakly Interacting Massive Particles.

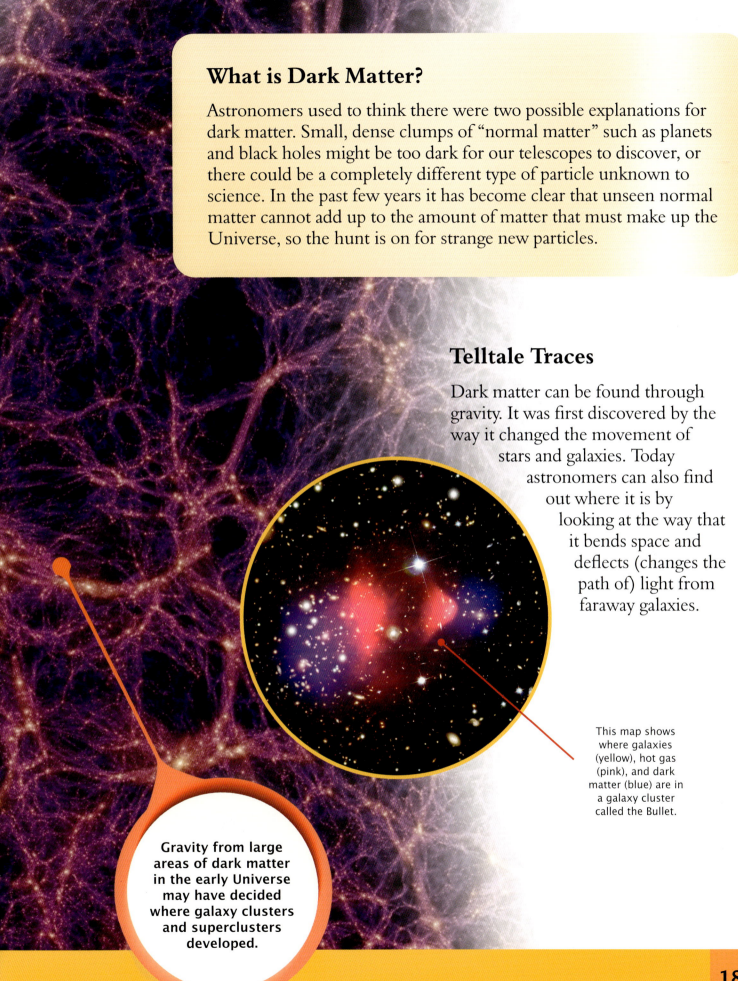

What is Dark Matter?

Astronomers used to think there were two possible explanations for dark matter. Small, dense clumps of "normal matter" such as planets and black holes might be too dark for our telescopes to discover, or there could be a completely different type of particle unknown to science. In the past few years it has become clear that unseen normal matter cannot add up to the amount of matter that must make up the Universe, so the hunt is on for strange new particles.

Telltale Traces

Dark matter can be found through gravity. It was first discovered by the way it changed the movement of stars and galaxies. Today astronomers can also find out where it is by looking at the way that it bends space and deflects (changes the path of) light from faraway galaxies.

This map shows where galaxies (yellow), hot gas (pink), and dark matter (blue) are in a galaxy cluster called the Bullet.

Gravity from large areas of dark matter in the early Universe may have decided where galaxy clusters and superclusters developed.

Alien Life

Are we alone in the Universe? It is one of the biggest questions in astronomy. Discoveries of planets around countless stars and welcoming environments in our Solar System mean that life could be common. But intelligent aliens are a very different matter.

Full of Life?

New discoveries have shown that some bacteria (tiny forms of life) can live in environments that we thought were uninhabitable (impossible to live in). We also now know that the basic chemicals for life are found across our galaxy. If life will automatically happen wherever the conditions are right, then there should be a lot of it in our galaxy.

Life would probably start out as simple life forms. However, that does not mean that it would develop into the same forms that it has on Earth.

EUROPA PROFILE

Moon of: Jupiter
Diameter: 3,100 km (1,900 miles)
Mass: 0.008 Earths
Orbit: 3.55 days
Description: With a deep-water ocean and undersea volcanoes beneath its icy crust, there could possibly be life on Europa.

DID YOU KNOW? Beneath their surface, at least six of the Solar System's moons probably have oceans, where life could develop as it did on Earth.

The human-like aliens described by many "alien abduction" victims are more like fairytale monsters than realistic alien life.

Our planet has few resources that any aliens who could travel here would want to take.

Alien Invaders

For many years, people have been fascinated by the idea that aliens might want to take over our planet. In reality, an invasion is very unlikely. Travel between star systems is such a huge challenge that it may simply be impossible to do. Hopefully any life forms that were able to reach that level of technology would feel no need to behave in this way toward others.

Alien invasions are the stuff of movies. Any extraterrestrial species (life forms that are not from Earth) with the technology to travel between the stars probably would not need to take over other planets.

187

Chapter 9

Stars

Almost every light you see in the night sky is a star (apart from satellites or aircraft). Stars are the only objects in the Universe that truly shine, or make their own light. Everything else, from planets to glowing clouds of gas, is only reflecting or absorbing (taking in) starlight.

Star Power

A star is a huge ball of extremely hot gas, called plasma (see page 12), that shines by changing light chemical elements (usually hydrogen) into heavier ones (usually helium). The process is called nuclear fusion, but astronomers still talk about stars "burning" their fuel supplies.

Measuring Stars

Even powerful telescopes cannot turn most stars into anything more than pinpricks of light, but astronomers can still find out an amazing amount. The wavelengths of light that a star releases can tells us about its surface temperature and chemical make-up. The star's movement in the sky compared to other stars can show its mass and perhaps its distance from Earth.

The *Gaia* satellite uses tiny changes in the position of stars to work out how far away they are.

Sirius, the Dog Star, is the brightest star in the sky and one of the closest (8.6 light-years away). It has a faint twin star called Sirius B.

The stars visible with the naked eye can be just a few light-years away or more than a thousand.

A star's brightness in the sky is called its magnitude. The brighter a star, the lower its magnitude.

Stars vary in brightness. Dwarfs are a thousand times fainter than the Sun, and giants are a million times brighter.

DID YOU KNOW? Sirius B is the white dwarf (see page 191) left behind by a star that was once brighter than Sirius itself.

Types of Star

The fact that stars have very different brightnesses and vary in hue from red to blue tells us that they are very different from each other. A star's brightness depends on the amount of energy it releases. Its tint tells us the temperature of its surface—red stars are cool, yellow stars hotter, and blue stars the hottest of all.

The Main Sequence

When you look at a large enough number of stars, a pattern starts to show. Cool red stars are fainter and hot blue ones are much brighter. Bright red stars are very rare, and so are faint blue ones. The link between temperature and energy output lasts for most of a star's lifetime. Astronomers call it the "main sequence" relationship.

The Witch Head Nebula is a cloud of dust and gas close to Rigel that shines by reflecting the star's light.

RIGEL PROFILE

Star type: Blue supergiant
Distance: 860 light-years
Constellation: Orion
Mass: 23 Suns
Brightness: At least 120,000 Suns
Surface temperature: 12,100 °C (21,800 °F)

DID YOU KNOW? The Sun is about halfway through its 10 billion years on the main sequence.

Rigel is a blue supergiant star that marks the knee of the constellation Orion (the Hunter).

Life Spans of Stars

Exactly where a star sits on the "main sequence" depends on its mass, just how much fuel it has, and how fast it burns. Low-mass stars called red dwarfs burn their fuel very slowly and so can shine for tens of billions of years. Middling ones like our Sun use up their fuel in about 10 billion years. Really massive stars burn fast and bright, lasting just a few million years.

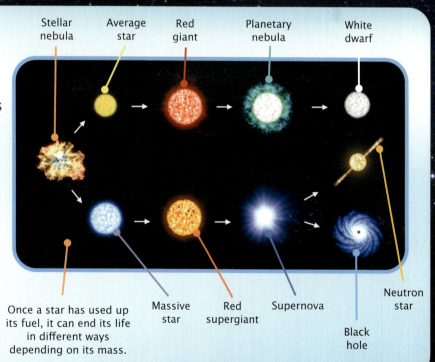

Stellar nebula · Average star · Red giant · Planetary nebula · White dwarf

Once a star has used up its fuel, it can end its life in different ways depending on its mass. · Massive star · Red supergiant · Supernova · Neutron star · Black hole

191

Star Birth

Stars are born in clouds of gas and dust called nebulae. They begin their lives as collapsing knots of gas that grow hotter and denser for perhaps a million years, until conditions at the core are able to turn hydrogen into helium.

Infrared shines through the dust to show glowing gas, warmed by newborn stars.

Brought into Being

Star-birth nebulae are some of the most beautiful sights in the Universe. As the stars inside begin to shine, they make the gas nearby glow. Different elements create red, green, yellow, and other hues. Streams of particles blowing off the surface of the stars shape their surroundings into all kinds of shapes.

An infrared view of part of the Horsehead Nebula region of Orion.

HORSEHEAD NEBULA PROFILE

Nebula type: Dark nebula
Catalogue number: Barnard 33
Distance: 1,500 light-years
Constellation: Orion
Size: Around 3 light-years long
Description: A dark cloud of gas and dust made visible by brighter gas glowing in the background.

STAR-FORMING NEBULAE

Carina

This nebula is the largest and brightest in the sky, but is only visible in southern skies.

Eagle

Stars are born inside these towers of gas and dust in the constellation Serpens, the Snake.

Horsehead

Seen as a whole, the famous Horsehead Nebula in Orion looks like a chesspiece.

The Horsehead is just one part of a much larger star factory.

DID YOU KNOW? Much of the constellation of Orion is filled with star–forming gas clouds, including the famous Orion Nebula (see page 206).

Star Death

When a star runs out of hydrogen to burn in its core, it is the beginning of the end. Stars have different ways to keep shining for a while longer, but they all run out of energy in the end. What happens next depends on the mass of the star.

Red Giants

As its main fuel supply runs out, a star goes through many internal (inside) changes. Its core actually gets hotter and it starts to burn hydrogen closer to the surface. This makes the star brighter, but it also makes it grow very large, so its surface is farther away from the hot core and cools. It is now a red giant.

Betelgeuse in the constellation Orion is a red supergiant star.

The Cat's Eye Nebula was first observed by William Herschel in 1786.

Supernova explosions are rare, but can outshine an entire galaxy for a short while.

Different Deaths

A star with about the mass of the Sun never makes it past the red giant stage. As it grows, it starts to vibrate (quickly grow bigger and smaller again). In the end, it throws off its outer layers, creating a gas cloud known as a planetary nebula. High-mass stars, however, keep burning fuel and making heavier elements in their cores. When they become unstable, they explode—an event called a supernova.

DID YOU KNOW? Planetary nebulae are short-lived compared to other objects in space—while some stars shine for billions of years, they glow for just 10,000 years.

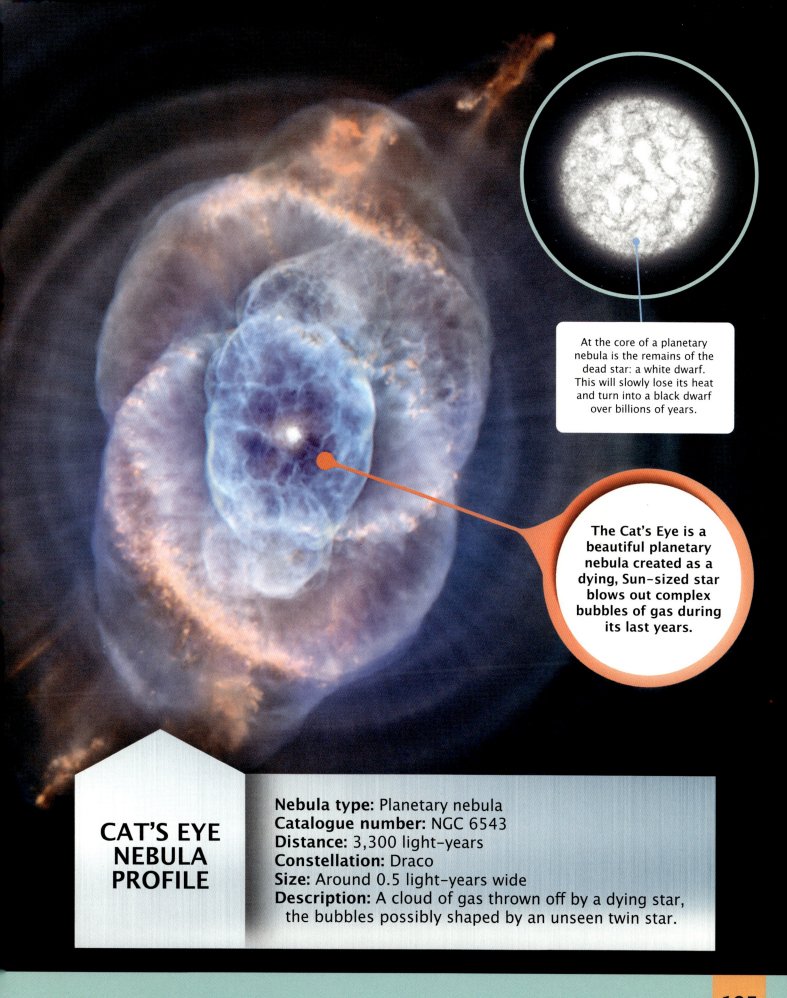

At the core of a planetary nebula is the remains of the dead star: a white dwarf. This will slowly lose its heat and turn into a black dwarf over billions of years.

The Cat's Eye is a beautiful planetary nebula created as a dying, Sun-sized star blows out complex bubbles of gas during its last years.

CAT'S EYE NEBULA PROFILE

Nebula type: Planetary nebula
Catalogue number: NGC 6543
Distance: 3,300 light-years
Constellation: Draco
Size: Around 0.5 light-years wide
Description: A cloud of gas thrown off by a dying star, the bubbles possibly shaped by an unseen twin star.

Neutron Stars

Neutron stars are all that is left behind when a supernova tears apart a dying star with a mass between 10 and 20 times that of our Sun. The neutron star is a sphere (ball) the size of a city.

Cosmic Lighthouses

As a star's core breaks into a neutron star, its rotation speeds up a lot. At the same time, its magnetic field grows much stronger, until it forces all of the star's radiation into two thin beams. The neutron star has become a flashing cosmic lighthouse called a pulsar.

The fastest pulsars spin hundreds of times per second.

Inside a Neutron Star

During a supernova explosion, a giant star's core is compressed (squeezed) with so much force that its atoms break down completely. Subatomic particles (smaller than an atom) called protons and electrons, with positive and negative electric charges, are then forced together to make uncharged neutrons. The neutrons stop the star breaking apart by knocking into each other.

The searing-hot surface of a neutron star gives off most of its energy as X-rays.

DID YOU KNOW? The Crab Pulsar formed in a supernova that was recorded by stargazers around the world in 1054 CE.

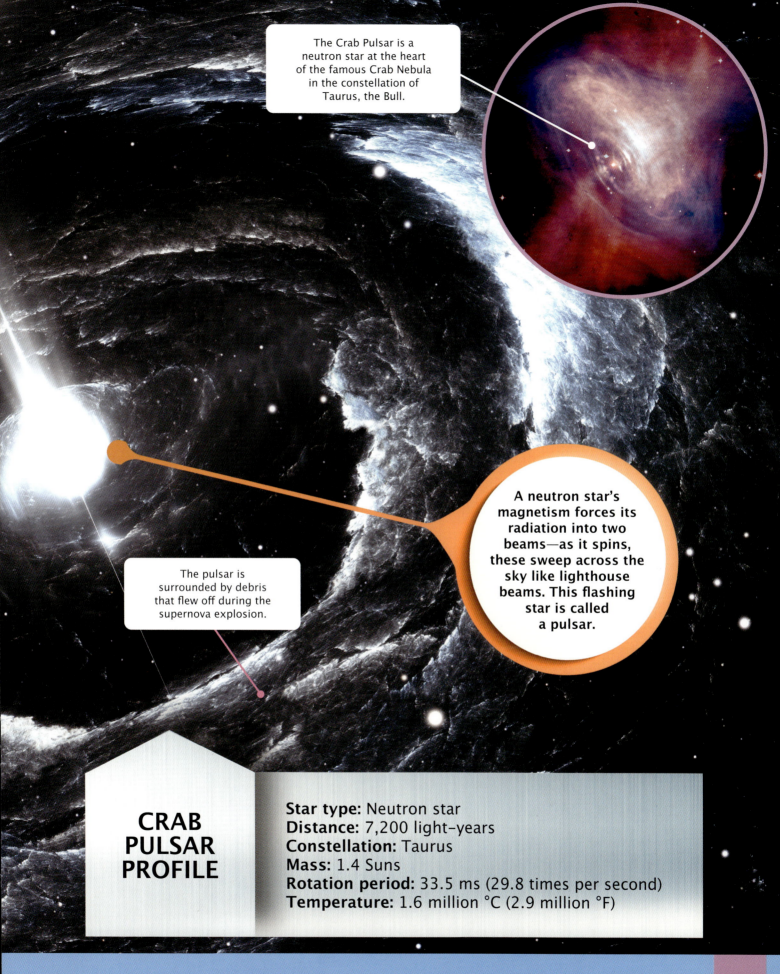

The Crab Pulsar is a neutron star at the heart of the famous Crab Nebula in the constellation of Taurus, the Bull.

A neutron star's magnetism forces its radiation into two beams—as it spins, these sweep across the sky like lighthouse beams. This flashing star is called a pulsar.

The pulsar is surrounded by debris that flew off during the supernova explosion.

CRAB PULSAR PROFILE

Star type: Neutron star
Distance: 7,200 light-years
Constellation: Taurus
Mass: 1.4 Suns
Rotation period: 33.5 ms (29.8 times per second)
Temperature: 1.6 million °C (2.9 million °F)

Black Holes

The strangest objects in the Universe, black holes can be formed by the death of the largest stars of all. With gravity so strong that not even light can escape, they pull anything that passes too close to its doom. A blast of radiation is the only sign the object was ever there.

Birth of a Black Hole

When the most massive stars—more than 20 times the mass of the Sun—explode as a supernova, they do not stop collapsing at the neutron star stage. Instead, the neutrons themselves are torn apart and the core shrinks to a tiny size. The gravity of all that matter, squeezed into so tiny an area, deforms space. A black hole is born.

A computer image shows two black holes joining together.

A black hole itself is invisible, but outside its event horizon is a disk of superhot material that releases X-rays and other energy as it spirals inwards.

CHANDRA X-RAY OBSERVATORY PROFILE

Telescope type: X-ray space telescope
Launched: 1999
Mirror diameter: 1.2 m (3.9 ft)
Mass: 4,790 kg (10,560 lb)
Description: NASA's main X-ray observatory, which has discovered many new black holes.

DID YOU KNOW? The smallest black holes have a mass 3 times that of the Sun, while the largest supermassive black holes may have a mass of 300 billion Suns.

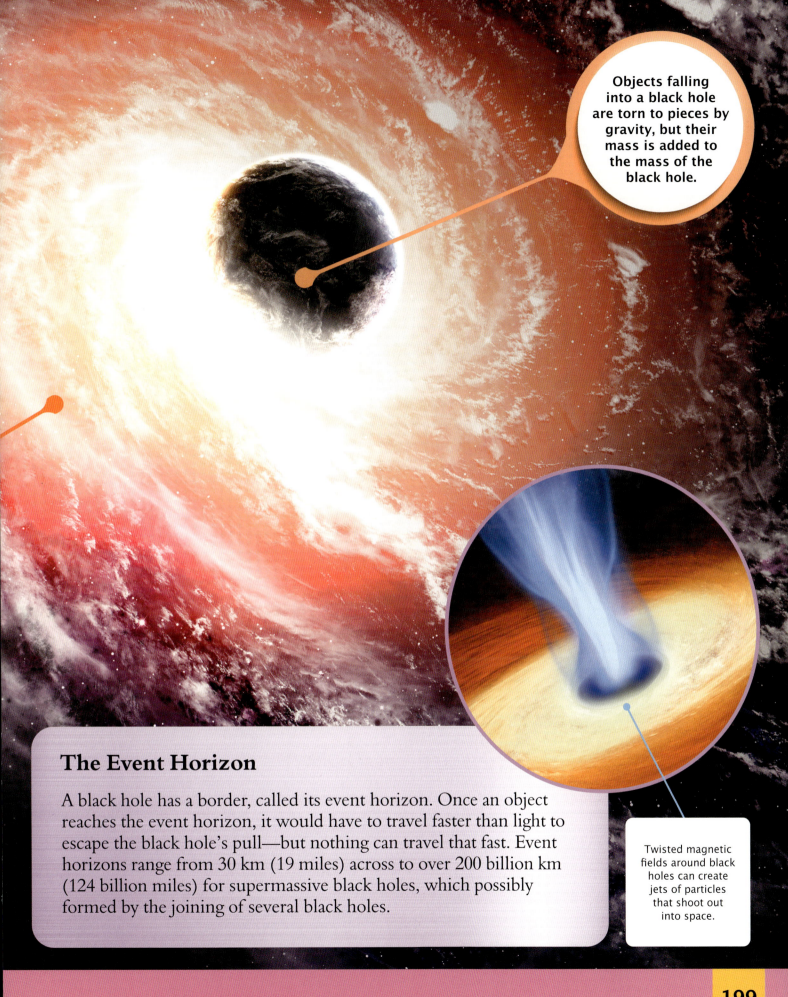

Objects falling into a black hole are torn to pieces by gravity, but their mass is added to the mass of the black hole.

Twisted magnetic fields around black holes can create jets of particles that shoot out into space.

The Event Horizon

A black hole has a border, called its event horizon. Once an object reaches the event horizon, it would have to travel faster than light to escape the black hole's pull—but nothing can travel that fast. Event horizons range from 30 km (19 miles) across to over 200 billion km (124 billion miles) for supermassive black holes, which possibly formed by the joining of several black holes.

Interstellar Space

The space between stars is far from empty: It is full of gas, dust, and particles that form the raw material for new stars. In this way, our galaxy and others are like massive recyclers, remixing used material and repackaging it into new stars.

Cosmic Recycling

Since the birth of the Universe, the death of each star has added more heavy elements to the light ones—hydrogen and helium—that formed soon after the Big Bang. These heavier elements, such as oxygen and carbon, are formed as dying stars fuse atoms together as they use them as fuel. Elements such as oxygen and carbon make up our planet and play a key role in life itself. We are all made of star stuff.

The Veil Nebula is a growing bubble of debris released by a supernova explosion more than 5,000 years ago.

Cycles of Star Birth

Astronomers think that star birth is often started when shockwaves from earlier supernova explosions meet clouds of star-forming material. Growing supernova debris also adds heavy elements to the star-forming nebula. Some elements end up in the new stars, while others form planets.

Heavy elements form the dark dust in star-forming nebulae.

WESTERN VEIL NEBULA PROFILE

Nebula type: Supernova remnant
Catalogue number: NGC 6960
Distance: 1,470 light-years
Constellation: Cygnus
Size: Around 90 light-years wide
Description: The remains of a supernova that covers 36 times the area of a Full Moon.

Gas in the expanding nebula is heated to temperatures of 150,000 °C (270,000 °F).

The remains of the supernova are made up of elements including hydrogen, oxygen, and carbon. These will one day find their way into new stars.

DID YOU KNOW? Stars that have large amounts of heavy elements from interstellar space shine more brightly, but have shorter lifespans.

Star Groups

Because stars are born together in "nurseries" of star-forming nebulae, they are usually found in loose groups called open clusters. Over tens of millions of years, these star clouds slowly drift apart, but some stars stick together all their lives.

Binaries and Multiples

Sometimes, the slowly spinning clumps of gas that form stars split into two or more regions. Each of these can then give birth to a star, leading to a pair or group of stars locked in orbit around each other. This is called a binary or multiple system. Because their stars were born at the same time, these systems can tell us a lot about the life cycles of stars.

Albireo in the constellation Cygnus, the Swan, is a beautiful binary pair of blue and orange stars.

Starlight reflects off nearby dust to surround the Pleiades with a blue glow.

PLEIADES PROFILE

Star cluster type: Open cluster
Catalogue number: Messier 45
Distance: 450 light-years
Constellation: Taurus
Size: Around 30 light-years wide
Description: A cluster of at least 1,000 stars that formed together about 100 million years ago.

DID YOU KNOW? Five of the brightest stars in the famous constellation of Ursa Major (the Great Bear) began life in the same open cluster.

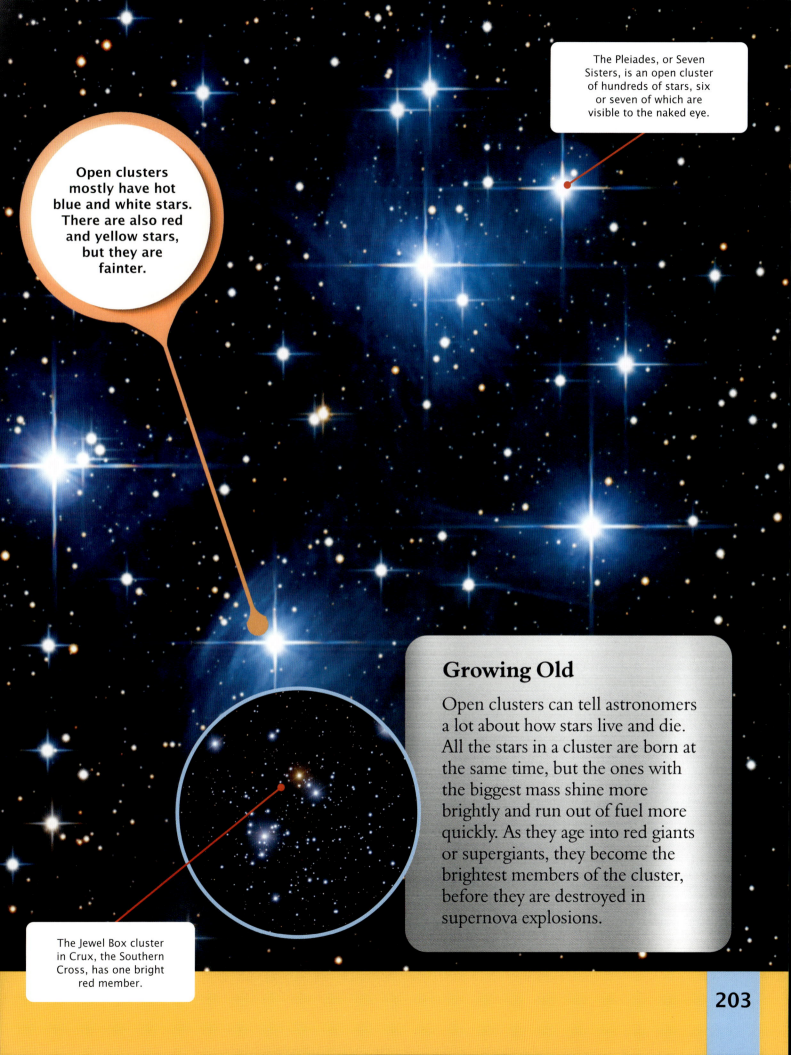

Open clusters mostly have hot blue and white stars. There are also red and yellow stars, but they are fainter.

The Pleiades, or Seven Sisters, is an open cluster of hundreds of stars, six or seven of which are visible to the naked eye.

The Jewel Box cluster in Crux, the Southern Cross, has one bright red member.

Growing Old

Open clusters can tell astronomers a lot about how stars live and die. All the stars in a cluster are born at the same time, but the ones with the biggest mass shine more brightly and run out of fuel more quickly. As they age into red giants or supergiants, they become the brightest members of the cluster, before they are destroyed in supernova explosions.

Globular Clusters

Very different from open star clusters, globular clusters are tight, compact balls with tens or hundreds of thousands of stars closely packed together. The stars in globular clusters are ancient compared to most others.

Some astronomers think that Omega Centauri might be the core of a galaxy torn apart by the Milky Way.

Distant Blobs

Globular clusters are much more difficult to see in the sky than open clusters and are many thousands of light-years away from Earth. They are only found around the middle of our galaxy and above and below its disk in a region called the halo. Their small size (usually a few tens of light-years across) means they look like fuzzy blobs.

Messier 13 in the constellation of Hercules is the brightest globular cluster in the northern sky.

Globular Beginnings

The old stars in globular clusters are red and yellow, and less massive than the Sun. There are no young hot stars, and no star-forming gas. Astronomers think that globulars formed during ancient galaxy collisions that created huge star clusters. While heavier stars in these clusters aged and died, the longer-lived, red and yellow stars survived until today.

OMEGA CENTAURI PROFILE

Star cluster type: Globular cluster
Catalogue number: NGC 5139
Distance: 15,800 light-years
Constellation: Centaurus
Size: Around 150 light-years wide
Description: The largest and densest of the Milky Way's globular clusters, with about 10 million stars.

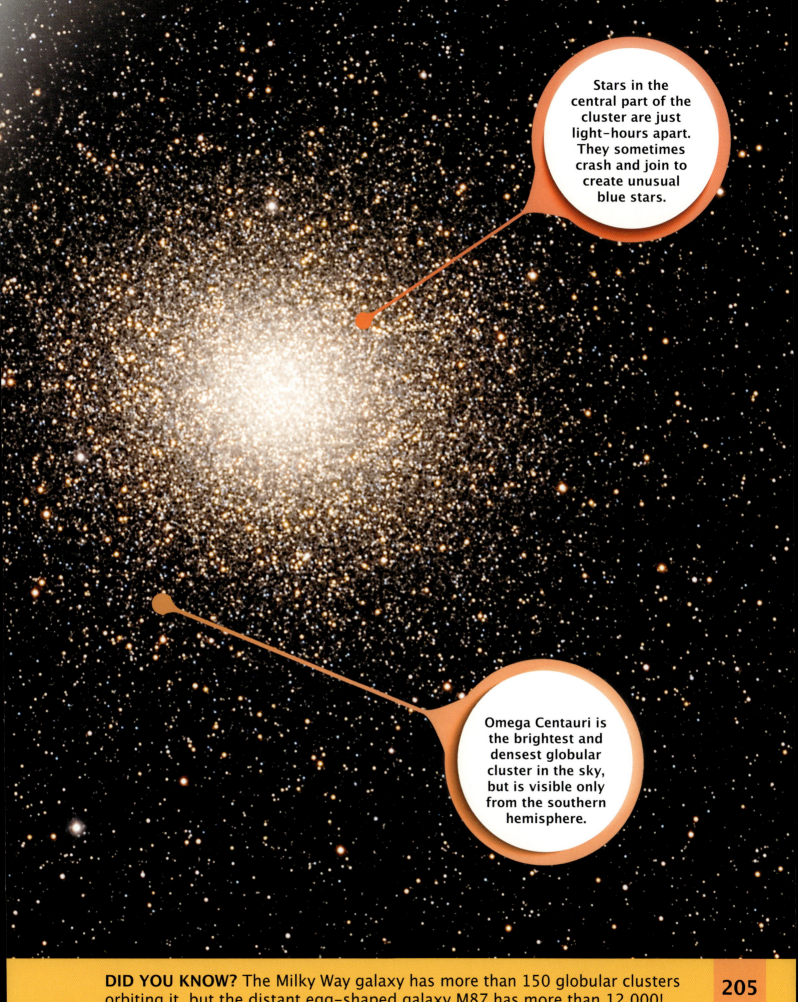

Stars in the central part of the cluster are just light-hours apart. They sometimes crash and join to create unusual blue stars.

Omega Centauri is the brightest and densest globular cluster in the sky, but is visible only from the southern hemisphere.

DID YOU KNOW? The Milky Way galaxy has more than 150 globular clusters orbiting it, but the distant egg-shaped galaxy M87 has more than 12,000!

Exoplanets

Since 1992, astronomers have discovered more than 5,000 exoplanets, which are planets orbiting stars outside our Solar System. They have also found signs of many more being born. These distant worlds are fascinating because, if they are the right temperature for flowing water, they might be suitable for life.

Planets form in nebulae that are rich in dust made from heavier elements, such as that in the Orion Nebula.

How Planets are Born

As stars form, they are often surrounded by a flattened disk called a protoplanetary disk. Over time, the material in this disk starts to clump together until some clumps have enough gravity to pull in more gas and dust from their surroundings. Once this has happened, they quickly grow into protoplanets, which crash together and form planets.

The *Hubble Space Telescope* discovered that many newborn stars in the Orion Nebula are surrounded by protoplanetary disks.

DID YOU KNOW? The closest star to Earth, a red dwarf called Proxima Centauri, is orbited by three exoplanets, one of which is Earth-like and could have surface water.

Planet hunters have found a lot of "hot Jupiters"—giant exoplanets orbiting very near their stars.

Planet Hunting

Astronomers use two main methods to look for planets. One way is to look for the tiny wobbles in a star's movement that are caused by an orbiting planet pulling it in different directions. Another is to watch for tiny dips in a star's brightness that happen when a planet is passing in front of it. With both methods it is easier to find planets that orbit close to their star, as well as giant planets rather than smaller ones.

This image of a planetary system called HR8799 was taken by the Keck Observatory. The system was found through direct imaging, which uses infrared wavelengths to observe planets.

ORION NEBULA PROFILE

Nebula type: Emission nebula (formed of clouds of electrically charged gas that emit light)
Catalogue number: Messier 42
Distance: 1,340 light-years
Constellation: Orion
Size: Around 25 light-years wide
Description: The heart of a star-forming region.

207

Chapter 10

Astronomers

Astronomers are scientists who study the Universe. They use observation, experiment, and mathematics to make discoveries. There are two main branches of astronomy: observational, which is based on watching space objects; and theoretical, which develops ideas to explain space objects.

> Stonehenge, on England's Salisbury Plain, was built in stages between 3100 and 2000 BCE.

Early Observational Astronomers

For early astronomers from ancient India to Mexico, the stars were signs from the gods or even the gods themselves. Despite these beliefs, many early astronomers were careful observers of space objects. By around 1400 BCE, astronomers in Egypt were recording the locations of stars. By 800 BCE, Babylonian astronomers—who lived in the region of modern Iraq—were using mathematics to predict eclipses of the Sun and Moon.

> Dating from 1800 to 1600 BCE, this Babylonian clay tablet lists Venus's risings and settings. It is written in cuneiform, which used wedge-shaped marks to form numbers and words.

> It is likely that people gathered at Stonehenge at the summer and winter solstices for ceremonies that celebrated the Sun and changing seasons.

DID YOU KNOW? The 4th-century BCE Chinese astronomers Gan De and Shi Shen are among the earliest astronomers that we know by name today.

In 1568, Portuguese astronomer Bartolomeu Velho published this model of the Universe as described by Ptolemy. The Earth is surrounded by circles representing the orbits of the Moon, Mercury, Venus, Sun, Mars, Jupiter, Saturn, and stars.

Early Theoretical Astronomers

The ancient Greeks started to figure out theories based on observation and mathematics, rather than on religion. In the 3rd century BCE, the Greek astronomer Aristarchus of Samos devised the correct theory that the planets rotate around the Sun. However, around 400 years later, one of the world's most famous theoretical astronomers had a different theory: Claudius Ptolemy used mathematics to prove that the Sun and other planets rotate around Earth. His theory was not scientifically disproved for hundreds of years.

Ancient astronomers aligned the stones to frame sunrise on the summer solstice (the longest day) and sunset on the winter solstice (the shortest day), when the Sun shone from opposite directions.

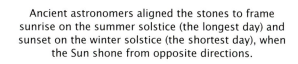

PTOLEMY PROFILE

Dates: c.100–170 CE
Nationality: A Greek living in Roman-ruled Egypt
Achievements: His theory that the Sun, other planets, and stars revolve around an unmoving Earth dominated astronomy for hundreds of years. This is known as the geocentric model of the Universe ("geo" means Earth).

Abd al-Rahman al-Sufi

The 10th-century astronomer al-Sufi lived at a time when Middle Eastern astronomy and mathematics were flourishing. He was employed by the local ruler, called an emir, in Isfahan, which is in today's Iran.

Book of the Fixed Stars

Al-Sufi is best known for his *Book of the Fixed Stars*, in which he drew 48 star constellations. He had studied the works of Ptolemy (see page 209), who listed the constellations agreed by the ancient Greeks. In his own book, al-Sufi was the first person to compare the Greek and Arabic constellations, which overlapped and differed in complex ways.

This 15th-century illustration of the Centaurus and Lupus constellations was copied from al-Sufi's *Book of the Fixed Stars*.

This page from *Book of the Fixed Stars* shows the Gemini constellation. Al-Sufi included star charts that gave each star's brightness and location. He wrote in Arabic, the language used by astronomers and scholars across the Middle East and North Africa.

Another Galaxy

In 964, al-Sufi wrote about his observations of the Andromeda Galaxy. Since he was working 644 years before the invention of the telescope, he could see it only with his naked eye. He described it as a "small cloud." However, this was the first known written mention of a galaxy beyond the Milky Way.

The Andromeda Galaxy is faintly visible to the naked eye in the constellation of Andromeda. At 2.5 million light-years from Earth, it is one of the most distant objects visible without a telescope.

The ancient Greeks saw Lupus ("wolf") and Centaurus ("centaur": a half-human, half-horse creature) as two constellations, but ancient Arab astronomers viewed them as one constellation: al-Shamareekh, meaning the branches of a date palm.

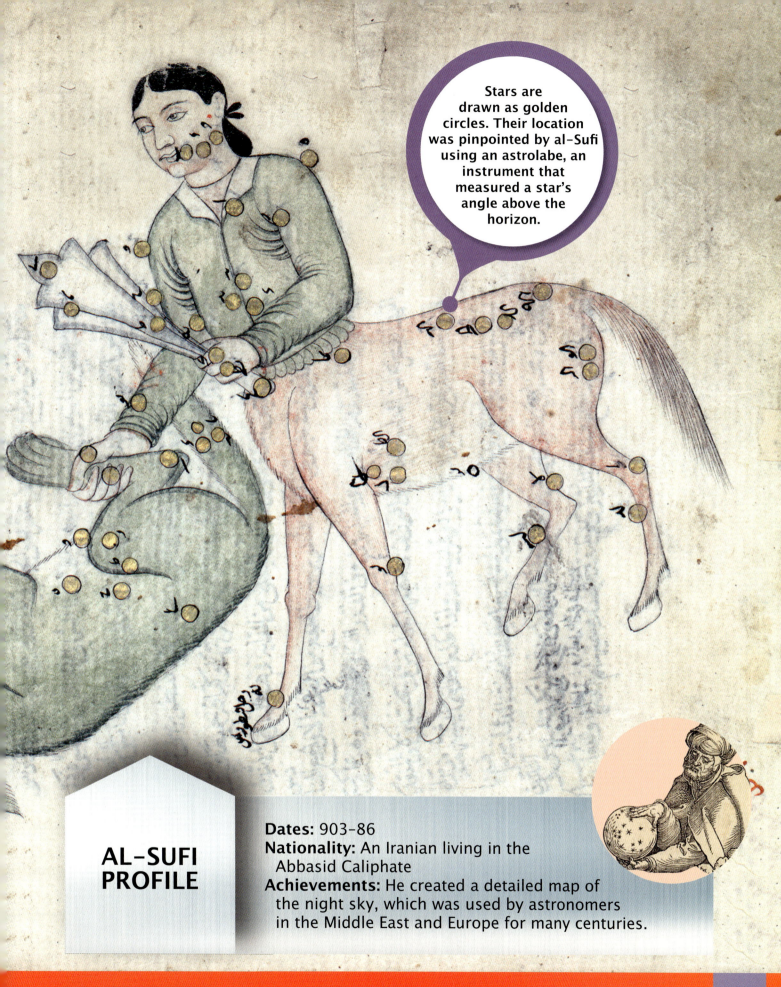

Stars are drawn as golden circles. Their location was pinpointed by al-Sufi using an astrolabe, an instrument that measured a star's angle above the horizon.

AL-SUFI PROFILE

Dates: 903–86
Nationality: An Iranian living in the Abbasid Caliphate
Achievements: He created a detailed map of the night sky, which was used by astronomers in the Middle East and Europe for many centuries.

DID YOU KNOW? Many stars—including Aldebaran ("follower") and Algol ("ogre")—have Arabic names due to the influence of Arabic-speaking medieval astronomers.

Galileo Galilei

Often called "the father of modern astronomy," Galileo was the first to use a telescope to make important discoveries. He adopted the scientific method, which is used by all modern scientists: using observation and experiment to answer questions.

Moons of Jupiter

When Galileo heard of the invention of the telescope by spectacle-maker Hans Lipperhey in 1608, he started to make his own. In late 1609 or early 1610, he pointed his telescope toward Jupiter, discovering the planet's four largest moons: Ganymede, Callisto, Io, and Europa. This made him the first person to see a moon orbiting another planet. His discovery proved the importance of the telescope as a tool for astronomers.

Using his telescope in 1610, Galileo was the first person to view Venus's phases: As Earth and Venus orbit the Sun, different portions of Venus's sunlit side are visible from Earth, making the planet seem to change shape in a similar manner to the Moon.

In 1609, Galileo (standing in the middle) demonstrated his telescope to the ruler of Venice.

GALILEO PROFILE

Dates: 1564–1642
Nationality: Italian
Achievements: He helped to prove the theory that the Sun is at the heart of the Solar System, which is known as the heliocentric model ("helios" means Sun).

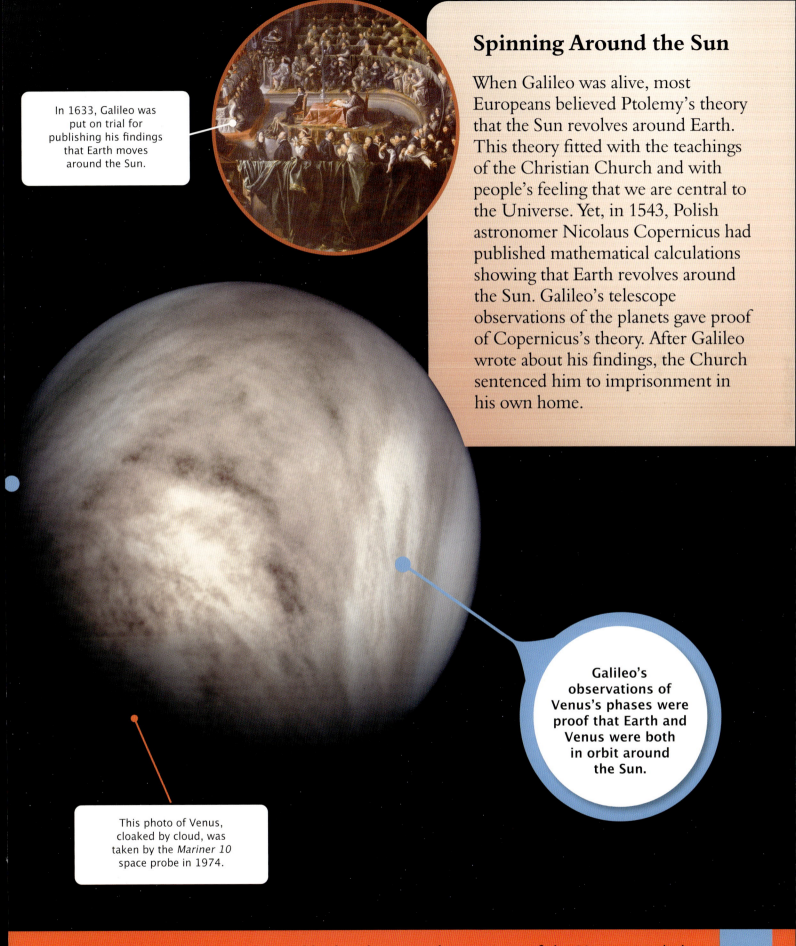

In 1633, Galileo was put on trial for publishing his findings that Earth moves around the Sun.

Spinning Around the Sun

When Galileo was alive, most Europeans believed Ptolemy's theory that the Sun revolves around Earth. This theory fitted with the teachings of the Christian Church and with people's feeling that we are central to the Universe. Yet, in 1543, Polish astronomer Nicolaus Copernicus had published mathematical calculations showing that Earth revolves around the Sun. Galileo's telescope observations of the planets gave proof of Copernicus's theory. After Galileo wrote about his findings, the Church sentenced him to imprisonment in his own home.

Galileo's observations of Venus's phases were proof that Earth and Venus were both in orbit around the Sun.

This photo of Venus, cloaked by cloud, was taken by the *Mariner 10* space probe in 1974.

DID YOU KNOW? In 1609, Galileo's telescope observations of the Moon revealed that it was not smooth, as previously thought, but mountainous and cratered.

Isaac Newton

This astronomer, mathematician, and physicist figured out the laws of gravity and motion. His breakthroughs explained the movements of space objects from planets to comets—and proved once and for all that the Sun is at the middle of the Solar System.

Laws of Gravity

It is said that Newton devised his laws of gravity after he saw an apple fall from a tree to the ground. He figured out that a force attracts every object to every other object. He called the force *gravitas*, the Latin for "weight." The more massive (or weighty) the object, the stronger the pull of its gravity. Since Earth is more massive than an apple, its gravity is stronger. In the same way, since the Sun is more massive than Earth, its gravity is stronger.

Newton's laws of gravity explained why an apple falls to Earth and why a planet is held in orbit around a star.

Laws of Motion

In 1686, Newton devised three laws of motion. The first law states: An object will not change its motion unless a force acts on it. This explains why a spacecraft carries on flying through space at the same speed, even if it never blasts its engines. The second law states: The greater an object's mass, the greater the force needed to make it accelerate (gain in speed). This explains why, the heavier a rocket is, the larger the force needed to launch it. The third law states: For every action, there is an equal and opposite reaction.

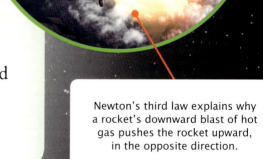

Newton's third law explains why a rocket's downward blast of hot gas pushes the rocket upward, in the opposite direction.

NEWTON PROFILE

Dates: 1643-1727
Nationality: British
Achievements: His realizations about how gravity behaves were the basis of astronomy until the 20th century, when they were built on by Albert Einstein's theory of relativity (see page 220).

Newton helped us understand the Moon's orbit around Earth by using the example of firing a cannonball from a very high mountain.

If the cannonball were fired slowly, it would simply fall to Earth. If the cannonball were fired very fast—at more than 10,000 m (33,000 ft) per second—it would overcome the pull of Earth's gravity and travel away from Earth. Yet if the cannonball were fired at 7,300-10,000 m (24,000-33,000 ft) per second, its speed would balance the pull of gravity and the cannonball would orbit Earth, like the Moon.

DID YOU KNOW? Newton figured out the laws of gravity while sheltering at his mother's home from the Great Plague of 1665-6.

Caroline Herschel

Caroline Herschel was the first woman to be paid a salary for her work in astronomy, making her the earliest female professional astronomer. In the beginning, she was known only as the younger sister of astronomer William Herschel, but she began to win her own fame as an astronomer.

> This emission nebula (glowing gas cloud) shines red as it is heated by the young stars of the surrounding cluster.

Servant or Astronomer?

In 1760, when Caroline was 10 years old, she caught the disease typhus, which damaged the sight in her left eye and stopped her growth, so her adult height was 1.3 m (4.3 ft). Caroline's mother decided that her daughter would never marry and should be a servant instead. Luckily, Caroline's brother William invited her to live with him. He was a gifted astronomer who, in 1781, discovered the planet Uranus. As Caroline worked with him and adjusted his home-made telescopes, she became a skilled observational astronomer.

This 19th-century illustration shows Caroline bringing William tea as he polishes a telescope mirror. Yet, by 1787, her contribution to astronomy was so important that she was paid a yearly wage by Britain's King George III.

Finding Comets

Between 1786 and 1797, Caroline discovered eight comets, seven of them using telescopes and one with her naked eyes. Although William lived at a time when husbands, fathers, and brothers often took credit for women's achievements, he proudly referred to these discoveries as "my sister's" comets. One of the comets bears Caroline's name today: 35P/Herschel–Rigollet, which has a 155-year orbit.

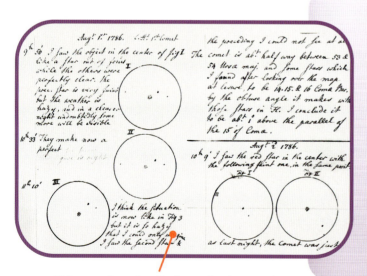

This page from Caroline's notebooks records the discovery of her first comet.

DID YOU KNOW? Caroline has a crater on the Moon named after her—C. Herschel—while William has craters named after him on the Moon, Mars, and Saturn's moon Mimas.

Less than 12 million years old, these blue stars form the star cluster NGC 7380, which was discovered by Caroline Herschel in 1787.

Star cluster NGC 7380 is around 8,500 light years away, in the Cepheus constellation.

HERSCHEL PROFILE

Dates: 1750–1848
Nationality: German–British
Achievements: She discovered 8 comets and made a catalogue of 2,500 nebulae and star clusters, including 500 that were previously unknown.

Annie Jump Cannon

In 1901, Annie Jump Cannon figured out a system for classifying stars. With small changes, her system is still used today, helping astronomers to describe and understand stars quickly and easily.

> In the Orion constellation, the red M-type star Betelgeuse marks the shoulder of the hunter Orion.

Star Light

The light given off by stars is made up of all the shades of the rainbow (see page 16), but hotter stars give off more light in the blue part of the spectrum, while cooler stars give off more red light. Cannon worked at the United States' Harvard College Observatory, where the light emitted by stars was split into its separate shades by a prism, which bent the light like raindrops bend sunlight so we can see a rainbow.

Cannon's job was to examine the pattern of light emitted by each star, which was captured on a photographic plate.

O stars are bright and often massive. They emit much of their light in the blue part of the spectrum and have temperatures over 30,000 °C (54,000 °F).

Star Types

Cannon devised what is known as the Harvard system of star classification. Stars are given the letters M, K, G, F, A, B, or O. M is the coolest and reddest, while O is the hottest and bluest.

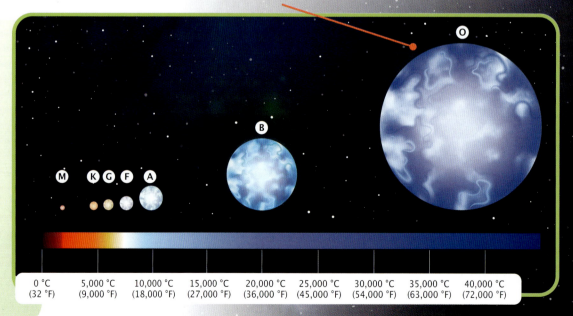

CANNON PROFILE

Dates: 1863–1941
Nationality: American
Achievements: She developed the Harvard system of star classification and also discovered around 300 variable stars, which are stars whose brightness, as seen from Earth, changes over time.

The stars of Orion's belt—Alnitak, Alnilam, and Mintaka—are blue B- and O-type stars.

The blue, B-type star Rigel marks Orion's knee.

DID YOU KNOW? In Annie Jump Cannon's Harvard star classification system, the Sun is a yellowish G-type star.

Albert Einstein

One of the most famous scientists who ever lived, Einstein figured out theories that changed the way we understand gravity. He also suggested the very complex idea that space and time are merged as spacetime.

The Theory of Relativity

We usually think of space and time as constant and separate—a yard is always a yard and a minute is a minute. Yet in his "theory of relativity," Einstein explained that measurements of space and time are relative, which means they change when taken by people moving at different speeds. Space and time are also combined as spacetime—which is best understood as a mathematical fact rather than as something we can see. Einstein explained that the gravity of a massive object, such as a planet, bends spacetime. These curves in spacetime create the gravitational pull toward the planet.

> In 1915, decades before anyone knew that black holes existed, the mathematics in Einstein's theory of relativity predicted that they did.

Since the Sun is more massive than Earth, its gravity curves spacetime more than Earth's gravity. These curves affect both space (distances) and time (the speed at which clocks run).

Famous Equation

In 1905, Einstein came up with an equation: $E = mc^2$. It was part of his realization that mass (anything that takes up space, such as a ball or an atom) can be turned into energy—and energy can be turned into mass. In the equation, E stands for "energy," m is for "mass," and c is the "speed of light" (299,792,458 m per second). The equation calculates the amount of energy made by converting a certain amount of matter. That energy—whether in the form of light or X-rays (see page 16)—moves at the speed of light.

> Einstein's equation explains how mass, such as atoms of hydrogen in the Sun's core, is converted into huge amounts of energy—which we see as light and feel as heat.

DID YOU KNOW? Einstein and his wife were Jewish, so in 1933 they left Germany to avoid Adolf Hitler's persecution of Jewish people.

EINSTEIN PROFILE

Dates: 1879–1955
Nationality: German–American
Achievements: He overturned ideas about the structure of the Universe with his theory of relativity, which explains that gravity is caused by mass bending the fabric of spacetime.

A few months after Einstein published his theory, German astronomer Karl Schwarzschild used his equations to show that an area with immense mass could create a bottomless pit in spacetime—a black hole.

Even though Einstein's mathematics—and Schwarzschild's calculations—predicted black holes, Einstein did not think they could exist in "the real world."

Edwin Hubble

When Edwin Hubble realized that there are other galaxies beyond the Milky Way, he started a new field of study—extragalactic ("beyond the galaxy") astronomy. He was also a pioneer in the field of cosmology, which is the study of the structure and history of the Universe.

The Triangulum Galaxy is around 2.7 million light years from Earth.

Other Galaxies

When Hubble started work at the United States' Mount Wilson Observatory in 1919, most astronomers believed the Milky Way was all that was in the Universe. Then, in 1924–26, Hubble realized that the "Andromeda Nebula" and "Triangulum Nebula" were not clouds of gas, known as nebulas, inside the Milky Way. He figured out they were so far away they must be other galaxies—today known as the Andromeda and Triangulum Galaxies.

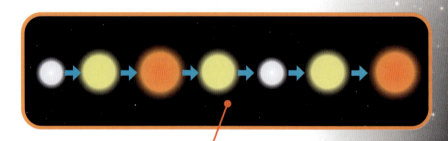

Hubble figured out the distance to other galaxies using Cepheid variable stars (pictured) within them. These stars have a known brightness, because their brightness is directly linked to regular changes in their size. By comparing the stars' known brightness with how bright they seem from Earth, the distance to them can be calculated.

HUBBLE PROFILE

Dates: 1889–1953
Nationality: American
Achievements: He proved that the Universe was far larger than believed, then found evidence that it is expanding, which disproved the previously held idea of a static Universe.

DID YOU KNOW? During planning, the Hubble Space Telescope was known as the Large Space Telescope, but it was renamed in 1983, seven years before its launch.

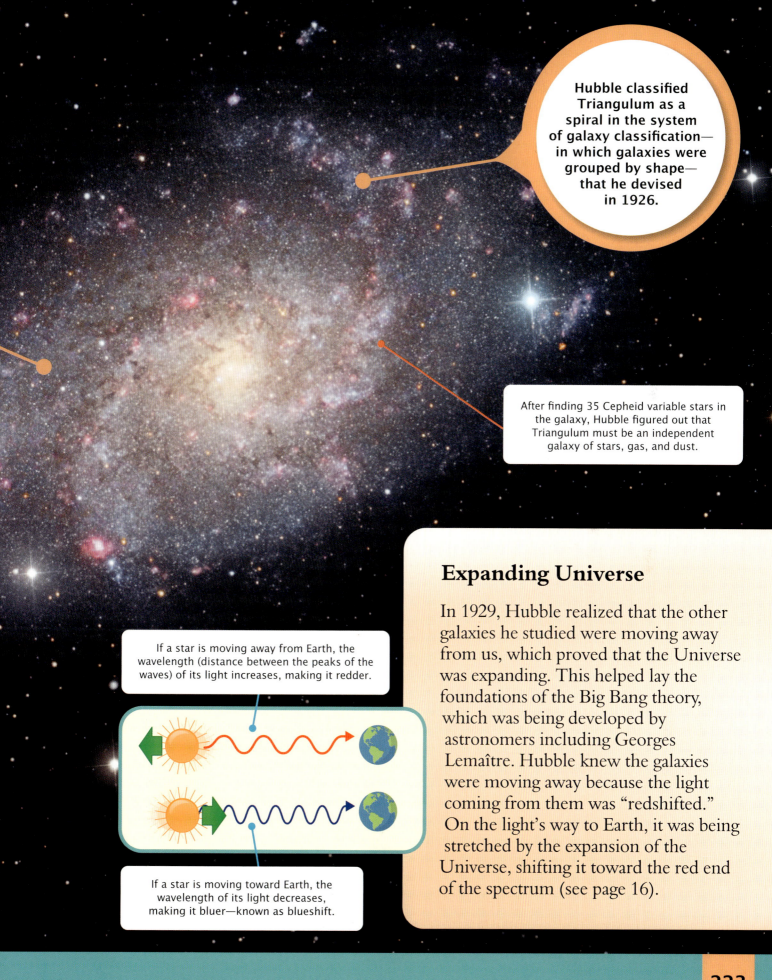

Hubble classified Triangulum as a spiral in the system of galaxy classification—in which galaxies were grouped by shape—that he devised in 1926.

After finding 35 Cepheid variable stars in the galaxy, Hubble figured out that Triangulum must be an independent galaxy of stars, gas, and dust.

If a star is moving away from Earth, the wavelength (distance between the peaks of the waves) of its light increases, making it redder.

If a star is moving toward Earth, the wavelength of its light decreases, making it bluer—known as blueshift.

Expanding Universe

In 1929, Hubble realized that the other galaxies he studied were moving away from us, which proved that the Universe was expanding. This helped lay the foundations of the Big Bang theory, which was being developed by astronomers including Georges Lemaître. Hubble knew the galaxies were moving away because the light coming from them was "redshifted." On the light's way to Earth, it was being stretched by the expansion of the Universe, shifting it toward the red end of the spectrum (see page 16).

Katherine Johnson

Johnson calculated the flight paths for the United States' early human spaceflights. She was one of the first African-American women to work as a scientist at the National Aeronautics and Space Administration (NASA).

Astrodynamics

From 1958 until her retirement in 1986, Johnson made astrodynamic calculations for NASA's crewed space flights, including flight paths, emergency escape routes, and launch windows (the time periods when a rocket can be launched to reach its target). Astrodynamics is the study of how spacecraft move through space as they blast their engines and are pulled by the gravity of stars and planets. Based on Newton's laws of gravity and motion, astrodynamics requires countless exact calculations.

Katherine Johnson was a gifted mathematician.

Putting Men in Space

Johnson calculated the flight path for the 1961 flight of Alan Shepard, the first American in space. She knew the flight path would be an upside-down U-shaped curve known as a parabola, so—keeping in mind Earth's rotation—she precisely calculated where Shepard would land so he could be rescued quickly. When NASA switched to using computers to calculate John Glenn's historic orbit around Earth in 1962, he refused to fly unless Johnson checked the calculations, saying: "If she says they're good, then I am ready to go."

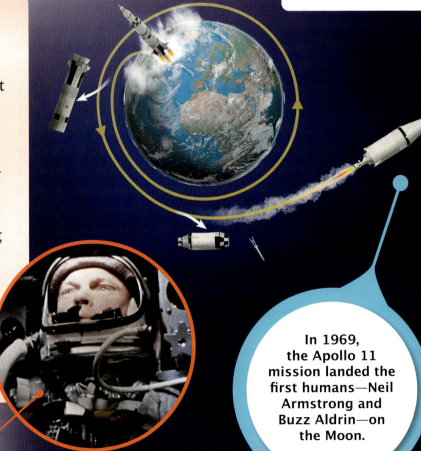

This photo shows John Glenn onboard *Friendship 7* as he became the first American to orbit Earth.

In 1969, the Apollo 11 mission landed the first humans—Neil Armstrong and Buzz Aldrin—on the Moon.

After reaching space, the Apollo spacecraft separated from its rocket, its protective fairing, and the Lunar Module. Then the Lunar Module was reattached to the nose of the Command and Service Module.

Johnson figured out flight paths for the Lunar Module (which landed on the Moon) and the Command and Service Module (which stayed in orbit around the Moon) so the two would meet again to return the astronauts.

JOHNSON PROFILE

Dates: 1918–2020
Nationality: American
Achievements: She made astrodynamic calculations that enabled key human spaceflights, including those that put the first American in space and the first humans on the Moon.

DID YOU KNOW? Johnson's home town did not offer schooling for Black children after eighth grade, so her family moved 190 km (118 miles) so she could go to high school.

225

Stephen Hawking

Hawking set out a theory of the Universe that combined Einstein's theories about gravity (which govern large objects) with the laws of quantum mechanics (which govern tiny atoms). His long equations described the whole history of the Universe.

Big and Small Ideas

Hawking used mathematics to examine the structure of the Universe at the biggest scale and the smallest scale. Along the way, he proved that the Big Bang started from an infinitely small point, called a singularity. He suggested that the Big Bang first created space, which was followed not quite instantly by time.

Hawking believed that there is not one Universe, but many similar universes, forming a multiverse.

Each universe may be separated from the rest by an inflating ocean.

In 1974, Hawking predicted that black holes shrink—and eventually vanish—as they release energy now known as "Hawking radiation." This radiation has not yet been observed.

DID YOU KNOW? Hawking believed that there is likely to be life on other planets, but was unsure whether extraterrestrial life forms would be friendly to humans.

When Hawking was diagnosed with motor neurone disease, he was told he would survive no more than two years. However, he lived and worked for another 55 years.

Motor Neurone Disease

When he was 21, Hawking was diagnosed with motor neurone disease, which gradually damages the nerve cells, called motor neurons, that control muscles. The disease slowly paralyzed him. After he was unable to control the muscles that enable speech, he communicated through an electronic speech-generating machine. At first, he operated this with a handheld switch, but he later used a single muscle in his cheek.

Hawking came to believe that each universe must obey the same laws of gravity and quantum mechanics as our own. However, the details of how each universe took shape would be random, with different stars, planets, and living things.

HAWKING PROFILE

Dates: 1942–2018
Nationality: British
Achievements: He devised theories of cosmology that explained the structure and history not just of our Universe but of the whole possible multiverse.

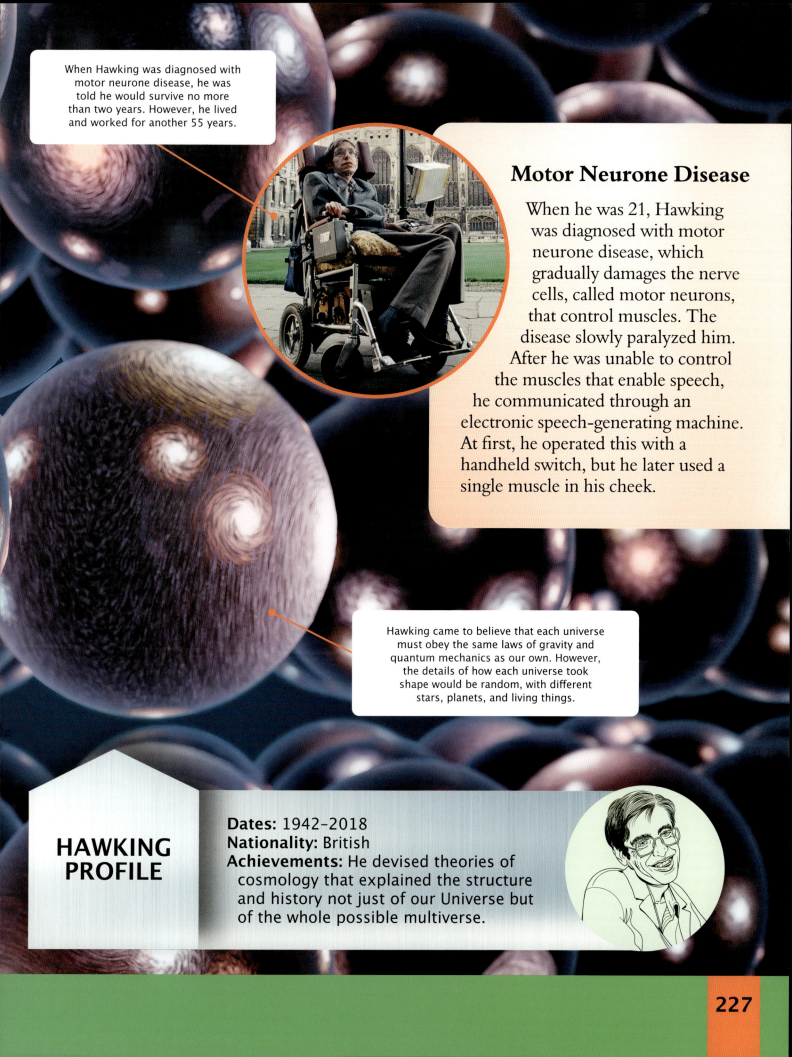

227

Jocelyn Bell Burnell

When she was 24 years old, Bell Burnell discovered a strange new object, which was soon named a pulsar. This is a spinning neutron star that blasts energy from its poles. Tiny, tightly packed neutron stars are usually the remains of massive stars that have exploded as a supernova.

Strange Signal

In 1967, Jocelyn Bell Burnell was studying results from a radio telescope she had just helped to build in Cambridge, England. She noticed that unusual radio waves were coming from a distant location. Her supervisor dismissed the findings, but Bell Burnell was convinced the waves were important, as they made a pulse, exactly every 1.337 seconds.

Just 10 km (6 miles) across but with a mass greater than the Sun, pulsar PSR B1257+12—also known as Lich, after an undead creature from fantasy novels—rotates 161 times per second.

Photographed here in 1977, Bell Burnell is studying a printout of radio waves.

BELL BURNELL PROFILE

Born: 1943
Nationality: Northern Irish
Achievements: She discovered a previously unknown object, a pulsar. Although the first pulsar Bell Burnell found, now named CP 1919, emits its energy as radio waves, pulsars have now been found that emit visible light, X-rays, and gamma rays.

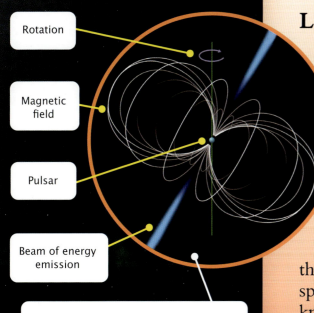

- Rotation
- Magnetic field
- Pulsar
- Beam of energy emission

The energy emitted from a pulsar's poles can be detected only when the beam of emission is pointing toward Earth as the star turns, which explains why the energy gives the appearance of a regular pulse.

Little Green Men

At first, Bell Burnell wondered if the pulses of radio waves might be a message from extraterrestrial beings on a distant planet, so she playfully named the signal LGM-1, for "little green men." It was only when she discovered a second, similar source of pulsing radio waves that the idea of "little green men" was abandoned. She and colleagues including Thomas Gold reached the conclusion that the source of the radio waves must be a rapidly spinning, highly magnetized neutron star, now known as a pulsar (see page 196).

Astronomers think Lich's three planets formed from a disk of leftover material after two dying stars, known as white dwarfs, collided and collapsed to form the pulsar.

The first exoplanets ever discovered were the two outer planets that orbit Lich, in 1992.

DID YOU KNOW? The name "pulsar" (short for "pulsating radio source") was suggested by a journalist for the UK's *Daily Telegraph* newspaper, named Anthony Michaelis.

Andrea Ghez

In 2003, Ghez proved that a supermassive black hole, called Sagittarius A*, lies at the middle of the Milky Way. A black hole is completely black, so we cannot see it directly—but Ghez found evidence it was there.

> This illustration shows the heart of the Milky Way, where hot gas is circling a supermassive black hole.

Special Sagittarius

In the 1980s, astronomers began to suspect there was a huge black hole at the heart of the Milky Way. This was due to the strange radio waves coming from the constellation of Sagittarius, which lies in the direction of the middle of the galaxy. This radio source was named Sagittarius A*. Astronomers thought the energy was probably being emitted by material circling the black hole really fast.

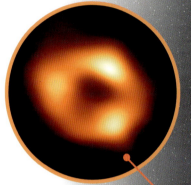

The Event Horizon Telescope created this image of Sagittarius A* in 2022. It shows radio waves emitted by glowing gas as a bright orange ring around a central dark area, which must be the black hole itself. Created after Ghez had found mathematical proof, this image was the first visual evidence of the black hole.

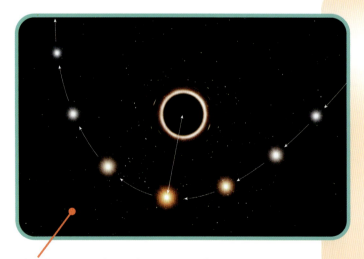

This illustration shows the star S2's elliptical orbit around the supermassive black hole. When closest to the black hole, at a distance of 20 billion km (12.4 billion miles), the immense gravitational pull makes the star glow redder.

Watching Stars

Our view of the middle of the Milky Way is masked by thick dust, so it was difficult to view until advances in infrared imaging, which enables us to see heat-emitting objects through dust. Using the W. M. Keck Telescope in Hawaii, Ghez watched the stars orbiting the middle of the galaxy. The speed and distance of the stars' orbits made it possible to calculate they were orbiting something with a mass of 4 million Suns. Since this immense object was emitting no light, it could only be a supermassive black hole.

The black hole is surrounded by a small cluster of very quickly orbiting stars, known as the S-stars.

Usually very quiet, Sagittarius A* does not suck in much material, but occasionally it destroys a passing gas cloud.

GHEZ PROFILE

Born: 1965
Nationality: American
Achievements: She presented mathematical proof for the existence of a supermassive black hole in the Milky Way Galaxy, as well as estimating its mass.

DID YOU KNOW? Astronomers estimate that Sagittarius A*'s event horizon (see page 199) is around 23.5 million km (14.6 million miles) wide.

Chapter 11

Astronauts

More than 600 people from over 40 countries have reached space, which is usually defined as beginning 100 km (62 miles) above Earth's surface. Most astronauts have journeyed no farther than Earth's orbit, but a few have flown around the Moon or walked on it.

Becoming an Astronaut

Until 1990, everyone who journeyed into space was paid and trained by a national space agency, such as the United States' National Aeronautics and Space Administration (NASA) or Russia's Roscosmos. Since then, some astronauts have been unpaid tourists or paid and trained by a private business. Up until 1978, all astronauts were from either the United States or the Soviet Union (which included today's Russia). Most of those early astronauts were already military test pilots, who had experience of flying newly designed planes.

Stephanie Wilson was photographed training for her third spaceflight, mission STS-131, which carried supplies to the *International Space Station* on board NASA's Space Shuttle *Discovery* in 2010.

Like other early NASA astronauts, Charles Duke (left) and John Young were test pilots with qualifications in aeronautics (the design of air- and spacecraft). In 1971, they were photographed in Florida while training to drive a lunar buggy for their mission to the Moon in April 1972.

GAGARIN PROFILE

Dates: 1934-68
Nationality: Soviet
Mission: Vostok 1 (April 12, 1961), which was the first mission to carry a human into space and the first crewed flight to orbit Earth. The Vostok 3KA space capsule reached a height of 327 km (203 miles). The mission lasted 108 minutes.

A life-size copy of the Space Shuttle flight deck was created at Johnson Space Center, in Texas, so astronauts could train for launch and landing.

First in Space

The Soviet Union's Yuri Gagarin was the first human in space, in April 1961. As his Vostok 3KA space capsule was launched by a Vostok-K rocket, Gagarin said, "Let's go!" into his radio. Ten minutes after liftoff, the final rocket stage detached from the capsule, which then made one orbit of Earth. Since no one knew what the flight would do to Gagarin's body, his capsule worked automatically. Yet Gagarin remained conscious and calm throughout.

Descent module

Service module

After completing an orbit, Gagarin's service module (containing the engines) released the descent module (containing Gagarin), which fell toward Earth, heating to around 1,480 °C (2,700 °F) as it battered through the atmosphere.

The descent module would be destroyed by landing, so at a height of 7 km (4.3 miles) Gagarin ejected and parachuted to the ground.

Today, Wilson is part of NASA's Artemis program, which hopes to send the first woman to the Moon soon.

DID YOU KNOW? The farthest any astronaut has journeyed is the far side of the Moon, around 400,170 km (248,655 miles) from Earth, on the Apollo 13 mission in 1970.

Alan Shepard

Freedom 7 was launched on top of a Redstone rocket from Cape Canaveral Space Force Station, in Florida.

Less than a month after Gagarin's spaceflight, American astronaut Alan Shepard became the second person in space. He did not complete an orbit of Earth in his *Freedom 7* space capsule, but he did reach a height of 187 km (116 miles).

Lift Off!

During the 1950s and 1960s, the United States and Soviet Union were locked in the Space Race, when the rival nations tried to better the other's achievements in space exploration. The United States had hoped to be first to put a human in space, but Shepard's flight was delayed several times for safety reasons, then by bad weather. Finally, his Mercury capsule, which he named *Freedom 7*, was launched 23 days after Gagarin's flight.

Landing!

As planned, Shepard's spacecraft—just 1.9 m (6.2 ft) across—did not go into orbit, as it was not moving fast enough to overcome the pull of Earth's gravity. During Shepard's 15-minute flight, his capsule was lifted by its rocket, which separated around 2 minutes after launch. The capsule continued to fly higher for another 3 minutes, then—like a ball thrown into the sky that peaks, then drops—*Freedom 7* fell back to Earth, around 487 km (303 miles) from where it set off.

Shepard was the first astronaut to have some control over the direction and height of his spacecraft, which enabled him to test the capsule for future, orbital flights.

This photo of Alan Shepard was taken by a movie camera inside *Freedom 7*. He is pictured just as he is about to raise a protective shield in front of his face during descent, moments after opening the capsule's parachute.

SHEPARD PROFILE

Dates: 1923–98
Nationality: American
Mission 1: Mercury–Redstone 3 (May 5, 1961), which made him the first American in space.
Mission 2: Apollo 14 (January 31–February 9, 1971), which made him the fifth person to walk on the Moon.

Inside *Freedom 7*

US marines rescued Shepard a few minutes after his splashdown.

Unlike Gagarin, Shepard was able to remain in his capsule throughout his flight: As planned, *Freedom 7* splashed down off the coast of Florida, slowed by parachutes during its descent.

DID YOU KNOW? Alan Shepard was 1.8 m (5 ft 11 in) tall, the maximum height allowed for astronauts flying in the tiny Mercury spacecraft.

Valentina Tereshkova

The first woman in space was the Soviet Union's 26-year-old Valentina Tereshkova, in 1963. She remains the only woman ever to make a solo spaceflight. Unlike most early astronauts, she was a factory worker, not an aircraft pilot, before being selected as an astronaut.

> The descent module was covered in a tough mineral called asbestos, which stopped it bursting into flames from the heat of descent.

Looking for Parachutists

After Gagarin and Shepard's flights in 1961, the Soviet space agency thought that the United States was starting to train female astronauts, although it was actually 17 years before NASA trained women (see page 240). A search was begun to find Soviet women to train. It was decided that they must be parachutists, as they would need to parachute from their descent module. Tereshkova, who enjoyed parachuting in her spare time, was selected in 1962.

During Tereshkova's 16-month training, she learned how to pilot her capsule. She also endured tests of her response to spinning, shaking, and being alone.

TERESHKOVA PROFILE

Born: 1937
Nationality: Soviet
Mission: Vostok 6 (June 16-19, 1963), which was the first mission to carry a woman into space. Each orbit of Earth by the Vostok 3KA capsule lasted around 88 minutes, at up to 231 km (144 miles) high. During the flight, Tereshkova turned the capsule using her controls.

Inside a Vostok 3KA

DID YOU KNOW? The Soviet space agency gave Tereshkova food, water, and toothpaste for her flight, but they forgot to pack a toothbrush.

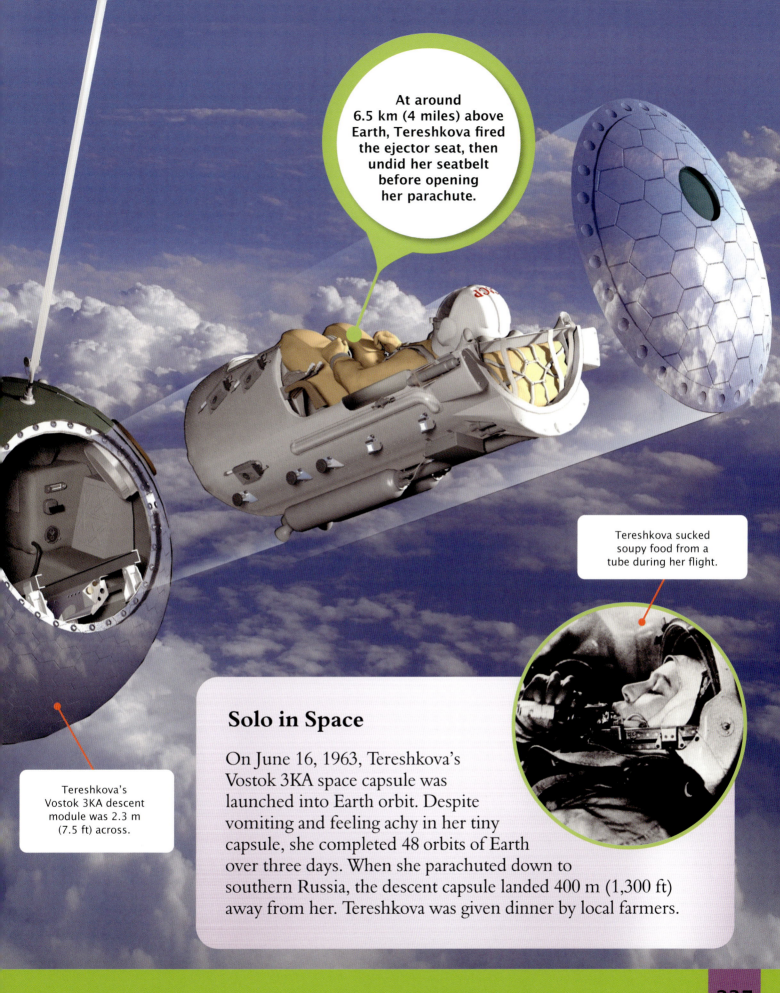

At around 6.5 km (4 miles) above Earth, Tereshkova fired the ejector seat, then undid her seatbelt before opening her parachute.

Tereshkova sucked soupy food from a tube during her flight.

Tereshkova's Vostok 3KA descent module was 2.3 m (7.5 ft) across.

Solo in Space

On June 16, 1963, Tereshkova's Vostok 3KA space capsule was launched into Earth orbit. Despite vomiting and feeling achy in her tiny capsule, she completed 48 orbits of Earth over three days. When she parachuted down to southern Russia, the descent capsule landed 400 m (1,300 ft) away from her. Tereshkova was given dinner by local farmers.

Neil Armstrong

At 2.56 a.m. on July 21, 1969, Armstrong was the first person to walk on the Moon, followed 19 minutes later by Buzz Aldrin. Before being selected as a NASA astronaut, Armstrong was a test pilot, flying more than 200 models of aircraft, from fighter jets to passenger planes.

First Spaceflight

Armstrong's first spaceflight was Gemini 8, which aimed to test the docking of two aircraft in orbit, an activity required for future Moon landings. The plan was to carry out four dockings of the Gemini capsule flown by Armstrong and his crewmate, David Scott, with an uncrewed Agena spacecraft, which was already in orbit around Earth. The first docking was successful, but the mission was emergency aborted after Armstrong had to use up vital fuel to correct the Gemini's dangerous rolling, caused by a stuck thruster (small rocket engine).

This photo was taken on March 16, 1966, by a camera on board Gemini 8 as it neared the Agena.

Armstrong took this photo during his moonwalk, showing his own shadow on the lunar surface.

Apollo lunar module

ARMSTRONG PROFILE

Dates: 1930–2012
Nationality: American
Mission 1: Gemini 8 (March 16–17, 1966), which carried out the first docking of two orbiting spacecraft.
Mission 2: Apollo 11 (July 16–24, 1969), which landed the first two humans on the Moon.

The lunar module had a descent stage, which was left on the Moon, and an ascent stage, which was abandoned in orbit around the Moon after returning Armstrong and Aldrin to the command and service module.

Man on the Moon

Late on July 20, 1969, Armstrong and Aldrin landed their lunar module on the Moon, leaving Michael Collins in orbit in the Apollo 11 command and service module (see page 152). Either Armstrong or Aldrin could have been first to walk on the Moon, but NASA felt it should be Armstrong because of his calm personality. As Armstrong climbed down the lunar module's ladder, he opened a hatch and turned on the TV camera inside, so his first steps and words were beamed almost live to 600 million people watching on Earth.

Armstrong's words as he stepped onto the Moon were: "One small step for [a] man, one giant leap for mankind." Although he meant to say "a" before "man," the word could not be heard by viewers. This photo of Armstrong was taken by Aldrin on the way home.

Neil Armstrong spent 2 hours and 31 minutes walking on the Moon's Sea of Tranquility, while Aldrin moonwalked for 1 hour and 33 minutes.

DID YOU KNOW? Armstrong, Aldrin, and Collins were kept in isolation for three weeks after returning from the Moon, in case they had been contaminated by tiny living things.

Sally Ride

The first American woman in space was Sally Ride, in 1983. She was only the third ever woman to reach space, after Valentina Tereshkova in 1963, and Svetlana Savitskaya in 1982, both from the Soviet Union.

Astronaut Group 8

In 1978, NASA selected a new group of 35 trainee astronauts, called Group 8. This was the first group that included women (six in total) as well as men considered to belong to "minorities": three men were African American and one was Asian American. All the women were picked as mission specialists, a title held by astronauts who—rather than being pilots—had special skills in science or medicine. Sally Ride was selected because she was a physicist.

Ride floats on the flight deck of Space Shuttle *Challenger* during STS-7, because both she and the orbiting spacecraft are actually falling around Earth, making her seem to be weightless.

Sally Ride (front row, eighth from the left) was the first of the Group 8 women to reach space. Guion Bluford (back row, first on the left) became the first African American in space in 1983.

RIDE PROFILE

Dates: 1951–2012
Nationality: American
Mission 1: STS-7 (June 18–24, 1983), which put into orbit two communications satellites, then released and retrieved the SPAS-1 experiment satellite.
Mission 2: STS-41-G (October 5–13, 1984), which was the first to carry two women: Ride and her Group 8 classmate Kathryn Sullivan both journeyed on Space Shuttle *Challenger*.

Space Shuttle

DID YOU KNOW? NASA engineers designed a make-up kit for Ride to use in space, but she had no interest—or time—to use it on her missions.

There were more than 1,000 dials, buttons, and switches on a Space Shuttle's flight deck, each carrying out or monitoring functions from an emergency abort to opening the landing gear.

Release and Retrieve

Ride's first spaceflight was on Space Shuttle *Challenger* on mission STS-7. One of her jobs was to manipulate the Space Shuttle's robotic arm so that it released a satellite, called SPAS-1, then retrieved it a few hours later. Mounted on the satellite were 10 experiments that, as SPAS-1 flew freely, carried out research into the making of metal alloys (mixtures of metals) in space.

Taken by a camera on board SPAS-1, this was the first photo taken of a Space Shuttle in orbit. It shows the open doors to the Shuttle's cargo bay, which had contained two other satellites that had already been released.

Over the course of her two missions, Ride spent more than 343 hours in space.

241

Mae Jemison

Mae Jemison was spurred on to become an astronaut by the 1983 spaceflights of Sally Ride and Guion Bluford. In 1992, she succeeded in becoming the first African American woman in space.

Star Trekker

Jemison decided she wanted to be an astronaut when she was a little girl. When she was 10 years old, she was inspired by a new TV show, called *Star Trek*, about a crew of astronauts exploring the Universe. The show made a decision that was groundbreaking in 1966: to have an African American actor—Nichelle Nichols—in a central role. Determined to make her own dreams a reality, Jemison graduated from high school when she was 16, then gained degrees in chemical engineering, African American studies, and medicine.

Nichelle Nichols (back left) played smart, resourceful astronaut Lieutenant Uhura in *Star Trek*.

Jemison spent 7 days, 22 hours, and 30 minutes in space, as she orbited Earth 126 times.

Science in Space

Jemison was selected by NASA in 1987. She was in the first group of astronauts to begin training after Space Shuttle *Challenger* broke apart in 1986, killing its crew. In 1992, Jemison departed on Space Shuttle *Endeavour* as a mission specialist. Loaded in the Shuttle's cargo bay was a science laboratory called Spacelab-J, where Jemison carried out medical experiments.

For the first time in space, Jemison made saline solution (sterile, salty water) that could be used to clean wounds.

DID YOU KNOW? On her spaceflight, Jemison began radio communications with the greeting "Hailing frequencies open," which was a line often said by Uhura on *Star Trek*.

A joint project between the US and Japan, Spacelab-J contained the materials and equipment for 43 experiments into materials and living things.

One experiment was designed by a girls' school in the United Kingdom: to grow crystals to see how they behaved in weightlessness. The crystals grew in random, twisting directions.

Inside Spacelab

JEMISON PROFILE

Born: 1956
Nationality: American
Mission: STS-47 (September 12-20, 1992), which was a science mission and the fiftieth mission of the Space Shuttle program. The crew of seven included the first African American woman in space and the first and only married couple, Mark Lee and Jan Davis.

Yang Liwei

By 2003, astronauts from many countries had flown on United States or Russian spacecraft. However, in that year, China became the third country to send a human into space on a spacecraft it built and launched itself. That astronaut was a fighter pilot called Yang Liwei.

Reaching Space

Starting in 1999, China launched four uncrewed Shenzhou space capsules. By 2003, the Chinese space program was ready for a human flight. Although the Shenzhou capsule had room for three crew, Yang was alone when he was launched by a Long March 2F rocket. Two minutes after launch, he reported "very uncomfortable" shaking of the capsule. It was later understood this was caused by a problem with the rocket, which was corrected for future launches. At a height of 343 km (213 miles) above Earth, 10 minutes after launch, Yang entered orbit.

Yang spoke to his wife by radio during the flight, reassuring her: "I feel very good, don't worry."

Heavenly Palace

After completing his mission, Yang became a director at the China Manned Space Agency, which is in charge of the nation's human spaceflights. The agency has successfully sent many more crewed flights into space, with the first Chinese spacewalk—by Zhai Zhigang and Liu Boming—in 2008. The first module of a long-term Chinese space station was launched in 2021: It is called Tiangong, which means "heavenly palace."

Like the *International Space Station*, Tiangong was built in orbit from pre-made parts. It has room for a crew of three to live and carry out experiments. This illustration shows a docked Shenzhou crewed spacecraft and the arrival of a Tianzhou cargo spacecraft.

DID YOU KNOW? English-speakers call space visitors "astronauts," but Russia calls them "cosmonauts" and China calls them "taikonauts" or "yuhangyuan" (journeyers in space).

YANG PROFILE

Born: 1965
Nationality: Chinese
Mission: Shenzhou 5 (October 15, 2003), which was the first Chinese crewed mission. Yang made 14 orbits of Earth over 21 hours. Slowed by parachutes and downward-blasting rockets, the Shenzhou capsule landed in northern China.

Shenzhou spacecraft

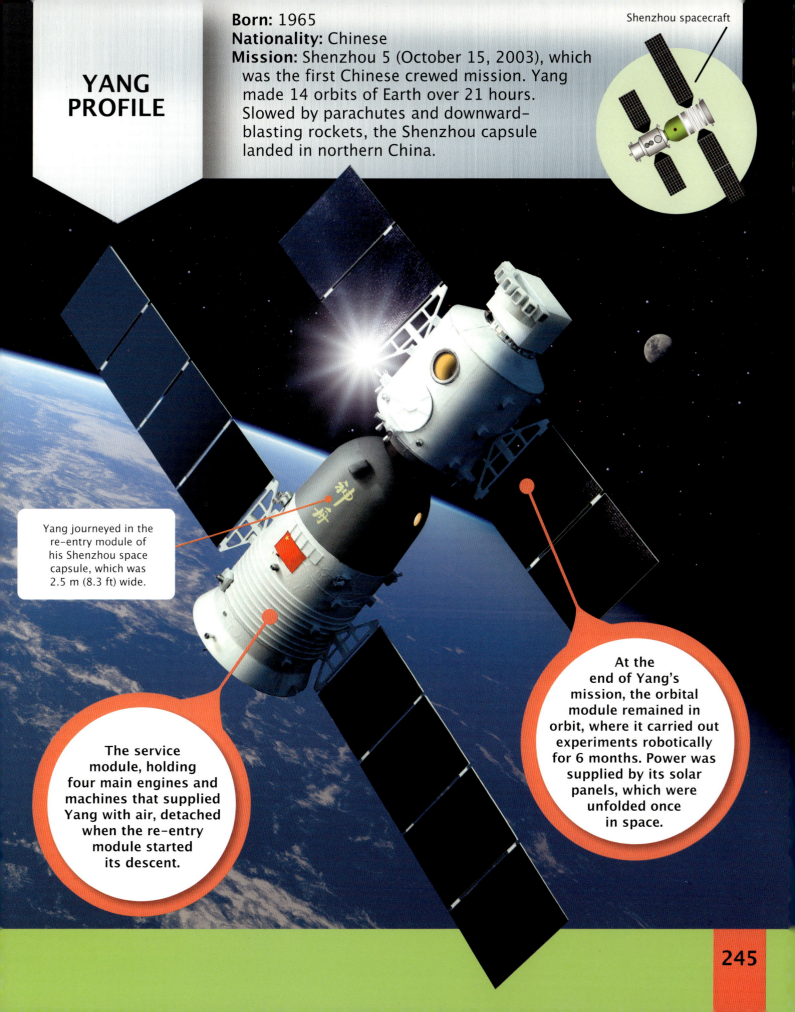

Yang journeyed in the re-entry module of his Shenzhou space capsule, which was 2.5 m (8.3 ft) wide.

The service module, holding four main engines and machines that supplied Yang with air, detached when the re-entry module started its descent.

At the end of Yang's mission, the orbital module remained in orbit, where it carried out experiments robotically for 6 months. Power was supplied by its solar panels, which were unfolded once in space.

245

Peggy Whitson

Each crew that works on board the *International Space Station* (*ISS*) has a commander, who makes sure that everyone is safe and well. Astronaut Peggy Whitson was the first woman to command the ISS, in 2007–8.

ISS Commander

When Whitson first visited the *ISS* in 2002, she helped to construct modules and external equipment while spacewalking. When she returned to the space station in 2007, it was as commander. During her time as the most senior astronaut on the *ISS*, she encouraged the whole crew to attend a Friday movie night to help them relax. In 2017, she became the first woman to command the ISS a second time.

On her 2016–17 visit to the *ISS*, Whitson looks at Earth from the Cupola observation pod of the Tranquility module.

On January 30, 2008, Whitson replaces a motor on the *ISS* during a spacewalk.

WHITSON PROFILE

Born: 1960
Nationality: American
Mission 1: Expedition 5 (June 5–December 7, 2002), the fifth long-term stay by a crew on the ISS.
Mission 2: Expedition 16 (October 10, 2007–April 19, 2008).
Mission 3: Expeditions 50, 51, 52 (November 17, 2016–September 3, 2017).
Mission 4: Axiom 2 (May 21–31, 2023).

DID YOU KNOW? The astronaut who has spent longest in space is Russia's Gennady Padalka, with 879 days over five missions to the Russian space station *Mir* and the *ISS*.

Record Breaker

During Whitson's three missions for NASA, she spent 665 days in space, more than any other American or woman. After retiring from NASA in 2018, she joined the business Axiom Space. In 2023, she commanded an Axiom flight to the *ISS* on a Crew Dragon (see page 248). She added another 10 days to her time in space and became the oldest woman to orbit Earth, aged 63.

In 2023, Whitson's Crew Dragon was launched by a SpaceX Falcon 9 rocket, taking her to the *ISS* for the fourth time.

During her first three missions, Whitson spent 60 hours and 21 minutes doing 10 spacewalks, more than any other woman.

Before being selected as a NASA astronaut, Whitson was a biochemist, which is a scientist who studies chemical processes in living things.

Sian Proctor

In 2021, Proctor became the first Black woman to pilot a spacecraft. She was a commercial astronaut, which means she flew on a spacecraft built by a private business and was also trained by the business rather than by a government space agency.

Crew Dragon Pilot

Proctor was pilot of a Crew Dragon space capsule owned by the American business SpaceX. Since 2020, Crew Dragons have been carrying astronauts to and from the *International Space Station*, the first private spacecraft to do so. However, Proctor's mission, named Inspiration4, was not to dock with the *ISS* but to orbit Earth, which the capsule did at a height of up to 585 km (364 miles), which is higher than the *ISS*.

While in orbit, Proctor painted, wrote poetry, and helped her crewmates with experiments.

A New Era

Inspiration4 was the first orbital spaceflight that carried only commercial astronauts, making it the start of a new era in spaceflight. The mission raised money for St Jude Children's Hospital, in Tennessee, United States. Proctor's crewmates were businessman Jared Isaacman, who paid for the mission and donated money to the hospital; Christopher Sembroski, who won his place in the hospital's raffle; and Hayley Arceneaux, who worked at the hospital.

While in orbit, Jared Isaacman (second from left) gives an update on the mission's status by radio. Arceneaux (upside down), who survived bone cancer as a child, was the first person in space with a prosthetic leg bone.

PROCTOR PROFILE

Born: 1960
Nationality: American
Mission: Inspiration4 (September 16–18, 2021), which was the first crewed spaceflight to orbit Earth with only civilians on board. Each orbit of the space capsule lasted around 90 minutes.

Crew Dragon

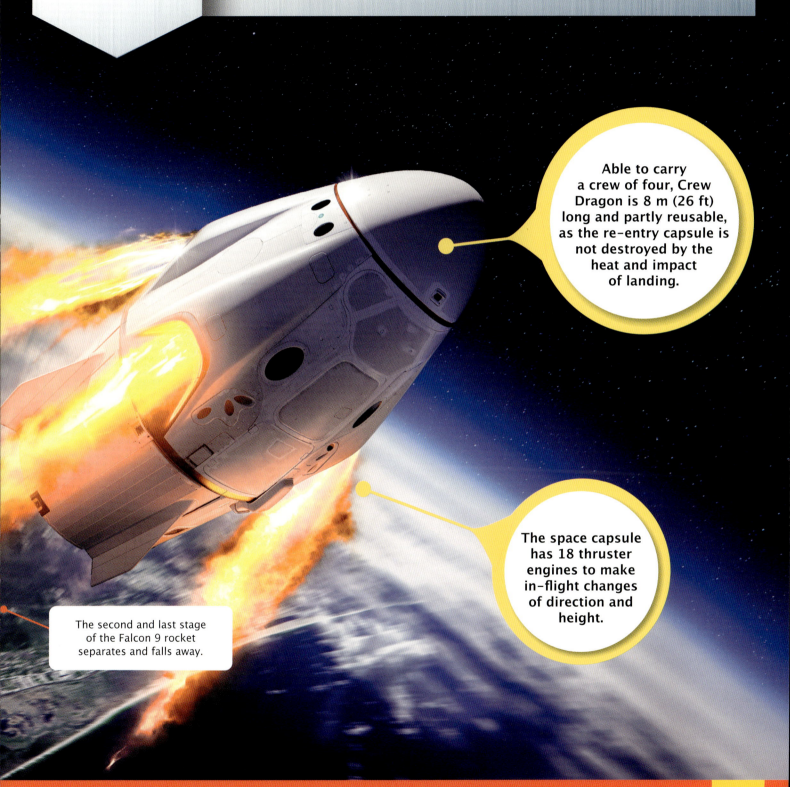

Able to carry a crew of four, Crew Dragon is 8 m (26 ft) long and partly reusable, as the re-entry capsule is not destroyed by the heat and impact of landing.

The space capsule has 18 thruster engines to make in-flight changes of direction and height.

The second and last stage of the Falcon 9 rocket separates and falls away.

DID YOU KNOW? In 2001, American businessman Dennis Tito became the first space tourist, when he paid for his trip to the *ISS* on a Russian Soyuz spacecraft.

Glossary

ACTIVE GALAXY
A galaxy with a compact region at its core that emits immense radiation, caused by material circling a supermassive black hole.

ASTEROID
A small rocky or metal object that orbits the Sun.

ASTEROID BELT
A ring-shaped region, between the orbits of Mars and Jupiter, that contains many asteroids.

ASTRONOMER
A scientist who studies planets, stars, and space itself.

ASTRONOMICAL UNIT (AU)
The average distance from Earth to the Sun: around 150 million km (93 million miles).

ATMOSPHERE
The gases surrounding a planet, moon, star, or other space object, held by its gravity.

ATOM
The smallest unit of matter. An atom has a central nucleus, containing particles called protons and neutrons, usually surrounded by one or more electrons.

AURORA
Lights in the sky made by particles from the Sun exciting gases in the atmosphere.

AXIS
An imaginary line through the middle of a planet, moon, star, or other space object, around which the object rotates.

BINARY STAR
One of a pair of stars orbiting each other.

BLACK HOLE
A superdense point in space with such strong gravity that no matter or light can escape from it.

CARBON DIOXIDE
A substance made of carbon and oxygen atoms. Carbon dioxide is a gas at room temperature.

CENTAUR
A small icy object that is orbiting the Sun in the region of the outer planets.

CHROMOSPHERE
An inner layer of the Sun's atmosphere.

COMET
A small icy object with an elliptical orbit that takes it both close to and far from the Sun. Close to the Sun, its melting ices form a glowing coma and tails of gas and dust.

CONSTELLATION
A group of stars that seem to make a shape in the night sky, as well as the area of sky around those stars.

CORE
The inner region of a planet, moon, star, or other space object.

CORONA
The outer layer of the Sun's atmosphere.

COUNTERCLOCKWISE
Also known as anticlockwise; the opposite direction from the way the hands of a clock turn.

CRUST
The outer layer of a planet or moon.

DARK MATTER
A strange, invisible substance that forms most of the mass in the Universe.

DAY
The time taken for a planet or moon to rotate on its axis until the Sun appears to return to the same position in the sky.

DENSE
Tightly packed.

DIAMETER
A straight line through the middle of a sphere.

DWARF PLANET
An object orbiting a star that is massive enough for its gravity to pull it into a ball-like shape, but is not massive enough to clear other objects out of its path.

ECLIPSE
When a body such as a star, planet, or moon is obscured by passing into the shadow of—or behind—another body.

ECLIPTIC
The plane of Earth's orbit around the Sun. The Sun and other planets appear to travel along the curving ecliptic through Earth's sky.

ELECTRIC CHARGE
A property of electrons and protons. Electrons are negatively charged and protons are positively charged. Electricity is a flow of electrically charged particles.

ELECTROMAGNETIC RADIATION
A type of energy that travels at the speed of light. Radiations are given different names depending on the amount of energy they carry, from low-energy radio waves, through microwaves, infrared, visible light, ultraviolet, and X-rays, to the highest-energy gamma rays.

ELECTROMAGNETISM
A basic force of nature that influences all particles that carry electric charge or a magnetic field.

ELECTRON
A subatomic particle (a particle found in atoms). An electron is negatively charged and located outside an atom's nucleus. Electricity is mostly driven by the flow of electrons from one place to another.

ELEMENT
A pure substance, made of one type of atom, that cannot be broken down into simpler substances.

ELLIPTICAL
Shaped like a stretched circle.

ELLIPTICAL GALAXY
An egg-shaped galaxy made up mostly of old red and yellow stars.

ENERGY
The power to do work that produces light, heat, or motion.

EXOPLANET
A planet outside our Solar System.

FLUID
A substance that can flow, typically a liquid, but can also be a dense gas or plasma.

FORCE
A push or pull on an object that changes its movement.

FRICTION
The force that resists the movement of one object past another.

GALAXY
Millions or trillions of stars, as well as gas and dust, all held together by gravity.

GAS
A substance, such as air, that can move freely and has no fixed shape.

GIANT PLANET
A planet much larger than Earth, made up mostly of gas, liquid, and slushy frozen chemicals.

GLOBULAR CLUSTER
A dense ball of ancient, long-lived stars, found in orbit around galaxies, such as the Milky Way.

GRAVITY
A force that pulls all objects and particles toward each other. The greater an object's mass, the greater the pull of its gravity.

HELIOSPHERE
A bubble blown by the solar wind.

HELIUM
The second most common and second lightest atom in the Universe. Helium is a gas at room temperature.

HEMISPHERE
Half of a sphere, such as a planet or moon.

HYDROGEN
The most common and lightest atom in the Universe. Hydrogen is a gas at room temperature.

IMPACT CRATER
A bowl-shaped dip on a planet or moon caused by a collision with an asteroid or other object.

INFRARED
A type of energy that humans can feel as heat.

IRREGULAR GALAXY
A galaxy with no clear shape, usually rich in gas, dust, and star-forming regions.

KUIPER BELT
A ring-shaped region of icy objects beyond the orbit of Neptune.

LAVA
Melted rock that has spilled from a volcano.

LIGHT-YEAR
The distance light travels in 1 year: 9.46 trillion km (5.88 trillion miles).

LUNAR ECLIPSE
When the Full Moon passes into Earth's shadow so direct sunlight does not reach its surface.

MAGMA
Melted rock beneath the surface of a planet or moon.

MAGNETISM
A force caused by the movement of electric charge, resulting in pulling and pushing forces between objects.

MAIN SEQUENCE
The longest phase in a star's life, when it shines by turning its main fuel source of hydrogen into helium at its core. During this time, the star's brightness and temperature are related—the brighter the star is, the hotter its surface and the bluer it looks.

MANTLE
A layer inside a planet or moon that lies between the core and crust.

MASS
A measure of the amount of matter in an object; often called "weight."

MATTER
A physical substance, in the form of a solid, liquid, gas, or plasma. See also *Dark matter*.

METALLIC
Behaving like a metal by allowing electricity to flow through it.

METEOR
A streak of light in the sky, caused by a space object burning up in Earth's atmosphere.

METEORITE
A space object that has fallen to Earth's surface.

METEOROID
A small rocky or metal object in space, less than 1 m (3.3 ft) wide.

MILKY WAY
Our home galaxy, a spiral with a bar across its core.

MOLECULE
A group of atoms that are bonded together.

MOON
A rounded object orbiting a planet.

MULTIPLE STARS
A system of two or more stars in orbit around one another.

NAKED EYE
Human sight, without the help of a telescope or other device.

NEBULA
A cloud of gas or dust in space. Nebulae are the raw materials from which stars are made.

NEUTRON
A subatomic particle (a particle found in atoms) with no charge, located inside the nucleus.

NEUTRON STAR
The core of a supermassive star, left behind by a supernova explosion.

NUCLEUS
The middle of an atom, where its positive electric charge and nearly all its mass are concentrated in a cluster of protons and neutrons.

OORT CLOUD
A spherical (ball-shaped) shell of objects, surrounding the Solar System to a distance of about 2 light-years.

ORBIT
The curved path of an object around a star, planet, or moon.

OXYGEN
The third most common atom. Oxygen is a gas at room temperature and is essential for life.

PARTICLE
A tiny portion of matter.

PHOTON
A particle that carries energy.

PHOTOSPHERE
The visible "surface" of the Sun.

PLANE
An imaginary flat surface.

PLANET
An object orbiting a star that is massive enough for its gravity to pull it into a ball-like shape and to remove other large objects from its path.

PLANETARY NEBULA
A cloud of glowing gas thrown off by a dying red giant star.

PLASMA
An electrically charged gas made of free electrons and atoms that have lost electrons.

POLE STAR
A star that lies close to Earth's north or south pole, and so stays more or less fixed in the sky as Earth rotates.

PROTON
A positively charged subatomic particle (a particle found in atoms), located inside the nucleus.

PULSAR
A fast-spinning neutron star whose intense magnetic field forces its radiation into two narrow beams that sweep around the sky like a lighthouse. From Earth, a pulsar appears as a quickly flashing star.

QUASAR
A distant active galaxy with a very bright core.

RADIATION
Energy that moves from one place to another, in the form of waves and particles.

RADIOACTIVE
Relating to a substance that releases energy as its atoms decay.

RADIO WAVE
A type of energy that can be used for sending information. The information is "coded" into a radio wave by changing the wave's shape.

RED DWARF
A small, faint star with a cool red surface and less than half the mass of the Sun.

RED GIANT
A huge, very bright star near the end of its life, with a cool, red surface. Red giants are stars that have used up the fuel supply in

their core and are going through big changes in order to keep shining for a little longer.

ROBOTIC
Relating to a machine programmed to carry out some of its activities independently.

ROCKET
A vehicle that drives itself forward through a controlled chemical explosion and can therefore travel in the vacuum of space. Rockets are the only practical way to launch spacecraft and satellites.

ROCKY PLANET
An Earth-sized or smaller planet, made up mostly of metal, rocks, and minerals, sometimes with a thin outer layer of gas and water.

ROOM TEMPERATURE
A comfortable indoor temperature of around 20°C (68°F).

ROTATION
Turning around an axis.

ROVER
A robot that can travel across the surface or a planet or moon.

SATELLITE
Any object that orbits a larger object. Moons are natural satellites usually made of metal, rock, or ice. Artificial (human-made) satellites are machines in orbit around Earth, the Sun, or another planet.

SOLAR ECLIPSE
When the Moon passes directly in front of the Sun, casting its shadow onto Earth.

SOLAR PANEL
A device that turns sunlight into electricity.

SOLAR SYSTEM
The Sun along with all the planets and other objects in orbit around it.

SOLAR WIND
A flow of charged particles from the Sun.

SOVIET UNION
A country that, from 1922 to 1991, included Russia and surrounding nations.

SPACE AGENCY
A government organization that works on space exploration.

SPACE CAPSULE
A wingless spacecraft.

SPACECRAFT
A vehicle that travels into space.

SPACE PROBE
An uncrewed spacecraft that explores the Solar System and beyond, while sending back signals to Earth.

SPECTRUM
The spread-out band of light with different hues, created by passing light through a prism, as well as the entire range of electromagnetic radiation.

SPIRAL GALAXY
A galaxy with a hub of old yellow stars (sometimes crossed by a bar) surrounded by a flattened disk of younger stars, gas, and dust. Bright newborn stars make a spiral pattern across the disk.

STAR
A glowing ball of plasma, held together by its own gravity.

SUN
The star at the middle of our Solar System, around which Earth and the other planets orbit.

SUPERNOVA
An enormous explosion marking the death of a star much more massive than the Sun.

SUPERNOVA REMNANT
An expanding (growing) cloud of shredded, superhot gas left behind by a supernova explosion.

TELESCOPE
A device used to observe distant objects by detecting the light or other energy they give off or reflect. An optical telescope uses mirrors and lenses to collect and focus light.

ULTRAVIOLET
A type of energy, given off by objects including the Sun.

UNIVERSE
All of space and its contents; everything that is known to exist.

VOLCANO
A hole in a planet or moon's surface through which lava can spill out.

WAVELENGTH
The distance between the peaks of waves of energy.

WHITE DWARF
The dense, burnt-out core of a star like the Sun, collapsed to the size of Earth but still intensely hot.

YEAR
The time taken for a planet to complete one orbit around the Sun.

ZODIAC
Twelve constellations surrounding the Sun's yearly path around Earth's sky. The planets and Moon are usually found within these constellations.

Index

active galaxies 182–183
Aldrin, Edwin "Buzz" 152, 224, 238, 239
aliens *see* Life
al-Sufi, Abd al-Rahman 210–211
Andromeda (constellation) 130, 210
Andromeda Galaxy 111, 180, 181, 210, 222
Apollo 8 mission 135, 139
Apollo 11 mission 26–27, 136, 139, 152–153, 224–225, 238–239
Apollo 13 mission 233
Apollo 14 mission 235
Arceneaux, Hayley 248
Ariel (moon) 82, 83
Aristarchus of Samos 209
armillary sphere 113
Armstrong, Neil 152, 224, 238–239
Arrokoth (Kuiper Belt Object) 95
Artemis space program 233
Asteroid Belt 9, 88, 89, 90–93
asteroids 6, 11, 88, 90–93, 102, 103, 105, 106, 107, 164, 165, 179
astronauts 127, 134, 135, 136, 138–139, 141, 144–145, 146, 147, 149, 166, 232–249
astronomers 208–231
Astronomical Units (AU) 250
astronomy 110–133, 182, 184, 185, 188, 207
atmospheres 14, 34–35, 36, 37, 38, 39, 41, 50, 56–57, 60, 62, 69, 70–71, 74, 78, 81, 84–85, 96, 102, 116, 118, 124, 126, 128, 134, 136, 140, 150, 166
atoms 12, 14, 36, 170, 220
auroras 18, 34, 36–37, 74

Babylonian astronomy 208
Bell Burnell, Jocelyn 228–229
Betelgeuse (star) 194
Big Bang 170–173, 174, 200, 223, 226

binary stars 202
black holes 25, 124, 178, 179, 182, 183, 185, 191, 198–199, 220–221, 226, 230–231
blueshift 223
Bluford, Guion 240, 242
Book of the Fixed Stars 210–211

Callisto (moon) 72, 78, 163, 212
Cannon, Annie Jump 218–219
Carina (constellation) 130
Carina Nebula 193
Cassini-Huygens mission 77, 160, 161, 162–163
Cat's Eye Nebula 194–195
centaurs 88, 100
Centaurus (constellation) 210–211
Cepheid variable stars 222
Ceres (dwarf planet) 88, 90, 92–93
Chandra X-Ray Observatory 198
Charon (moon) 97
Chinese space program 244–245
Collins, Michael 152, 239
comets 6, 11, 88, 100–101, 102, 103, 104, 164, 166, 216
commercial astronauts 248–249
conjunctions 70
constellations 38, 111, 113, 128, 130–133, 177, 178, 180, 183, 190, 191, 192, 193, 194, 195, 197, 201, 202, 204, 207, 210–211
Copernicus, Nicolaus 113, 114, 213
cosmic background radiation 173
Crab Pulsar 197

dark matter 169, 184–185
DART (probe) 106–107
Dawn (probe) 92
day and night 33
Deep Impact (probe) 164–165
Deimos (moon) 66–67
detached objects 88, 108–109
Dimorphos (moon) 106–107
Duke, Charles 232
dwarf planets 9, 88, 89, 92–93, 94, 96–97, 98–99, 108–109, 164
Dysnomia (moon) 98, 99

Eagle Nebula 121, 193
Earth 8, 9, 24, 26–37, 44–45, 135, 150, 151, 168
atmosphere 26, 34–39
formation 26

orbit 28, 32–33
rotation 32, 33
structure 28–31
eclipses
lunar 47
solar 20–21
ecliptic 54
Egyptian astronomy 208
Einstein, Albert 215, 220–221, 226
electromagnetic spectrum 16–17, 118–119
electrons 12, 36
emission nebulae 216–217
energy and mass 220
equinoxes 33
Eris (dwarf planet) 88, 98–99
Euclid (space telescope) 184
Europa (moon) 72, 78, 163, 186, 212
Event Horizon Telescope 230
exoplanets 128, 206–207, 229
Extremely Large Telescope 117

Falcon 9 (rocket) 247, 249
Freedom 7 (space capsule) 234, 235
Friedmann, Alexander 170
Friendship 7 (space capsule) 224

Gagarin, Yuri 138–139, 142, 232, 233, 234, 235
Gaia (space telescope) 188
galaxies 6–7, 111, 112, 127, 130, 168, 169, 170, 171, 172, 174–183, 184, 185, 186, 194, 200, 204, 205, 210, 222, 223
galaxy clusters 6, 7, 130, 174, 180, 185
Galilei, Galileo 72, 76, 114, 115, 212–213
Galileo (probe) 160, 161, 163
gamma rays 16, 118, 124, 125
Ganymede (moon) 9, 72–73, 78, 163, 212
Gemini (constellation) 210
Gemini 8 mission 238
Gemini Telescopes 116–117
geocentric model 113, 209, 213
Ghez, Andrea 230–231
Glenn, John 224
globular clusters 204–205
Gold, Thomas 229
Gonggong (dwarf planet) 88
gravity 7, 8, 10, 25, 44–45, 49, 134, 145, 167, 168, 174, 176, 180, 185, 198, 199, 206, 214–215, 220–221
Great Red Spot 70
Greek astronomy 112–113, 209

254

Hale-Bopp (comet) 100
haloes 38
Harvard system of star classification 218–219
Haumea (dwarf planet) 88, 94
Hawking, Stephen 226–227
Hayabusa (probe) 165
heliocentric model 209, 212, 213
heliosphere 22–23, 161
Herschel, Caroline 216–217
Herschel, William 120, 177, 194, 216
Hipparchus 112–113
Horsehead Nebula 192–193
Hubble, Edwin 170, 172, 222–223
Hubble Space Telescope 74, 81, 82, 87, 98, 126–127, 174–175, 206, 222

Iapetus (moon) 79
Ida (asteroid) 91, 163
impact craters 42, 43, 50, 52–53, 58, 61, 73, 83, 92, 93, 104–105, 107, 114, 166
infrared 16, 118, 120–121, 180, 192, 230
International Space Station 134, 148–149, 232, 246–247, 248
interstellar medium 22
interstellar space 200–201
Io (moon) 72, 78, 163, 212
Itokawa (asteroid) 164, 165

James Webb Space Telescope 128–129
Jemison, Mae 242–243
Jewel Box (star cluster) 203
Johnson, Katherine 224–225
Juno (probe) 160–161
Jupiter 9, 10, 49, 51, 54, 68, 69, 70–73, 88, 160–161, 163, 186, 212

Keck Telescopes 116, 230
Kepler Space Telescope 128
Kuiper Belt 9, 87, 88, 89, 94–97, 100

Lacaille, Nicolas-Louis de 132
Laika 139
Large Magellanic Cloud 180–181
Lemaître, Georges 170, 223
Lich (pulsar) 228–229
life 35, 62, 73, 78, 92, 123, 156, 186–187, 226
Lippershey, Hans 212
Low Earth Orbit (LEO) 134, 150

lunar buggy 232
Lupus (constellation) 210–211

M13 (globular cluster) 204
M81 (galaxy) 119
M106 (galaxy) 182, 183
Maat Mons 58–59
Magellan (probe) 58–59, 158–159
magnetic fields 18–19, 22, 36–37, 38, 39, 40, 74, 154, 161, 163, 196, 199, 229
main sequence stars 190, 191
Makemake (dwarf planet) 88
Mariner probes 52, 63, 65, 158, 159
Mars 9, 48, 49, 60–67, 156–157, 166–167
Mars Express (probe) 62
Mauna Kea Observatory 94
Mercury 9, 20, 24, 36, 48, 49, 50–53, 54, 158
Mercury-Redstone 3 mission 235
MESSENGER (probe) 50, 52, 158
meteorites 102, 104–105
meteor showers 34, 102–103
Meteosat 150–151
microwaves 16, 119, 173, 184
Milky Way Galaxy 6–7, 23, 70, 114, 127, 130, 132, 177, 178–179, 180, 188, 204, 205, 230–231
Mir (space station) 146–147
Moon, the 20–21, 26–27, 40–47, 78, 104, 110, 114, 125, 135, 152–153, 166, 215, 224–225, 238–239
  maria ("seas") 42–43
  orbit 27, 40, 41, 46, 215
  phases 46
Moon landing *see* Apollo 11 mission
moons 9, 10, 11, 49, 66–67, 72–73, 78–79, 82–83, 86–87, 91, 94, 97, 98, 99, 106–107, 109, 114, 162–163, 186
motion, laws of 214
multiple star systems 202
multiverse 226–227

National Aeronautics and Space Administration (NASA) 224–225, 232, 233, 234–235, 236, 238–243, 246–247
near-Earth objects 102, 106–107, 165
NEAR (Near Earth Asteroid Rendezvous) Shoemaker (probe) 165

nebulae 6, 7, 119, 121, 180–181, 190, 192–193, 200–201, 202, 206–207
  planetary nebulae 194–195
Neowise (comet) 101
Neptune 9, 25, 49, 68, 69, 84–87, 160–161
neutron stars 191, 196–197, 228–229
New Horizons (probe) 95, 96, 161, 164
Newton, Isaac 8, 137, 214–215
noctilucent clouds 38–39
nuclear fusion 12, 24, 25

observational astronomy 208
Olympus Mons 61, 64
Omega Centauri (globular cluster) 205
Omega Nebula 120–121
Oort Cloud 88, 89, 109
open star clusters 202–203
Orcus (dwarf planet) 88
Orion (constellation) 190–191, 193, 194, 218–219
Orion (space capsule) 134–135, 157
Orion Nebula 193, 206

Parker Solar Probe 154
Phobos (moon) 66–67
photons 14–15, 16
Pioneer Venus (probe) 58, 159
planetary nebulae 194–195
planets 6, 8–11, 26–87, 112, 113, 119, 128, 168, 206–207
  axial tilts 32, 33, 63, 75, 80
  definition 9
  formation 11, 48, 68
  orbits 8–9, 50
  rotations 55, 80
Pleiades (open star cluster) 110, 202–203
Pluto (dwarf planet) 9, 88, 89, 94, 96–97, 98
Polaris (star) 130, 131
Proctor, Sian 248–249
Project Mercury 224, 234–235
Proteus (moon) 87
Ptolemy, Claudius 130, 132, 209, 210, 213
pulsars 196–197, 228–229

255

quantum mechanics 226
Quaoar (dwarf planet) 88
quasars 170, 182

radio telescopes 122–123
radio waves 16, 59, 118, 122, 123, 126, 128, 151, 153, 155, 159, 182, 183, 228–229, 230
red dwarfs 6, 191, 206
red giants 190, 191, 194, 203
redshift 223
Redstone (rocket) 234
relativity, theory of 220–221
Ride, Sally 240–241, 242
Rigel (star) 190–191
ring systems 69, 70, 73, 75, 76–77, 81, 82, 84, 94
rockets 136–137, 140, 141, 142–143, 144, 152, 167, 214, 234, 249
Roscosmos 232
rovers 60, 153, 156–157
rupes 52, 53

Sagittarius A★ 230–231
Salyut (space station) 146
satellites (artificial) 34, 39, 120, 126, 128, 138, 139, 141, 150–151, 154, 156, 158, 159, 160, 162, 163, 165, 168, 184, 188
Saturn 9, 49, 54, 68, 69, 70, 74–79, 160–162
Saturn V (rocket) 136
Savitskaya, Svetlana 240
Scattered Disk 88, 98–99, 100
Schwarzschild, Karl 221
Scott, David 238
seasons 32
Sedna (dwarf planet) 88, 108–109
Shenzhou (space capsule) 244–245
Shepard, Alan 224, 234–235
shooting stars 102–103
singularities 226
Sirius (star) 132, 189
Solar and Heliospheric Observatory (SOHO) (probe) 154–155
Solar Orbiter (SolO) (probe) 154
solar radiation 16–17
Solar System 8–109, 112–113, 152–165, 209, 212–213, 214–215
solar wind 22, 23, 37, 60, 100, 154, 161
solstices 32–33, 208–209

Soviet space program 232, 233, 234, 236–237
Soyuz (rocket) 142–143, 144
Soyuz (space capsule) 146
spacecraft 134–167, 233, 236–237, 238, 240–241, 243, 245, 248–249
Spacelab 242–243
space probes 152–166
Space Shuttles 140–141, 147, 232–233, 240–241, 242–243
space stations 146–149, 244, 246–247
spacetime 220–221
SpaceX Crew Dragons 247, 248–249
Spitzer Space Telescope 121
Sputnik 1 and *2* (satellites) 139, 151
star clusters 127, 181, 202–203, 204–205, 217
Stardust (probe) 164
stars 6, 7, 10, 11, 12–25, 110, 112, 113, 118, 119, 120, 121, 123, 124, 127, 128, 130–133, 168, 169, 170, 172, 174, 175, 176, 177, 178, 179, 180, 181, 182, 183, 184, 185, 186, 187, 188–205, 206, 207, 210–211
  birth 192–193, 200
  death 191, 194–199
  magnitude 189
  types 190–191, 218–219
Star Trek 242
Stonehenge, England 208–209
Sullivan, Kathryn 240
Sun, the 6, 8, 10, 11, 12–25, 34, 35, 38, 39, 45, 112, 113, 114, 123, 124, 125, 128, 131, 133, 148, 154–155, 167, 190, 191
  atmosphere 14, 15, 19, 21, 22, 154
  cycle 18–19
  death 24–25
  formation 10–11
  structure 12, 14–15
sundogs 38
sunlight 12, 13, 16–17, 32, 33, 35, 80
Sunrise (telescope) 124–125
supernova remnants 200–201
supernovas 25, 124, 191, 194, 196, 197, 200–201, 203

Tarantula Nebula 180–181
tectonic plates 30–31
telescopes 110, 114–117, 120–129, 168, 178, 184, 188, 212

Tereshkova, Valentina 236–237
terraforming 166–167
theoretical astronomy 208, 209
Tiangong space station 244
tidal locking 40
tides 44–45
Titan (moon) 78–79, 162–163
Titania (moon) 82–83
Tito, Dennis 249
transits 20
Triangulum Galaxy 222–223
Triton (moon) 86–87
trojans 88

ultraviolet 16, 118–119, 124, 125, 154
Universe 168–187
  expansion 223
Uranus 8, 49, 68, 69, 80–83, 120, 160–161, 216

V2 (rocket) 136
Valles Marineris 64–65
variable stars 219, 222
Veil Nebula 200–201
Venera 13 (lander) 159
Venus 9, 20, 24, 48, 49, 54–59, 158–159, 208, 212–213
Viking 1 (space probe) 60
volcanoes 30–31, 42, 58–59, 64, 72, 92, 163
Vostok missions 138–139, 142, 232, 233, 236–237
Voyager probes 70, 82, 84, 85, 87, 161, 163

water 34, 35, 56, 60, 62–63, 72, 73, 86, 92, 93, 94, 96, 98, 156, 166, 167, 183, 186, 206
weather 35, 49, 57, 60, 63, 70, 74, 75, 84
white dwarfs 189, 191, 195, 229
Whitson, Peggy 246–247
Wilson, Stephanie 232–233
Witch Head Nebula 190

X-rays 16, 118, 124, 125, 156, 179, 196, 198

Yang, Liwei 244–245
Yerkes Observatory 114–115
Young, John 232

zodiac 39, 113, 130, 131, 133
zodiacal light 39